BEING AND ACTION *CORAM DEO*

T&T Clark New Studies in Bonhoeffer's Theology and Ethics

Series Editors
Jennifer McBride
Michael Mawson
Philip G. Ziegler

BEING AND ACTION *CORAM DEO*

Bonhoeffer and the Retrieval of Justification's Social Import

Koert Verhagen

LONDON • NEW YORK • OXFORD • NEW DELHI • SYDNEY

T&T CLARK
Bloomsbury Publishing Plc
50 Bedford Square, London, WC1B 3DP, UK
1385 Broadway, New York, NY 10018, USA
29 Earlsfort Terrace, Dublin 2, Ireland

BLOOMSBURY, T&T CLARK and the T&T Clark logo are trademarks of
Bloomsbury Publishing Plc

First published in Great Britain 2021
Paperback edition published 2023

Copyright © Koert Verhagen, 2021

Koert Verhagen has asserted his right under the Copyright, Designs and
Patents Act, 1988, to be identified as Author of this work.

For legal purposes the Acknowledgments on pp. viii–ix constitute an extension of
this copyright page.

Cover image: bpk / Rotraut Forberg

All rights reserved. No part of this publication may be reproduced or transmitted
in any form or by any means, electronic or mechanical, including photocopying,
recording, or any information storage or retrieval system, without prior
permission in writing from the publishers.

Bloomsbury Publishing Plc does not have any control over, or responsibility for, any
third-party websites referred to or in this book. All internet addresses given in this
book were correct at the time of going to press. The author and publisher regret any
inconvenience caused if addresses have changed or sites have ceased to exist, but can
accept no responsibility for any such changes.

A catalogue record for this book is available from the British Library.

Library of Congress Cataloging-in-Publication Data
Names: Verhagen, Koert, author.
Title: Being and action Coram Deo : Bonhoeffer and the retrieval of justification's
social import / Koert Verhagen.
Description: London ; New York : T&T Clark 2021. | Series: T&T Clark new
studies in Bonhoeffer's theology and ethics | Includes bibliographical references. |
Identifiers: LCCN 2021011795 (print) | LCCN 2021011796 (ebook) | ISBN 9780567700193
(hardback) | ISBN 9780567703491 (paperback) | ISBN 9780567700209 (pdf) |
ISBN 9780567700216 (epub)
Subjects: LCSH: Bonhoeffer, Dietrich, 1906-1945. | Justification (Christian theology) |
Theological anthropology–Lutheran Church. | Christian ethics–Lutheran authors. | Lutheran
Church–Doctrines. | Church and social problems–Lutheran Church.
Classification: LCC BX4827.B57 V47 2021 (print) | LCC BX4827.B57 (ebook) |
DDC 234/.7–dc23
LC record available at https://lccn.loc.gov/2021011795
LC ebook record available at https://lccn.loc.gov/2021011796

ISBN: HB: 978-0-5677-0019-3
PB: 978-0-5677-0349-1
ePDF: 978-0-5677-0020-9
eBook: 978-0-5677-0021-6

Series: T&T Clark New Studies in Bonhoeffer's Theology and Ethics

Typeset by Deanta Global Publishing Services, Chennai, India

To find out more about our authors and books visit www.bloomsbury.com and
sign up for our newsletters.

To my wife, Diana, and my two boys, Everett and Duncan

CONTENTS

Acknowledgments	viii
INTRODUCTION	1
Chapter 1 BACKGROUNDING BONHOEFFER: MARTIN LUTHER ON JUSTIFICATION'S IMPORT FOR ANTHROPOLOGY	5
Chapter 2 JUSTIFIED IN CHRIST AND THE CHURCH: THE SHAPE OF BONHOEFFER'S EARLY ANTHROPOLOGY	27
Chapter 3 JUSTIFICATION AGAINST *WELTANSCHAUUNG*: BONHOEFFER'S EVALUATION OF COMPETING ANTHROPOLOGIES	51
Chapter 4 FROM ANTHROPOLOGY TO ETHICS: A PAULINE CASE FOR CONTINUITY IN BONHOEFFER	77
Chapter 5 JUSTIFICATION AND WITNESS-BEARING: DISCIPLESHIP AS EMBODIED PARTICIPATION IN CHRIST	93
Chapter 6 RECONCILING CHURCH AND WORLD: JUSTIFICATION'S COORDINATION OF THE ULTIMATE AND PENULTIMATE	123
Chapter 7 JUSTIFICATION AGAINST WHITE SUPREMACY: RETRIEVAL AS CRITICAL CORRECTIVE	139
Bibliography	157
Index	169

ACKNOWLEDGMENTS

A few years before he passed away, my grandpa, Arie Dirk Verhagen, let me raid his book collection. He was a medical doctor with a PhD in medicine, but in his free time he was also an avid reader of theology. In the stack of books I took from him was a 1966 mass market paperback edition of *The Cost of Discipleship*. I would not crack that book until several years later after finishing my undergraduate degree, but when I did it was the proverbial spark that, once fanned, became the fire that resulted in this book.

Of course, Bonhoeffer would have fallen on deaf ears if it were not for my parents, Mark and Becky Verhagen, who, from the start, faithfully taught me to love God, people, and the church. They did not bat an eye when I switched from majoring in biology to philosophy in college, which is indicative of their constant love, support, and encouragement over the years. Similarly crucial has been the support of my sisters, Lydia Honken and Linnea Rico (and their respective families). In addition, I owe a huge debt of gratitude to my in-laws, Keith and Tess Duncan.

I count myself fortunate to have an equally robust academic family tree. At Taylor University, I was privileged to learn from three excellent philosophy professors, Kevin Diller, Brad Seeman, and Jim Spiegel, who invested in me both personally and intellectually. Likewise, at Gordon-Conwell, Donna Petter instilled in me a love for the Old Testament, Gordon Isaac introduced me to Bonhoeffer's wider Lutheran context, and Patrick Smith inducted me into the world of analytic theology. Just as important as my formal education during these years was the informal education I received sharing life, and sometimes living quarters, with Russell Johnson, Sam McKnight, Andrew Jones; all excellent theologians in their own right, and even better friends.

I am particularly thankful for my time spent as part of the Logos Institute for Analytic and Exegetical Theology (University of St. Andrews), participating in the interdisciplinary conversations it fosters. Its concerns have challenged and shaped my thinking in important ways, making this book better than it would have been otherwise. This is due in large part to the tireless work of Alan and Andrew Torrance. Alan offered incisive and insightful comments on early drafts. Andrew graciously read and commented on anything and everything I sent him, never hesitant to challenge my thinking in the friendly confines of St Andrews pubs. I am also grateful to a number of colleagues, friends, and mentors: Oliver Crisp, Tom McCall, and Mike Rea, Joshua Cockayne, Simon Dürr, Kim Kroll, Christa McKirland, Jeremy Rios, Jonathan Rutledge, and Taylor Telford.

Many thanks to Sinead O'Connor and Anna Turton at T&T Clark for all their help in seeing this book through to publication. I am likewise indebted to Mike

Mawson, Phil Ziegler, and Jenny McBride for seeing something in this text and inviting me to submit it for inclusion in their monograph series. Mike and Phil, in particular, provided crucial feedback as I worked to transform this study from a thesis into a book.

Finally, I owe more to Diana than I could adequately express in writing. She has shouldered the brunt of my endless hours in the office with characteristic grace and fierce loyalty, even as she mothers Everett and Duncan while working full-time. I have been blown away that time and again throughout this process she has had strength enough for both of us. Along with our boys, she has provided the joy that made it easy to put limits on my work, which in turn made the work more enjoyable.

Acknowledgment of Published Material

Portions of this book, in an earlier form, appear in the following journal article:

Koert Verhagen. "Justified *ex nihilo*: Retrieving Creation for Theological Anthropology with Luther and Bonhoeffer." *International Journal of Systematic Theology* 21, no. 2 (2019): 199–216.

INTRODUCTION

In March 1928, Dietrich Bonhoeffer delivered his first sermon while serving as the vicar for a church-community of German ex-patriots living in Barcelona.[1] As his text, he selected Rom. 11:6—"But if it is by grace, it is no longer on the basis of works, otherwise grace would no longer be grace."[2] Within moments of launching into the sermon Bonhoeffer asks the following questions:

> Why should we be concerned with talk about justification by grace alone when there are so many other more important and more serious things to talk about? One hears such remarks everywhere today. Are they really right? Should we have gone beyond that which was so serious and important to Paul and to early Christianity, by virtue of the two thousand years separating us from that era?[3]

Bonhoeffer's rhetorical questions, like those of any good preacher, reflect his perception of his congregants' theological thought patterns. However, this is not to say that these questions merely reflect the theological zeitgeist of 1928. Indeed, fifty-six years later Oswald Bayer frames the plight of the doctrine of justification in a similar manner: "When the Pauline and Reformation doctrine of justification is passed on without being understood, when it has become merely an empty formula, then we need not be surprised that it is passed on with some embarrassment, and with an apologetic tone."[4] Fifteen years after Bayer penned those words, the Joint Declaration on the Doctrine of Justification, written collaboratively by delegates from the Catholic Church and the Lutheran World Federation, thrust the doctrine

---

1. Eberhard Bethge, *Dietrich Bonhoeffer: A Biography*, ed. Victoria Barnett, Rev. Ed. (Minneapolis, MN: Fortress Press, 2000), 116.
2. *DBWE* 10:480. In what follows, when Bonhoeffer's works provide a rendering of the text, we shall follow that. Otherwise, biblical citations will be drawn from the NRSV.
3. *DBWE* 10:480-481.
4. Oswald Bayer, *Living by Faith: Justification and Sanctification* (Grand Rapids, MI: Eerdmans, 2003), xi. Likewise, Ernst Käsemann notes that in 1963 the Lutheran World Federation declared justification irrelevant. His disdain is evident when he writes: "The World Federation should then have been dissolved as out of date." See "Justification and Freedom," in *On Being a Disciple of the Crucified Nazarene: Unpublished Lectures and Sermons*, ed. Rudolf Landau and Wolfgang Kraus, trans. Roy A. Harrisville (Grand Rapids, MI: Eerdmans, 2010), 52.

back into the theological limelight. At the same time, the New Perspective on Paul was peaking in the realm of New Testament Studies, offering fresh challenges to Reformation interpretations of justification. One might say, then, that justification is making a comeback, even if there is little clarity on what exactly is coming back under that nomenclature.[5]

Yet, there is at least one aspect of the doctrine of justification that has received surprisingly little attention from theologians in recent years: namely, its social implications. Perhaps one reason for this is the fact that the New Perspective has, at times, come close to reducing justification to its social implications by treating it solely in relation to the reconciliation of Jews and Gentiles within the church. Protestant theologians, then, have doubled down on the soteriological import and theological centrality of the justification of the sinner.[6] Insofar as this dynamic has played out, it is, indeed, a thoroughly unhelpful impasse. On the one hand, justification is reduced to its communal-ecclesial or ethical import, while on the other hand, it is relegated to the sphere of individual salvation and pure doctrine. Thus, a situation arises in which justification's social implications are either understood as the heart of the doctrine or are largely neglected.

The challenge, then, is to articulate the social implications of justification in a manner that bridges the gap between doctrine and ethics and between soteriology and social action, while preserving the integrity of both. In the present study, we shall take up this challenge in dialogue with Bonhoeffer's theology.[7] Recalling the

---

5. Of course, there are pockets of Protestants who might push back on this characterization, suggesting that we not call it a comeback.

6. The substance of this characterization is drawn from John G. Flett's insightful and well-argued article, "Justification Contra Mission: The Isolation of Justification in the History of Reconciliation," *Zeitschrift Für Dialektische Theologie* Supplement Series 6 (2014): 105–27. Protestant suspicion in relation to the New Perspective can also be linked back to its origins—namely, the Reformation. In its dispute with Rome, a deep suspicion of any association between justification and the ethical took root. To this effect, in a section of his systematics titled "Justification if Forensic, not Ethical," Herman Bavinck is careful to separate justification not only from any ethical presupposition (contra Rome), but also from too close an association with any ethical purpose or implication (*Reformed Dogmatics: Holy Spirit, Church, and New Creation*, ed. John Bolt, trans. John Vriend, vol. 4 [Grand Rapids, MI: Baker Academic, 2008], 204–9). In drawing the latter line, Bavinck is less decisive and more cautious. Yet, it still illustrates well how ethical implication and ethical presupposition might be problematically conflated in the Protestant imagination when it comes to justification by faith.

7. Only one other study has given sustained attention to something like the social implications of justification in Bonhoeffer's thought. Michael DeJonge's recent work, *Bonhoeffer on Resistance: The Word Against the Wheel* (Oxford: Oxford University Press, 2018), explores the political dimensions of Bonhoeffer's theology with special reference to the Lutheran provenance of his thought throughout. As such, justification plays an important role. However, DeJonge's method is primarily historical and his focus is expressly political-

aforementioned rhetorical questions he posed, the research that follows constitutes an attempt both to sketch the contours of his response to these questions and, ultimately, to provide an endorsement of it: "Most certainly not [*Ganz gewiß nicht*]; in fact quite the opposite is the case."[8] In this emphatic denial, Bonhoeffer marks himself as a theologian of justification, as we shall see in the first and second chapters. However, Bonhoeffer's thought is also particularly ripe for such a project because of the remarkable coherence between the life he lived and the words he wrote. Not only was he deeply committed to the truth that justification comes only by grace through faith, but his biography also demonstrates a consistent drive to express this truth concretely in the church and for the world.

For Bonhoeffer, Christian doctrine must bear witness to the living Christ who calls people to a specific form of life. The implication here is that doctrine is genuinely Christian only when it is christologically oriented and its concrete bearing on human existence is taken seriously. However, this is not to suggest that Bonhoeffer reduces doctrine to ethics. Indeed, Bonhoeffer would agree with Barth and Jüngel that "a theory of praxis stands in need of dogmatics, not ethics."[9] Thus, a basic assumption of this study is that Philip Ziegler is correct when he writes:

[B]eing disposed over by sin "in Adam" and being disposed over by grace "in Christ" represent two total determinations of human being and so also, for that same reason, of all thought and speech that would do justice to the truth of that being. They provide comprehensive rubrics under which all humanity—and so also all human moral knowing and acting—must be ranged and understood if *theological* understanding is our aim.[10]

theological, whereas the method of this thesis is theological and its focus is anthropological and ethical in nature. It is also worth mentioning Brian Gregor's *A Philosophical Anthropology of the Cross: The Cruciform Self* (Bloomington: Indiana University Press, 2013). Given that Gregor's presentation of a theological anthropology of the cross interacts extensively with Luther and Bonhoeffer, there are a number of similarities between his project and the first two chapters of this thesis, especially. However, Gregor's philosophical-theological method and the variety of interlocuters with whom he engages lead him to overlook key aspects of Bonhoeffer's theological anthropology which feature centrally in the present study, such as Bonhoeffer's real, historical dialectic.

8. *DBWE* 10:481; *DBW* 10:455. Translation altered.

9. Eberhard Jüngel, *Karl Barth: A Theological Legacy*, trans. Garrett E. Paul (Philadelphia, PA: Westminster Press, 1986), 96; cf. John Webster, "Justification, Analogy and Action: Barth and Luther in Jüngel's Anthropology," in *Barth's Moral Theology: Human Action in Barth's Thought* (Edinburgh: T&T Clark, 1998), 182–3.

10. Philip G. Ziegler, "'Completely Within God's Doing': Soteriology as Meta-Ethics in the Theology of Dietrich Bonhoeffer," in *Christ, Church, and World: New Studies in Bonhoeffer's Theology and Ethics*, ed. Michael Mawson and Philip G. Ziegler (London: Bloomsbury T&T Clark, 2016), 105.

Indeed, Ziegler's claim that soteriological considerations govern both Bonhoeffer's anthropology and his ethics points to the basic thematic structure of the thesis.

The study that follows will unfold in two overlapping parts which signal both development and continuity in Bonhoeffer's thought. The first part pertains primarily to anthropology and is the focus of the first three chapters. Here, we shall engage Bonhoeffer's early theology and indebtedness to Luther in order to suggest that justification fundamentally shapes his theological anthropology and, as such, informs his resistance to the *Weltanschauung* of National Socialism. Chapters 4 through 7 comprise the second part, marking a shift toward ethics. As such, they engage recent developments in Pauline theology as a framework for considering the continuity between Bonhoeffer's early theology and his later ethics of discipleship before turning to *Discipleship* and *Ethics* in order to consider how justification inflects his understanding of following after Christ in and for the world. Chapter 7, then, points suggestively to how reorienting the church to the social implications of justification by faith might play an important role in its confrontation of white supremacy.

Ultimately, the goal of this study is to consider an important way in which Bonhoeffer attempts to repeat the word which Christ speaks by the Holy Spirit, through Scripture, concerning justification by faith. Indeed, we shall see that by drawing on justification's social implications, Bonhoeffer offers fresh and vital insights regarding how the doctrine bears witness to the living Christ who calls to discipleship. To this end, Bonhoeffer's elaboration on his "*Ganz gewiß nicht*" in 1928 will set the tone as we begin:

> [O]ur first concern should be to take seriously, in fact, to take extremely seriously, what was once so important to Paul; and we will see that if there is anything at all on this earth that is not ultimately trivial or even comical, however seriously it may present itself, it is the fact of justification. This is so precisely to the extent it reveals God's honor and glory, God's seriousness and goodness. In it our gaze is opened to the entire world, to that which is vain and to that which is serious in that world; in it we understand both ourselves and . . . our God.[11]

---

11. *DBWE* 10:481.

Chapter 1

BACKGROUNDING BONHOEFFER

MARTIN LUTHER ON JUSTIFICATION'S IMPORT FOR ANTHROPOLOGY

I Introduction

Given Bonhoeffer's own intellectual formation, the question of the role of justification in his theology inevitably sends one back to Luther. Indeed, several recent studies have convincingly demonstrated the impossibility of properly understanding Bonhoeffer's theology apart from Luther, who, along with Paul, formed the theological vein in which Bonhoeffer sought to establish himself.[1] Beyond serving as Bonhoeffer's theological baseline, Luther also formulated his theological anthropology explicitly with reference to justification. This is more than can be said for Bonhoeffer, who, although clearly motivated by anthropological considerations, never outlines a theological anthropology as such. Thus, Luther's way of construing anthropology in terms of justification does not simply form an important explanatory backdrop against which Bonhoeffer's anthropology should be understood. Indeed, it also presents a framework within which to interpret the anthropological subtext of Bonhoeffer's early theological writings.[2] The following discussion will begin with a brief consideration of the case for Luther as Bonhoeffer's primary theological influence, before turning to consider how justification shapes what it means to be human in Luther's theology. This will provide a framework for assessing the extent to which justification constitutes a controlling anthropological concept in Bonhoeffer's own thought in the next chapter.

---

1. H. Gaylon Barker, *The Cross of Reality: Luther's Theologia Crucis and Bonhoeffer's Christology* (Minneapolis, MN: Fortress Press, 2015); Michael P. DeJonge, *Bonhoeffer's Reception of Luther* (New York/Oxford: Oxford University Press, 2017); Wolf Krötke, "Dietrich Bonhoeffer and Martin Luther," in *Bonhoeffer's Intellectual Formation: Theology and Philosophy in His Thought*, ed. Peter Frick (Tübingen: Mohr Siebeck, 2008), 53–82.

2. Following Clifford Green, Bonhoeffer's early theology is understood here as the period between 1927 and 1933. See Clifford J. Green, *Bonhoeffer: A Theology of Sociality*, Rev. Ed. (Grand Rapids, MI: Eerdmans, 1999), 4–7.

II Luther as Theological Influence on Bonhoeffer

To claim a significant role for Martin Luther in the shaping of Dietrich Bonhoeffer's theology is relatively uncontroversial. Yet, generally speaking, Bonhoeffer's interaction with dialectical theology, especially that of Karl Barth, has ruled the day in terms of exploration of his thought.[3] Perhaps this is partially due to the fact that it seems self-evident that Bonhoeffer—as a German Lutheran who was trained in the Luther Renaissance by the likes of Karl Holl and Reinhold Seeberg—bears the mark of Luther. If this is the case then it may be that Luther's influence on Bonhoeffer has often simply been assumed in Anglophone scholarship.[4] Whatever the case may be, a number of recent studies have emerged in English which demonstrate persuasively that Luther plays a central role in shaping Bonhoeffer's theology.[5] We shall comment briefly here on only three of them in order to confirm the legitimacy of reading Bonhoeffer's theology against the background of Luther's influence.

In a recent monograph, Michael DeJonge advances the twofold claim that first, "Bonhoeffer thought his theology was Lutheran" and second, that "he was justified in thinking so."[6] As such, DeJonge's work largely aids in locating Bonhoeffer firmly within the Lutheran confessional tradition, even if his participation in it was often creative in nature.[7] This, however, does not entail a reduction of all aspects of Bonhoeffer's theology to his Lutheran heritage. Rather, it grounds Bonhoeffer's

---

3. See, for example, Christiane Tietz, *Theologian of Resistance: The Life and Thought of Dietrich Bonhoeffer*, trans. Victoria Barnett (Minneapolis, MN: Fortress Press, 2016), 10. Here, Tietz acknowledges the significant influence that Luther had on Bonhoeffer but subordinates it to that of Barth.

4. German scholarship has been more explicit about the connection. See Klaus Grünwaldt, Christiane Tietz, and Udo Hahn, eds., *Bonhoeffer Und Luther: Zentrale Themen Ihrer Theologie* (Hannover: Amt der VELKD, 2007); Hans-Walter Krumwiede, *Glaubenszuversicht Und Weltgestaltung Bei Martin Luther: Mit Einem Ausblick Auf Dietrich Bonhoeffer* (Göttingen: Vandenhoeck & Ruprecht, 1983); Christian Gremmels, ed., *Bonhoeffer Und Luther: Zur Sozialgestalt Des Luthertums in Der Moderne* (München: C. Kaiser, 1983). However, in 2007, Kirsten Busch Nielsen noted the relative lack of attention to the connections between Luther and Bonhoeffer even in the German sphere ("Sünde," in *Bonhoeffer Und Luther: Zentrale Themen Ihrer Theologie*, ed. Klaus Grünwaldt, Christiane Tietz, and Udo Hahn [Hannover: Amt der VELKD, 2007], 111).

5. This need not conflict with or undercut claims regarding the significant impact that Barth, Harnack, etc. had on Bonhoeffer. However, it may, indeed, relativize certain aspects of those claims.

6. DeJonge, *Bonhoeffer's Reception of Luther*, 7. See also DeJonge's prior work on the role of Bonhoeffer's Lutheran self-understanding in *Act and Being* specifically, in Michael P. DeJonge, *Bonhoeffer's Theological Formation: Berlin, Barth, and Protestant Theology* (New York/Oxford: Oxford University Press, 2012).

7. DeJonge, *Bonhoeffer's Reception of Luther*, 8.

thinking in such a way as to suggest "that interpretations that forget about Luther's importance for Bonhoeffer tend toward misinterpretation."⁸ Thus, although DeJonge does not specifically address Bonhoeffer's anthropology—instead, he primarily focuses on defending Bonhoeffer's Christological appropriation of Luther's two kingdoms theology—his account implies that a proper understanding of it must take Luther's influence into consideration.⁹

Second, H. Gaylon Barker's *The Cross of Reality* explores the relationship between Bonhoeffer and Luther in terms of Christology and the *theologia crucis*. Like DeJonge, Barker is careful to note the dynamic nature of Luther's importance for Bonhoeffer, asserting: "Bonhoeffer's goal was not simply to replicate Luther's theology; however, what he finds in Luther is the key to unlocking the church's witness for this new time."¹⁰ According to Barker, then, one must read Bonhoeffer's Christocentrism with Luther in the background, yet always in a way that foregrounds Bonhoeffer's commitment to the importance of the church's concrete proclamation in the present.

Barker offers particularly convincing evidence for the connection between Bonhoeffer and Luther when he recounts comments made by Eberhard Bethge and Gerhard Ebeling in personal conversations he had with them. Bethge, Bonhoeffer's best friend and biographer, notes the compulsion Bonhoeffer felt in relation to Luther when he suggests: "Bonhoeffer had to find his own Luther."¹¹ Ebeling, a student of Bonhoeffer's at the preacher's seminary in Finkenwalde and a prominent Luther scholar in his own right, speaks to the deep, theological affinity between Bonhoeffer and Luther when he comments: "In my heart, I believe Bonhoeffer and Luther are one."¹² Barker elaborates further on his conversation with Ebeling, writing: "[He] believed it was Bonhoeffer's intention to 're-win' Luther over against the interpretations of the nineteenth century and of his time to come to the original Luther."¹³

Third and, finally, although Wolf Krötke's essay on Luther's presence in Bonhoeffer's theology is considerably shorter than the aforementioned monographs, he makes a concise and powerful argument for the importance of understanding Bonhoeffer in light of Luther. Rather than consolidating Bonhoeffer's dependence on Luther thematically, as DeJonge and Barker do, Krötke moves systematically through core tenets of Bonhoeffer's theology—Scripture, Christology, sin, justification and sanctification, ethics, and temptation. In doing so, he ranges across

---

8. DeJonge, *Bonhoeffer's Reception of Luther*, 11.
9. Dejonge treats Bonhoeffer's theological anthropology in a more substantive manner in an earlier work, but does not specifically consider it in relation to Luther's justification-inflected construal. See DeJonge, *Bonhoeffer's Theological Formation*, 56–82.
10. Barker, *The Cross of Reality*, 3.
11. Barker, *The Cross of Reality*, 18; cf. Eberhard Bethge, *Dietrich Bonhoeffer: A Biography*, ed. Victoria Barnett, Rev. Ed. (Minneapolis, MN: Fortress Press, 2000), 54.
12. Barker, *The Cross of Reality*, 18.
13. Barker, *The Cross of Reality*, 18–19.

Bonhoeffer's works, showing how Luther's influence shapes every theme. Krötke is honest about where Bonhoeffer departs from Luther, not shying away from identifying where Bonhoeffer's departures were less than successful. However, like DeJonge and Barker, he asserts that "Bonhoeffer considered [Luther] an authority with whom he desires to be in agreement even and especially when he goes beyond him . . . His orientation towards Luther's theology evidently constituted for him the objective orientation of the Protestant Church and theology as such."[14] Unlike DeJonge, Krötke balks at locating Bonhoeffer within Lutheran confessionalism, citing both his resistance to the Luther offered him by his Berlin professors and the freedom exercised in his incorporation of Luther into his theology. In light of this freedom, Krötke concludes his essay modestly, claiming that in Bonhoeffer "we often encounter Luther. In Bonhoeffer's theology and life we encounter—far from any Luther cult or Lutheran confessionalism—the heartbeat of one who has a living, Reformed faith in the midst of difficult circumstances."[15]

DeJonge, Barker, and Krötke all substantively ground their respective studies in Bonhoeffer's works, giving special attention to the way in which he was shaped by the so-called Luther Renaissance.[16] Yet, it is clear that Bonhoeffer relentlessly sought the "real" Luther, rather than settling for the one presented by Holl, Seeberg, Althaus, and others. Even so, Bonhoeffer had little interest in presenting "a harmonious 'picture of Luther.'"[17] Rather, "for him, Luther—who himself rejected such a picture—represented an unparalleled theological, intellectual, and spiritual impulse and source for his own experiences of faith and reality."[18]

From these studies, it might seem that the flexibility with which Bonhoeffer incorporated Luther's theological insights conflicts with the assertion that he sought the "original Luther." However, Bonhoeffer himself provides the key to reconciling these two apparently contradictory lines of thinking in *Letters and Papers from Prison*. There, in a letter to his parents on October 31, 1943, he writes: "Already one hundred years ago Kierkegaard said that Luther today would say the opposite of what he said back then. I think this is true—*cum grano salis*."[19] By this Bonhoeffer does not mean that he thinks Luther would abandon his core

---

14. Krötke, "Dietrich Bonhoeffer and Martin Luther," 53–4.

15. Krötke, "Dietrich Bonhoeffer and Martin Luther," 82.

16. For a definition of the Luther Renaissance, see James M. Stayer, *Martin Luther, German Saviour: German Evangelical Theological Factions and the Interpretation of Luther, 1917-1933* (Montreal and Kingston: McGill-Queen's University Press, 2000), 151n41. Although Stayer defines the Luther Renaissance in terms of the Holl school, over the course of the study he demonstrates the ways in which it resists strict definition.

17. Krötke, "Dietrich Bonhoeffer and Martin Luther," 57.

18. Krötke, "Dietrich Bonhoeffer and Martin Luther," 57.

19. *DBWE* 8:173. This signals Bonhoeffer's awareness of Luther's historical situatedness and as such, serves to further separate him from the Luther Renaissance, which tended to read Luther's theology as the logical unfolding of pure idea. On this, see Stayer, *Martin Luther, German Saviour*, 39.

doctrinal insights, but, rather, that his application of those insights would differ markedly. Thus, in Bonhoeffer's mind, faithfully retrieving the "original Luther" for the sake of the church in the present would, at times, necessarily entail taking up and articulating Luther's core insights in a highly flexible manner. Viewed in this way, slavish adherence to Luther and Lutheranism is, paradoxically, infidelity to Luther. As such, any account of Luther's influence on Bonhoeffer must move beyond sketching corresponding thoughts and ideas to a further articulation of what exactly Bonhoeffer does with those thoughts and ideas in order to put them to theological work for the church situation of his time.

Before moving on to consider Luther's treatment of justification by faith alone as an anthropological concept, it is worth noting that not only are DeJonge, Barker, and Krötke unified in identifying Luther as Bonhoeffer's theological baseline, but all three also identify the fundamental importance of Luther's doctrine of justification for understanding Bonhoeffer's theology. For DeJonge, if Bonhoeffer is, indeed, to be considered within Lutheran confessionalism then his definition of Lutheranism "is focused on justification, a particular account of the person of Christ, and the church community, where the last is defined both in terms of Christ's presence and the correlative concept of the preached and heard word."[20] Giving special attention to the role of the doctrine of justification in *Act and Being* and *Discipleship*, DeJonge concludes that justification is key to the structure of Bonhoeffer's theology.[21] Likewise, Barker asserts that, for Bonhoeffer, "the central theological question was that of justification, which, out of necessity, is tied to Christology, for salvation comes through Christ alone."[22] Finally, Krötke simply states that "Bonhoeffer gained his theological framework and categories from Luther's doctrine of justification."[23] Indeed, far from a static, theological substratum, Bonhoeffer's theological work was driven by the doctrine of justification in a comprehensive manner.[24]

---

20. DeJonge, *Bonhoeffer's Reception of Luther*, 10.
21. DeJonge, *Bonhoeffer's Reception of Luther*, 259.
22. Barker, *The Cross of Reality*, 74.
23. Krötke, "Dietrich Bonhoeffer and Martin Luther," 57. Krötke also suggests that Barth's theology at the time received its primary impetus from Luther's doctrine of justification, thereby keeping the lines between Bonhoeffer and Barth tight without undermining the centrality of Luther's thought for Bonhoeffer. Although literature on their relationship has grown considerably in recent years, the best treatment of Barth's influence on Bonhoeffer remains Andreas Pangritz, *Karl Barth in the Theology of Dietrich Bonhoeffer* (Grand Rapids, MI: Eerdmans, 2000).
24. Krötke, "Dietrich Bonhoeffer and Martin Luther," 71–2. For an attempt to substantiate this in the context of Bonhoeffer's entire body of work, see Hans Pfeifer, "The Forms of Justification: On the Question of the Structure in Dietrich Bonhoeffer's Theology," in *A Bonhoeffer Legacy: Essays in Understanding*, ed. A. J. Klassen (Grand Rapids, MI: Eerdmans, 1981), 14–47.

To sum up, it is clear that Luther looms in Bonhoeffer's theology as a dominant presence, especially in terms of Bonhoeffer's devotion to Luther's *solus Christus*.[25] Indeed, Krötke describes it as the "fundamental and crucial aspect in which Bonhoeffer was always in agreement with Luther."[26] Part and parcel of inheriting Luther's Christological priority, Bonhoeffer also adopted his emphasis on justification by faith as doctrinally central and basic. Although Bonhoeffer exercised freedom in his translation of Luther for his present context, these two aspects retain their primacy throughout. Just as Christology and justification are two sides of the same coin for Luther, so too are they for Bonhoeffer.[27] Given this connection it follows that, where Bonhoeffer grounds aspects of his theology christologically, one might also then reasonably inquire as to what work justification is doing for Bonhoeffer in that context.[28] It is this line of inquiry that we shall pursue in relation to the role of justification in Bonhoeffer's christologically oriented anthropology. However, we must first consider the anthropological significance that Luther attributes to justification in his own theology.

III Luther on Justification

Luther's ability to employ justification as an anthropological concept follows from his expansive vision for the doctrine. In turn, this scope stems both from Luther's theological convictions concerning Scripture and his own, powerful experience of being set free by this fundamental Pauline doctrine.[29] Later in his life Luther famously recounts the "before" and "after" of his pivotal "discovery" of justification by faith:

> I hated the word "righteousness of God," which, according to the use and custom of all the teachers, I had been taught to understand philosophically regarding the formal or active righteousness, as they call it, with which God is righteous and

---

25. See Marc Lienhard's insistence that, for Luther, justification and the *solus Christus* are "Two Faces of the Same Reality," in *Luther, Witness to Jesus Christ: Stages and Themes of the Reformer's Christology*, trans. Edwin H. Robertson (Minneapolis, MN: Augsburg Publishing House, 1982), 271.

26. Krötke, "Dietrich Bonhoeffer and Martin Luther," 56.

27. Barker, *The Cross of Reality*, 97.

28. Cf. Jonathan D. Sorum's argument that justification by faith provides a mediatorial framework within which to read the relationship between Christology and ethics in "Bonhoeffer's Early Interpretation of Luther as the Source of His Basic Theological Paradigm," *Fides et Historia* 29, no. 2 (1997): 35–51.

29. On the relationship between textual reasoning and personal experience, specifically in relation to Luther's anthropology, see Notger Slenczka, "Luther's Anthropology," in *The Oxford Handbook of Martin Luther's Theology*, ed. Robert Kolb, Irene Dingel, and Ľubomír Batka (Oxford: Oxford University Press, 2014), 214.

punishes the unrighteous sinner. . . . Nevertheless, I beat importunately upon Paul at that place, most ardently desiring to know what St. Paul wanted. At last, by the mercy of God . . . I began to understand that the righteousness of God is that by which the righteous lives by a gift of God, namely by faith. And this is the meaning: the righteousness of God is revealed by the gospel, namely, the passive righteousness with which merciful God justifies us by faith, as it is written, "He who through faith is righteous shall live." *Here I felt that I was altogether born again and had entered paradise itself through open gates.*[30]

Following this powerful, existential realization, Luther reports that he mentally began to scan through Scripture and found it to be in perfect alignment with the aforementioned understanding of God's righteousness and justification. Thus, for Luther, the centrality of justification was affirmed both textually and existentially.[31] Yet, even "centrality" as a descriptor falls short of Luther's comprehensive vision for and employment of justification. For Luther justification by faith is not merely central, but also foundational, like the keystone in an arch. Apart from justification, theology and the church will crumble.

This raises the question as to how exactly Luther understands justification, especially given its primacy in his thought. Yet, it is one that is virtually impossible to answer tidily. By most accounts, a simple definition might go something like this: justification is God's gracious gift of faith by which the human person receives or participates in the passive, alien righteousness of Christ.[32] However, for Luther, the import of this simple definition unfolds in such a way as to make it relevant for all aspects of theology and doctrine. Thus, Wolfhart Pannenberg writes: "There is no unanimity in evangelical theology itself concerning the particularity and meaning of the doctrine of justification. There is not 'the' Reformation doctrine of justification, nor is there even 'the' Lutheran doctrine of justification. There are more than a half-dozen of them."[33] Likewise, even as Olli-Pekka Vainio seeks to provide a unified articulation of the Lutheran doctrine of justification, he must acknowledge the existence of at least five models which had already emerged by 1580.[34] This variation is not solely the fault of those who followed after Luther, but is simply a consequence of Luther's theology itself. Affirming this, Bernard

---

30. *LW* 34:336–7. Emphasis added.

31. Klaus Schwarzwäller speaks of Luther's use of justification as a leading into Scripture and reality in "Justification and Reality," *Lutheran Quarterly* 24, no. 3 (2010): 292–3.

32. Cf. theses 27–9 of Luther's "The Disputation Concerning Justification" in *LW* 34:153.

33. Wolfhart Pannenberg, "Hintergründe Des Streites Um Die Rechtfertigungslehre in Der Evangelischen Theologie," vol. 3 (Bayirsche Akademie der Wissenschaften Philosophisch-Historische Klasse, München: Verlag der Bayerischen Akademie der Wissenschaften, 2000), 3.

34. See Olli-Pekka Vainio, *Justification and Participation in Christ: The Development of the Lutheran Doctrine of Justification from Luther to the Formula of Concord (1580)* (Leiden/Boston: Brill, 2008), 223–7.

Lohse writes: "One significant conclusion to be drawn is that for Luther the doctrine of justification did not involve some sort of definition or formula.... Any description of Luther's doctrine must guard against . . . summarizing it in mere formulas, however carefully defined."[35] This has led some Lutheran scholars to refer to justification as a meta-doctrine.[36] Indeed, Oswald Bayer asserts that "[t]he theme of justification is not one theme among many. It has principal significance. It touches on every theme. Justification concerns not merely one's own history, not only world history, but also natural history. It has to do with everything."[37]

Contrary to the expansive theological vision Luther maintained for the doctrine, treatments of justification often reflect the calcifying effects, post-Luther, of positioning justification within an *ordo salutis*.[38] When viewed in this way justification's soteriological implications are reduced to matters of personal salvation and relativized as such. While this certainly has the effect of making it a more manageable theological concept—one that is easier to define and situate in the context of a systematic theology—it comes at the expense of the scope and impact which Luther attributed to the doctrine. Thus, it might seem that doing justice to the role of justification in Luther's theology is inimical to the task of providing a formal definition of that doctrine.[39] In this way a sort of impasse is

---

35. Bernhard Lohse, *Martin Luther's Theology: Its Historical and Systematic Development*, ed. and trans. Roy A. Harrisville (Minneapolis, MN: Fortress Press, 1999), 259–60. See also Oswald Bayer, *Martin Luther's Theology: A Contemporary Interpretation*, trans. Thomas H. Trapp (Grand Rapids, MI: Eerdmans, 2008), xvii.

36. Mark Mattes, "Luther on Justification as Forensic and Effective," in *The Oxford Handbook of Martin Luther's Theology*, ed. Ľubomír Batka, Irene Dingel, and Robert Kolb (Oxford: Oxford University Press, 2014), 270. For what is, perhaps, a preferable construal, see Jonathan Linebaugh's work on justification as the "grammar of the gospel" in "The Gr,ammar of the Gospel: Justification as a Theological Criterion in the Reformation and in Paul's Letter to the Galatians," *Scottish Journal of Theology* 71, no. 3 (2018): 287–307.

37. Oswald Bayer, *Living by Faith: Justification and Sanctification* (Grand Rapids, MI: Eerdmans, 2003), xi.

38. Bayer, *Martin Luther's Theology*, 242. Bayer notes that although Luther's Small Catechism incorporates some aspects of the *ordo salutis*, it refrains from organizing them in a temporal sequence, instead preferring to attribute them to the unified, justifying action of the Holy Spirit.

39. This challenge is implied in the editor's introduction to Luther's "The Disputation Concerning Justification," which begins: "Though Luther was not a theological systematizer in the manner of Melanchthon or Calvin, he recognized that all aspects of evangelical theology were related to the one article of faith by which the church stands or falls" (Helmut T. Lehmann, "Editor's Introduction to the Disputation Concerning Justification," in *Luther's Works: Career of the Reformer IV* [Philadelphia, PA: Fortress Press, 1960], 147). The lack of clarity then seems to stem from the fact that, rather than systematically sketching how the doctrine of justification is central, Luther shows its centrality by bringing it to bear on most, if not all, doctrinal issues.

formed between the desiderata of clarity and the breadth and power with which Luther interpreted the doctrine of justification, the danger being that justification becomes so nebulous that it is reduced to an "empty formula . . . passed on with some embarrassment, and with an apologetic tone."[40]

Yet, this impasse is hardly irresolvable. After all, Lohse points out: "Only by a strict orientation to the subject matter does the oft-asserted principle apply that a link to the doctrine of justification must always be forged when evaluating separate questions of doctrine in Luther. When this does not occur, Luther's position is caricatured."[41] What he means by this is that justification assumes different articulations and inflections depending on the doctrinal subject matter to which it is linked. Thus, something approaching a total form of clarity might be achieved only via a comprehensive treatment of justification as it relates to the massive web of doctrinal content with which Luther dealt. However, this falls outside the scope of this project. Rather, the goal of this chapter is to achieve clarity on the manner in which justification shapes and grounds Luther's theological anthropology. In this way, the myriad other doctrines with which Luther linked justification can, for the most part, be left to the side. We shall then be able to approach some sort of clarity on justification's implications for anthropology, if not justification as a meta-doctrine.

Before moving on to more specifically anthropological considerations, we must note two possible ways of construing Luther's doctrine of justification which have been the subject of much recent debate—that is, the relationship between forensic and effective models.[42] On the one hand, Lutheranism has traditionally construed justification in strongly forensic terms. Since Luther, this forensic emphasis on the imputation of an alien righteousness has become tightly bound up with law court imagery as a means to demonstrate its mechanisms and significance. However, some critics have responded to such a construal of justification, labeling it a legal fiction. Although a full treatment of this complex topic falls outside of the scope of this study, two things are worth noting. First, legal language pertaining to justification seems to be a contribution of Lutheranism—especially Melanchthon—rather than Luther himself. Thus, Alister McGrath notes: "Whereas Luther consistently employed images and categories of personal relationship to describe the union of the believer and Christ, Melanchthon increasingly employed images and categories drawn from the sphere of Roman law."[43] As such, a retrieval of Luther's doctrine need not entail the granting of priority to law court imagery. Second, although law court imagery is hardly an essential aspect of Luther's doctrine of justification, the

---

40. Bayer, *Living by Faith*, xi.
41. Lohse, *Martin Luther's Theology*, 260.
42. On the tension between the Luther Renaissance and Dialectical Theology as a precursor to more recent debates, see Stayer, *Martin Luther, German Saviour*, 122.
43. Alister E. McGrath, Iustitia Dei, *A History of the Christian Doctrine of Justification*, vol. 2 (Cambridge: Cambridge University Press, 1986), 24. See also Vainio, *Justification and Participation in Christ*, 17.

presence of a forensic element is indisputable, so one cannot easily minimize or dismiss it.

On the other hand, however, unitive understandings of the atonement and soteriology have recently begun to ascend to theological pride of place. As such, Luther's account of justification has been pressed on whether it can adequately account for the effective or transformative aspects of justification. Again, one must give careful attention to where Luther ends and Lutheranism begins. Indeed, just as Luther's use of legal terminology tends to be overstated, so too is his focus on the extrinsic nature of justification at the expense of all else. McGrath notes that, while Luther never gives up on the extrinsic nature of imputed righteousness, he is also staunchly committed to the fact that "Christ is nonetheless really present within the believer, effecting his renovation and regeneration."[44] For Luther, Christ's mediatorial presence is an essential component of justification, and in this way he reflects the unitive emphasis of the Swiss reformers. Yet, this often goes unacknowledged since Lutheranism quickly abandoned this aspect of Luther's thought.[45] Thus, McGrath can say that, regarding the Christological dimension of justification, "the Reformed school is considerably closer to Luther (especially 1525 Luther) than Lutheranism."[46]

The recent contributions of Tuomo Mannermaa and the Finnish school of Luther interpretation, while contested, are helpful insofar as they have served to re-emphasize the centrality of union with Christ in Luther's understanding of justification. In his assessment of Luther's theology, Mannermaa asserts that its central idea is "that in faith human beings *really* participate in the person of Christ, and in the divine life and victory that comes with him. Or, to say it the other way around: Christ gives his person to us through faith. 'Faith' means participation in Christ, in whom there is no sin, death, or curse."[47] By way of this summary statement, the Finnish school—following Mannermaa—is attempting to counteract what they perceive as a one-sided emphasis on the forensic aspect of justification in the Lutheran tradition. Via an accent on the justificatory centrality of participation, Mannermaa identifies the striking similarity between Luther's doctrine of justification and Eastern Orthodoxy's emphasis on divinization. This is, he believes, not only more accurate to Luther's theology, but it also better accounts for the effective and transformative dimensions of justification.

However, while the Finnish school has been embraced by some prominent Lutheran theologians, like Robert Jenson and Carl Braaten,[48] others maintain it

---

44. McGrath, Iustitia Dei, 2:14; cf. *LW* 26:129.

45. See Tuomo Mannermaa, *Christ Present in Faith: Luther's View of Justification*, ed. Kirsi Irmeli Stjerna (Minneapolis: Fortress Press, 2005), 4. Mannermaa attributes this turn of events to the influence of Melanchthon.

46. McGrath, Iustitia Dei, 2:51.

47. Mannermaa, *Christ Present in Faith*, 16.

48. See their co-edited volume, *Union with Christ: The New Finnish Interpretation of Luther* (Grand Rapids, MI: Eerdmans, 1998).

sets up a false dichotomy between the forensic and effective aspects of justification. Reflecting the latter position, Robert Kolb suggests "that such attempts are both historically inaccurate and theologically unnecessary" since "the more 'forensic' Luther's teaching becomes, the more 'effective' it is, because nothing can be more real than that which God's word declares."[49] What exactly Kolb means by this is not entirely clear. His point seems to be, however, that by overstating the ontological reality of union with Christ, the Finnish school has simultaneously identified an important aspect of Luther's doctrine of justification (union) while obscuring another (declaration and imputation).

As stated earlier, an adjudication of the forensic/effective debate is beside the point of this study. However, the shape of the debate provides helpful context when seeking to evaluate how Bonhoeffer draws on Luther in relation to anthropology and justification. As we seek to show the ways in which Bonhoeffer takes up Luther's justification-based anthropology, we shall do so with an eye to how he, at different times and in different ways, accents both the forensic and the participative dimensions of justification by faith. Furthermore, an awareness of where the accent falls for Bonhoeffer will prove important in Chapter 4 when we turn to consider the manner in which he draws on the participative element in Paul's articulation of justification, incorporating it into his theology of discipleship.

IV Luther on Justification's Import for Anthropology

In his commentary on Psalm 51, Luther provides the following definition of theology: "The proper subject of theology is man guilty of sin and condemned, and God the Justifier and Savior of man the sinner. Whatever is asked or discussed in theology outside this subject, is error and poison."[50] This definition yields two important insights into Luther's understanding of the theological task. First, it is clear that Luther's approach foregrounds the human being's place in the task of theology, setting her in relation to God and marking this relationship as the subject matter of theology. Second, rather than attributing an independent importance to humanity, Luther uses the adjectives "justifying" and "sinning" to qualify God and humanity, respectively. In this way, he defines exactly the sort of relationship between God and humanity with which theology is concerned. As such, the connection between anthropology and justification is not an unfortunate side effect of his fixation on the doctrine of justification. Rather, it is a natural entailment of Luther's basic understanding of the theological endeavor.[51] Indeed, theology cannot be abstracted from its soteriological framing.

---

49. Robert Kolb, *Martin Luther: Confessor of the Faith* (Oxford: Oxford University Press, 2009), 128.
50. *LW* 12:311.
51. Cf. Bayer, *Martin Luther's Theology*, 37–9.

Far from being a later development, Luther's interpretation of justification as an anthropological concept is foundational to his early understanding of justification as such.[52] However, his fullest and most direct articulation of a justificatory anthropology occurs in the aptly titled *The Disputation Concerning Man* (hereafter, *DCM*), given in 1536. It is this disputation that will serve as the basis for our discussion here.[53] In *DCM*, Luther articulates three aspects of the human being which theology must hold firm, framing them in terms of the dispute between philosophy and theology.[54] Bayer notes that "[w]ith masterful conciseness Luther formulated the following theses concerning these three aspects in one single Latin sentence":[55]

> 21. Namely, that man is a creature of God consisting of body and a living soul, made in the beginning after the image of God, without sin, so that he should procreate and rule over the created things, and never die.
>
> 22. But after the fall of Adam, certainly, he was subject to the power of the devil, sin and death, a twofold evil for his powers, unconquerable and eternal.
>
> 23. He can be freed and given eternal life only through the Son of God, Jesus Christ (if he believes in him).[56]

Thus, for Luther, the human being is simultaneously one who is created, fallen, and reconciled through Jesus Christ alone. While these are obviously not mutually

---

52. McGrath, Iustitia Dei, 12. For a concise and helpful assessment of how Luther grows and changes as a theologian throughout his career, see Gordon Rupp, "*Miles Emeritus?* Continuity and Discontinuity Between the Young and the Old Luther," in *Luther: Theologian for Catholics and Protestants*, ed. George Yule (Edinburgh: T&T Clark, 1985), 75–86.

53. Although it is only a small slice of Luther's massive corpus, there is precedent for such an approach since no less a Luther scholar than Gerhard Ebeling devoted three volumes to this one disputation, with the third volume expanding to the point where it practically became a summary of Luther's theology. See Gerhard Ebeling, *Die Theologische Definition Des Menschen: Kommentar Zu These 20-40*, vol. 2:3, Lutherstudien (Tübingen: Mohr Siebeck, 1989). See also Eberhard Jüngel's development of a justification-based anthropology in "On Becoming Truly Human: The Significance of the Reformation Distinction Between Person and Works for the Self-Understanding of Modern Humanity," in *Theological Essays II*, ed. J. B. Webster, trans. Arnold Neufeldt-Fast and J. B. Webster (Edinburgh: T&T Clark, 1995), 216–40.

54. Theses 1 to 19 deal with philosophy, while 20 to 40 pertain to theology. For an overview of the relationship between theology and philosophy in Luther's wider theological work, see Lienhard, *Luther, Witness to Jesus Christ*, 346–9.

55. Bayer, *Martin Luther's Theology*, 154.

56. LW 34:138. On the way in which Bonhoeffer takes up these three theses in his assessment of Christian community in *Sanctorum Communio*, see Michael Mawson, "Theology and Social Theory: Reevaluating Bonhoeffer's Approach," *Theology Today* 71, no. 1 (2014): 76–7.

exclusive categories—indeed, Luther's *simul justus et peccator* testifies to this fact—neither should they be confused or conflated. According to Luther this is the great error of philosophy, since it supposes, under the auspices of reason, "that natural things have remained untainted after the fall."[57] It follows that, if natural faculties remain intact after the fall, then those faculties are not in need of Christ's redemption, and it is thereby possible to view the human solely through the lens of creation.[58] Thus, while Luther believes that it is necessary to take the human being's status as creature seriously—we shall see later that, for Luther, creation itself is a justificatory event—he also thinks that sin is a total reality for which justification by faith is the only remedy. As such, Luther gives his concise definition of the human person in *DCM*'s thirty-second thesis, provocatively asserting that Paul's formulation in Romans 3:28 "briefly sums up the definition of man, saying, 'man is justified by faith.'"[59] Despite the simplicity of the definition, there is much to unpack here, so in what follows we shall examine both the ontological and the epistemological dimensions of these central claims from *DCM*.

a The Ontological Dimension

Oswald Bayer offers the following interpretation of *DCM*'s thirty-second thesis: "What is fundamental anthropologically and ontologically, since [the thesis] states the essence of a human, his actual *being*, is that he can be justified only by faith."[60] The ontological assumption here, then, is that humans are created in such a way as to require justification and the corresponding means by which this requirement is met is faith. As such, being human does not necessarily entail that one *is* justified by faith in actuality. Neither does it mean that only those who are justified by faith in actuality are human. Rather, it means that human existence requires justification which only faith can provide.

The danger at this point is to suppose that, for Luther, God creates humans incomplete, with a soteriological void which needs to be filled. By interpreting the doctrine of creation in terms of justification by faith, however, Luther's definition of the human in *DCM* corresponds to a creational reality which, on account of sin, must be soteriologically recapitulated.[61] Although it certainly does not shape the

---

57. *LW* 34:139.

58. *LW* 12:308.

59. *LW* 34:139. Bayer helpfully suggests the following translation, which is a bit more clear in light of the definitional nature of Luther's thesis: "The human being is human in that he is justified by faith." Bayer, *Martin Luther's Theology*, 155.

60. Bayer, *Martin Luther's Theology*, 100.

61. Robert Kolb, "Luther's View of Being Human: The Relationship of God and His Human Creatures as the Core of Wittenberg Anthropology," *Word & World* 37, no. 4 (2017): 337. See also Oswald Bayer, "The Doctrine of Justification and Ontology," trans. Christine Helmer, *Neue Zeitschrift Für Systematische Theologie Und Religionsphilosophie* 43, no. 1 (2001): 45.

broader Protestant theological imagination, the connection between justification and creation is regularly commented on by Luther scholars. Particular attention is given to the first article of Luther's Small Catechism.[62] Here, his statement of belief regarding creation conspicuously employs the language of justification, especially in the final line:

> I believe that God has created me and all that exists; that he has given me and still sustains my body and soul, all my limbs and senses, my reason and all the faculties of my mind, together with food and clothing, house and home, family and property; that he provides me daily and abundantly with all the necessities of life, protects me from all danger, and preserves me from all evil. *All this he does out of his pure, fatherly, and divine goodness and mercy, without any merit or worthiness on my part.*[63]

Thus, along with his marked attention to the God-givenness of worldly life, Luther, in a clear allusion to justification, identifies human existence as an undeserved, categorical gift which is passively received.

Luther also weaves elements of justification into his exegetical lectures on the book of Genesis.[64] At times, he does so indirectly, such as when he asserts that a central aspect of humanity's unimpaired, pre-fall nature was their righteousness and uprightness.[65] Yet, he also draws more explicit parallels between the work of God in creation and Christ's redemptive work, stating: "This care and solicitude of God for us, even before we were created, may rightly and profitably be considered here.... There is a similar beneficence of God toward us in His spiritual gifts. Before we were brought to faith, Christ, our Redeemer, is above in the Father's house; He prepares mansions so that when we arrive, we may find a heaven furnished with

---

62. See Bayer, *Martin Luther's Theology*, 95; Lohse, *Martin Luther's Theology*, 341; Johannes Schwanke, "Luther's Theology of Creation," in *The Oxford Handbook of Martin Luther's Theology*, ed. Robert Kolb, Irene Dingel, and L'ubomír Batka (Oxford: Oxford University Press, 2014), 210. In a recent article, Schwanke identifies the dangers implicit in Luther's emphasis on the individual in creation and justification ("Martin Luther's Theology of Creation," trans. Carsten Card-Hyatt, *International Journal of Systematic Theology* 18, no. 4 [2016]: 401–4). While it falls outside the scope of this chapter, one could make the case that Bonhoeffer corrects this individualism in his *analogia relationis*.

63. Theodore G. Tappert, ed., *The Book of Concord: The Confessions of the Evangelical Lutheran Church*, trans. Theodore G. Tappert (Philadelphia, PA: Fortress Press, 1959), 345. Emphasis added. On this, see Bayer, *Martin Luther's Theology*, 95; Lohse, *Martin Luther's Theology*, 341; Schwanke, "Luther's Theology of Creation," 210.

64. Cf. Robert Kolb, "God and His Human Creatures in Luther's Sermons on Genesis: The Reformer's Early Use of His Distinction of Two Kinds of Righteousness," *Concordia Journal* 33, no. 22 (2007): 176–8.

65. *LW* 1:114.

every kind of joy (John 14:2)."⁶⁶ We can thus begin to see a sort of parallel for Luther according to which non-existence and sin are correlates, and God in Christ acts to overcome both, thereby establishing humanity in the righteousness of faith. As such, Johannes Schwanke notes that "[f]or Luther re-creation is of the same order as creation."⁶⁷ That is, both creation and re-creation ground human existence in God's categorical gift. Perhaps Luther's fullest explication of this dynamic is when, later in his Genesis lectures and again using confessional language, he writes:

> We believe in God, who is an almighty creator, who makes everything out of nothing, who makes out of evil good, out of the hopeless and lost redemption and salvation. Just as Paul writes in Romans 4:17, "He who creates new things out of nothing" and 2 Corinthians 4:6 "God, who said, light shall shine out of darkness." This means: Not out of a gleaming coal a little spark, but "out of darkness light"; also out of death life, out of sin righteousness, out of the slavery of the devil and hell heaven and the liberty of the children of God.⁶⁸

Here, Luther seizes on the parallel that Paul draws in Romans 4:17—between death and nothing on the one hand, and new things and life on the other.⁶⁹ In this way, he ties justification *qua* reality of redemption to justification *qua* reality of creation.

Yet, drawing such a tight parallel between justification by faith in creation, on the one hand, and justification by faith in redemption, on the other hand, raises the question: How, then, do they differ? One might suggest that, whereas creation is a work of God the Father, redemption is a work of God the Son, thereby making a Trinitarian distinction. However, Luther does not allow such a move since his lectures on Genesis clearly identify the Son as the primary operative in creation.⁷⁰ Instead, Luther's distinction seems to be a narratival one, which hangs on the intervening reality of sin between pristine creation and redemption. It is here that Luther's affirmation of creation entails a disjunction in the analogy between the material nothingness out of which God creates in the beginning and the sinful nothingness out of which God salvifically recreates. Soteriological justification is distinct from creational justification precisely because it is not a starting over *ex nihilo*. Instead, it is a recreation in which God in Christ affirms his identity as the God who is free for humanity, desiring to be in relationship with them.⁷¹

---

66. *LW* 1:39.
67. Schwanke, "Luther's Theology of Creation," 210.
68. *LW* 8:39.
69. Cf. Eberhard Jüngel, "The World as Possibility and Actuality: The Ontology of the Doctrine of Justification," in *Theological Essays*, trans. John Webster (Edinburgh: T&T Clark, 1989), 107.
70. *LW* 1:21, 50.
71. On the manner in which justification, construed in this way, grounds the dignity and worth of humanity, see Oswald Bayer, "Martin Luther's Conception of Human Dignity,"

By framing the human person in terms of creation, sin, and redemption in *DCM*, Luther is putting forward the three aspects or realities which structure the relationship in which humans stand to God. Teasing out what this relationality means in reference to creation, Ian McFarland writes: "Precisely because creation is the bestowal of existence where there was nothing existing before, it is not a process that can be described in terms of a sequence of events, it is rather a relationship. Nor is it a onetime act, but rather an enduring bond of intimate and complete dependence on God."[72] Through *creatio ex nihilo*, God justifies human existence by calling it into being, and the nature of this existence is relational insofar as it is God's categorical gift received by humans in the dependence of faith.[73] For Luther this relationality and dependence on God signals humanity's fundamental status as creatures *coram Deo*. While Luther identifies other *coram* relationships, human existence *coram Deo* serves as the relational and ontological starting point according to which all other relationships are ordered.[74] As such, humanity's relational ontology serves as the subject matter of Luther's justification-based anthropology and helps to explain its tripartite structure.[75] In other words, each aspect—creation, sin, and redemption—informs and contributes to the substance and definition of the human being as one who is justified *coram Deo* by faith.

Yet, how exactly are we to conceptualize the relationship between these three aspects insofar as they form the structure of humanity's relational ontology *coram Deo*? There are two primary ways to answer this question, represented, on the one hand, by Notger Slenczka and, on the other, by Bayer. Slenczka has suggested that they be interpreted in terms of the salvation-historical narrative, which entails a chronological understanding.[76] Such a reading places humanity "in relation to the past—the original image of God—and in relation to the future, in which [the]

---

in *The Cambridge Handbook of Human Dignity*, ed. Marcus Düwell et al., trans. Naomi van Steenbergen (Cambridge: Cambridge University Press, 2014), 102.

72. Ian A. McFarland, *From Nothing: A Theology of Creation* (Louisville, KY: Westminster John Knox Press, 2014), 58.

73. For an excellent essay that seeks to articulate a relational anthropology in a way that does justice to the doctrine of creation, see Christoph Schwöbel, "Human Being as Relational Being: Twelve Theses for a Christian Anthropology," in *Persons, Divine and Human: King's College Essays in Theological Anthropology*, ed. Christoph Schwöbel and Colin E. Gunton (Edinburgh: T&T Clark, 1999), 141-70. The current study is, largely, consonant with Schwöbel's proposal. However, by accenting justification and the relational dimensions implied by it, we are seeking to develop and lay bare the doctrinal logic undergirding relationality.

74. Gerhard Ebeling, *Luther: An Introduction to His Thought* (London: Collins, 1970), 199-200.

75. On Luther's relational ontology over against a scholastic substance ontology, see Gerhard Ebeling, "Luther's Understanding of Reality," trans. Scott Celsor, *Lutheran Quarterly* 27, no. 1 (2013): 56-75.

76. Slenczka, "Luther's Anthropology," 219.

human essence will be restored."[77] This interpretation is problematic insofar as both creation and ultimate redemption are pushed out of the present, and thus lose their ontological decisiveness. Bayer offers a more promising interpretation when he suggests that these three aspects are best understood as existing concurrently.[78] More specifically, it is a dynamic concurrence due to the inherent tension introduced by the disruptive realities of sin and grace.[79] Sin disrupts creation, introducing a new and total reality over against it. Likewise, grace disrupts sin, inaugurating the total, eschatological reality of new creation. In this way, on the anthropological level, we might say that Luther is proposing a threefold *simul* in which the human simply is, in relation to God, simultaneously creature, sinner, and reconciled in Christ alone. While teasing out exactly how this simultaneity unfolds is beyond the scope of this chapter, it is sufficient to note that holding these three aspects together prevents the undue consolidation of human ontology into any single aspect at the expense of the others. Thus, they function as theological checks and balances for one another.

At this point we have seen how Luther defines humanity in terms of justification by faith, thereby suggesting a relational anthropology in which human existence *coram Deo* is ontologically fundamental.[80] This relational ontology is presented in terms of a threefold simultaneity according to which the human is one who is created, sinful, and reconciled in Christ alone. However, while we have briefly outlined the contours of justification as a creational and redemptive reality earlier, we have yet to address how justification by faith can be considered ontologically basic for humans lost in sin.

Previously we noted that Luther's basic anthropological definition implies that humans require the sort of justification that only faith can provide. Insofar as faith is created (or re-created) by the Holy Spirit and in Jesus Christ, it is the substance of a properly ordered relational ontology.[81] However, sin intervenes as a total disruption of this reality.[82] While he speaks only of the radical effects

---

77. Slenczka, "Luther's Anthropology," 219.

78. On this, see Bayer, *Martin Luther's Theology*, 154–5.

79. Bayer, *Martin Luther's Theology*, 155. My thanks to Phil Ziegler who helpfully suggested the conceptuality of sin and grace as disruptive realities.

80. Cf. Eberhard Jüngel, "Humanity in Correspondence to God: Remarks on the Image of God as a Basic Concept of Theological Anthropology," in *Theological Essays*, trans. John Webster (Edinburgh: T&T Clark, 1989), 133; John Webster, "Justification, Analogy and Action: Barth and Luther in Jüngel's Anthropology," in *Barth's Moral Theology: Human Action in Barth's Thought* (Edinburgh: T&T Clark, 1998), 211.

81. Oswald Bayer, "Being in the Image of God," *Lutheran Quarterly* 27, no. 1 (2013): 77; cf. Bayer, "The Doctrine of Justification and Ontology," 46.

82. Luther distinguishes between actual sin and original sin, but we shall focus only on the latter in order to highlight its total effects. See L'ubomír Batka, "Luther's Teaching on Sin and Evil," in *The Oxford Handbook of Martin Luther's Theology*, ed. Robert Kolb, Irene Dingel, and L'ubomír Batka (Oxford/New York: Oxford University Press, 2014), 235.

of sin in terms of humanity's natural capacities in *DCM*, Luther fundamentally understands sin in terms of unbelief or unfaith.[83] Insofar as sin is a total reality, it undermines faith as the substance of humanity's relational ontology and in this way destroys humanity's justified existence *coram Deo*. Thus, sin introduces a new reality in which humanity rejects its relational ontology, turning in on itself in search of self-justification.

It is in this quest for self-justification that we begin to see the enduring ontological significance of justification by faith emerge. The reality of sin is not justification-less or faith-less, but, rather, it is self-justification and faith in self. Apart from God, humans grasp at justification by placing themselves in a faith relationship to someone or something other than God.[84] Ultimately though, even if humans place their faith in something other than themselves, they have set themselves up as the final arbiter concerning what or who is worthy of that faith. As such, Luther picks up on Augustine's description of sin as an incurvature of the self in on itself.[85] When Luther refers to sinful humans as *homo incurvatus in se* he is highlighting the relational nature of sin and its significance as a total ontological reality.[86] Rather than an ontology grounded extrinsically in one's relationship with God, the human being becomes locked within herself, creating her own gods, her own righteousness, and justifying her own existence.[87]

However, while sinful humanity's quest for self-justification demonstrates justification by faith's enduring ontological significance negatively as a need or privation, the doctrine of preservation does so positively.[88] Insofar as Luther's tripartite anthropology holds, the sinful human always remains the created human. Herein lies Luther's doctrine of preservation. There is no possibility for humanity to reverse the curved inwardness of their sinful, relational ontology. Yet, God, out of sheer mercy, preserves in anticipation of the justificatory, re-creative work of the incarnate Christ and the Holy Spirit. Thus, even though, for the human in sin, justification by faith is solely a divine possibility, it remains

---

83. *LW* 29:182.

84. See Bayer on the "dispute of justifications" in *Living by Faith*, 1–7.

85. While this is by no means the only sin-imagery Luther employs, it most clearly illustrates the effect of sin on humanity's relational ontology. For an excellent overview of Luther on sin, see Batka, "Luther's Teaching on Sin and Evil." For an in-depth study on Luther's use of *homo incurvatus in se*, see Matt Jenson, *The Gravity of Sin: Augustine, Luther and Barth on* homo incurvatus in se (London/New York: T&T Clark, 2006), 47–97.

86. Luther's use of this formula appears primarily in his *Commentary on Romans*. See *LW* 25:291, 313, 345, 426.

87. Cf. Karl Barth's discussion of humanity's self-justification apart from God in *The Epistle to the Romans*, trans. Edwin C. Hoskyns, 6th ed. (Oxford/New York: Oxford University Press, 1933), 44–5.

88. Contra Jüngel, who does not take preservation to be a form of relation, and as such, construes being in sin as relationlessness. See his "The World as Possibility and Actuality," 107–8.

ontologically decisive because it is this possibility—grounded in creation and realized in reconciliation—that marks God as being *for* humanity, thereby preserving human existence even as the sinful human turns in on and unmakes herself.

b The Epistemological Dimension

Up to this point we have discussed justification by faith as a basic ontological reality for humanity. However, a further problem that confronts us in Luther's short definition of the human being is the challenge of distinguishing the ontological question—what does it mean to be human?—from the epistemological question— how do we know what it means to be human? By defining the human person as one who is justified by faith Luther provides an answer to both.[89] In the context of *DCM*, Luther's apparent meaning is ontological, but by making this ontological claim within the context of the dispute between philosophy and theology he is also implicitly commenting on the epistemic framework necessary for providing a theological definition of the human being: namely, the framework of faith. By briefly considering why Luther believes philosophy is epistemically limited in such a way that it is insufficient to the task of describing the human being, we shall see how justification by faith can serve this dual function.

In contradistinction to the diatribes against reason for which Luther is famous,[90] *DCM* contains no less than seven theses (4–9, 24) extolling reason, in relation to other aspects of human life, as "the best and something divine."[91] While this cuts against the popular caricature of Luther as one for whom reason is nothing but a whore which faith must blind, it serves to establish the parameters within which Luther's sharpest polemics against reason take place.[92] For example, in his later commentary on Galatians, Luther goes so far as to suggest that "faith slaughters reason and kills the beast that the whole world and all the creatures cannot kill."[93] His feud with reason here stretches over several pages, yet it is notable—when comparing its enmity toward reason with the praise accorded to reason in *DCM*—

---

89. Cf. Piotr J. Malysz, "Luther and Dionysius: Beyond Mere Negations," *Modern Theology* 24, no. 4 (2008): 687.

90. While reason and philosophy are clearly not the same thing, Luther seems to identify reason as the primary tool which philosophy uses to evaluate reality, and as such uses them interchangeably. Thus, following Luther's lead in the eleventh thesis of *DCM* (*LW* 34:137), I shall also use them synonymously.

91. *LW* 34:137; cf. Ebeling, *Luther*, 91. However, Luther's esteem for reason also poses some serious theological challenges insofar as it is the primary basis on which Luther invests so much confidence in the state and created orders. On this, see Lohse, *Martin Luther's Theology*, 245–7.

92. See *LW* 37:221; 45:39.

93. *LW* 26:228.

that his polemic is entirely framed as a dispute between faith and reason.[94] Faith need not slaughter reason as such, but only reason in its impropriety and hubris. Insofar as this is the case, reason becomes the enemy only when it sets itself over against faith and God himself, and in so doing recommends justification by works.

Yet, in *DCM*, Luther praises reason only in relation to the created order and even then in a limited manner. Luther, choosing to speak philosophically about philosophy, works with Aristotle's four causes—efficient, material, formal, and final—as the four ways in which the human being can be known.[95] The material and formal causes roughly correspond to the body and soul, respectively, and are available to reason as objects of knowledge. However, even in this regard Luther is hesitant to give human reason free rein. This is presumably due to the debilitating effects of sin, which prevent one from distinguishing between true and distorted knowledge of humanity's formal and material causes.[96] Instead, he asserts that "we seem scarcely to perceive his material cause sufficiently," and similarly notes a complete lack of philosophical consensus in relation to the formal cause.[97] In this way, Luther acknowledges some space for philosophical anthropology, but one might be forgiven for a lack of optimism regarding its prospects. As for the efficient and final causes—corresponding to humanity's origin and goal, respectively— these are entirely inaccessible to reason, since they are given to knowledge only by means of revelation. Theology, then, exposes and posits three epistemic deficiencies in philosophy that seriously limit its ability to speak anthropologically: lack of knowledge of the efficient cause, ignorance of the reality of sin, and lack of knowledge of the final cause. Thus, Luther shows that a purely philosophical ontology of the human person—which he sums up in terms of "reason, sensation, and body" in the first thesis of *DCM*—is undermined from the outset.

These epistemic limitations cannot be overcome apart from faith.[98] Only from within the epistemic framework of faith is it possible to recognize the total reality of sin and its dire effects,[99] God in Christ as the creator and efficient cause,[100] and Christ as the final cause.[101] While this is perhaps obvious given the fact that Luther

---

94. See *LW* 26:227–34.
95. *LW* 34:138.
96. Cf. Bayer, *Martin Luther's Theology*, 186.
97. *LW* 34:138. In thesis 16 Luther takes aim specifically at Aristotle's *On the Soul* where he posits the soul as not only the formal cause, but also the efficient and final cause. On this account, Aristotle asserts that the soul "is the cause in the sense of being that from which motion is derived, in the sense of the purpose or final cause, and as being the substance of all bodies that have souls." Cited from *LW* 34:138n1.
98. Cf. Jüngel's assertion that theological anthropology "interprets humanity as defined *a priori* from outside itself, even though this 'outside' can only be recognized *a posteriori*" ("Humanity in Correspondence to God," 127).
99. *LW* 25:215.
100. *LW* 1:21, 50; 34:138. See also Bayer, *Martin Luther's Theology*, 116.
101. *LW* 1:64, 68; 34:140.

is proposing a specifically *theological* anthropology, it is rarely brought so clearly to the fore. Rather than offering a theological interpretation of reason, sensation, or the body, Luther boldly grounds human ontology in a reality that is in no way intrinsic to humanity. Instead, human ontology is defined extrinsically in terms of justification by faith, and this is a reality that can be known only when it is revealed to faith from the outside.

Luther's theological counterproposal mirrors his description of a philosophical approach to defining the human person in two important ways. First, on Luther's account of philosophical anthropology, reason functions both ontologically, as definitional of the human, and epistemologically, as the means by which human ontology is known. However, this is an insufficient analogue for faith, for the reasons noted earlier. Faith, as the means by which one is justified, is the substance of one's relationship with God, which Luther takes to be ontologically fundamental. Only from within this relationship, in which humanity exists *coram Deo*, can the human being be properly understood theologically.

Second, it is almost certainly not coincidental that this three-pronged critique of philosophical anthropology corresponds to Luther's tripartite definition of humanity—outlined earlier—on all three points. By way of a negative critique of philosophy then, Luther's theological definition of humanity proves robust exactly where philosophy's deficiencies are the most evident. This is because, whereas the structure of philosophy's human is evaluated according to the dictates of reason, the structure of theology's human is understood according to revelation received in and by faith. Whereas theology begins with a human ontology that is given in revelation and structures its anthropological thinking accordingly, philosophy constrains human ontology to what is epistemically accessible to reason. If fundamental aspects of human ontology are basically inaccessible to reason, as Luther asserts in *DCM*, then the external, revelatory Word of God about humanity is the only proper starting point for an anthropology that is not, in Luther's words, "fragmentary, fleeting, and exceedingly material."[102]

Thus, we see that Luther's critique of philosophy functions as a sort of proof that reason's epistemic framework is insufficient to evaluate human ontology. This is because, for Luther, the human being must first and primarily be understood *coram Deo*. Being before God is the basic reality of human ontology and the proper starting point for an epistemology that is sufficient to the task of anthropology. Faith, then, is both the substance of a justified relationship with God in Christ and the epistemic presupposition that makes a genuinely theological anthropology possible.

V Conclusion

In looking at Luther's use of justification by faith as an anthropological concept we have seen that it is fundamentally a relational concept. What this means is that

---

102. *LW* 34:138.

justification constitutes the shape and structure of one's relationship with God, with faith defining its substance. Thus, human ontology is extrinsically grounded and defined in terms of this relationship in which humanity exists *coram Deo*. The *coram Deo* relationship involves three aspects which are derived from the salvation-historical narrative: creation, sin, and reconciliation. These three aspects simultaneously inform humanity's relational ontology, but remain distinct and in tension with one another due to the disruptive realities of sin and grace. Despite this tension, God's being *for* humanity in Christ through justification by faith remains ontologically decisive—decisive for creation in the gift of existence *coram Deo*, for sin in preservation, and for reconciliation as repair, recapitulation, and re-creation. Finally, while creation, sin, and reconciliation stand in dynamic tension ontologically, reconciliation must be given epistemic pride of place in theological anthropology since it is only in and through faith that we can know anything of the realities of sin and creation. With these focal points of Luther's theological anthropology in mind, we shall now turn to Bonhoeffer's early theology in order to investigate the extent to which Bonhoeffer picks up on and works within this anthropological framework.

Chapter 2

JUSTIFIED IN CHRIST AND THE CHURCH

THE SHAPE OF BONHOEFFER'S EARLY ANTHROPOLOGY

I Introduction

A survey of Dietrich Bonhoeffer's early theological work reveals that his understanding of theology conforms to Luther's definition: "The proper subject of theology is man guilty of sin and condemned, and God the Justifier and Savior of man the sinner. Whatever is asked or discussed in theology outside this subject, is error and poison."[1] This is borne out both by Bonhoeffer's Christocentric approach and his vested interest in theological anthropology. To this definition, when thinking about Bonhoeffer, one must also add the church as a third term. Bonhoeffer's early theology weaves these three strands together in a tight braid, emphasizing the church as the place where Christ encounters humanity and, as such, the context in which theological anthropology becomes a genuine possibility.

Therefore, it is impossible to treat Bonhoeffer's theological anthropology in isolation. Instead, it can only be worked out in relation to its Christological basis, on the one hand, and its ecclesial context on the other. Similarly, we shall see that, for Bonhoeffer, the import of justification for human existence is thoroughly Christological and only fully grasped within the sphere of the church. As such, picking up where the last chapter left off, we shall focus on the ways in which Luther's justification-based anthropology provides a framework for assessing the shaping influence of justification on Bonhoeffer's theological anthropology. In doing so, we shall give special attention to the unique manner in which Bonhoeffer elaborates on Luther's model by fleshing out Christ's determinative import for the human person and highlighting the central significance of the church for human existence.[2] The goal of this chapter is not to give a thoroughgoing account of

---

1. *LW* 12:311.

2. By "elaborates on," I do not mean that Luther neglected Christology, or that he had a thin ecclesiology, since neither is the case. Indeed, Luther's Christology is essentially related to his sacramentology and ecclesiology (on this see Brian Lugioyo, "Martin Luther's Eucharistic Christology," in *The Oxford Handbook of Christology*, ed. Francesca Murphy [Oxford /New York: Oxford University Press, 2015], 267–83.) Rather, I simply mean that

Bonhoeffer's anthropology, but, rather, to show how the doctrine of justification shapes his thinking about humanity in important ways.

II Bonhoeffer's Early Anthropology

Given our focus on Luther's *Disputation Concerning Man* (*DCM*) in the previous chapter, it is natural to query whether Bonhoeffer himself was, indeed, familiar with this small piece of Luther's voluminous written corpus. Of course, reading something and engaging with it in the development of one's own thought are hardly the same thing. So, the primary proving ground for Luther's influence on Bonhoeffer remains in the sphere of thematic resonance. However, it is certainly worthwhile to note the historical evidence for Bonhoeffer's first-hand encounter with *DCM* as we begin to consider the extent to which, following on Luther, justification by faith structures his understanding of the human person.

While a student at the University of Berlin, Bonhoeffer found himself in the thick of the Luther Renaissance. He did not shy away from this reality, but, rather, set about the task of coming to grips with the sixteenth-century reformer who continued to loom large over and in German theology. This immersion in Luther, especially through his courses with Karl Holl, left an indelible mark on Bonhoeffer. According to Bethge, Bonhoeffer was especially influenced by the way that Holl located justification by faith at the center of theology,[3] although he doubted whether Holl gave sufficient attention to the Christological dimension of Luther's theology.[4]

While studying under Holl, Bonhoeffer wrote two lengthy essays on Luther: "Luther's Feelings about His Work as Expressed in the Final Years of His Life Based on His Correspondence of 1540-1546,"[5] and "Luther's Views of the Holy Spirit according to the *Disputationen* of 1535-1545 edited by Drews."[6] Only the latter essay will be discussed here, but it is worth noting that both focus on the latter portion of Luther's theological career. Although the degree to which Luther's understanding of justification by faith evolves over the course of his life is open to debate, Bonhoeffer was clearly well versed in his later theology, where *DCM* is situated. Thus, at the very least, Bonhoeffer was familiar with the shape of Luther's theology during the period out of which the reformer's mature theological anthropology emerges. Insofar as the central themes of *DCM* are reiterated elsewhere in Luther's later theology, Bonhoeffer's acquaintance with the broader

---

Bonhoeffer teases out the Christological and justificatory connection between anthropology and ecclesiology in a manner distinct from Luther.

3. Eberhard Bethge, *Dietrich Bonhoeffer: A Biography*, ed. Victoria Barnett, Rev. Ed. (Minneapolis, MN: Fortress Press, 2000), 85–6.
4. Bethge, *Dietrich Bonhoeffer*, 69.
5. DBWE 9:257–84.
6. DBWE 9:325–70.

literature adds historical heft to our central claim: namely, that his anthropology reflects the core concepts of *DCM*.

Yet, on the basis of his essay on Luther's understanding of the Holy Spirit, it is also possible to establish that Bonhoeffer at least read and was directly familiar with *DCM*. Indeed, although it is hardly the focus of the larger essay, Bonhoeffer footnotes one of *DCM*'s disputation fragments in his discussion of infant baptism.[7] Needless to say, this comment has little to do with theological anthropology, does not cite an issue central to the disputation itself, and hardly demonstrates Bonhoeffer's enduring interest in *DCM*. However, it does satisfy the minimal historical criteria of familiarity in terms of a direct encounter with the text of *DCM* itself. This familiarity is confirmed and substantiated when, six years later, Bonhoeffer again references *DCM*, this time in his lecture course entitled "The History of Twentieth-Century Systematic Theology."[8] Here, Bonhoeffer invokes Luther's *DCM* as an example of the inherent tension between theology and philosophy with which theologians must constantly reckon. Thus, it is not only clear that Bonhoeffer was directly familiar with the text of *DCM*, but also that this familiarity was enduring rather than punctuated.

At the end of the previous chapter we outlined the key components of Luther's theological anthropology, centering on its articulation in *DCM*. These components are derivative of Luther's central claim that justification by faith sums up what it means to be human, and include the essentially relational nature of human being *coram Deo*, the three-part narration of the *coram Deo* relationship (under the rubric of creation, fall, and reconciliation), faith as the epistemic condition for knowledge of humanity according to its tripartite structure in relation to God, and God's being for humanity in Christ as ontologically decisive. In what follows we shall address each of these aspects and the ways in which they surface in Bonhoeffer's early theology under the broader rubrics of Bonhoeffer's relational ontology and what he calls the historical dialectic. We shall then demonstrate the manner in which Christology and ecclesiology serve to inform how justification shapes his understanding of the human person.

a Relational Ontology

By interpreting justification as an anthropological principle, Luther locates human being *coram Deo*, thereby placing theological anthropology under the umbrella of soteriology. In doing so, he introduces the idea that humans are irreducibly social by virtue of their need for justification in relation to an other, and that the

---

7. *DBWE* 9:359. Here and throughout this essay, Bonhoeffer is working with Paul Drew's edited volume of Luther's disputations: Martin Luther, *Disputationen Dr. M. Luthers in den Jahren 1535–1545 an der Universität Wittenberg gehalten*, ed. Paul Drews (Göttingen, 1895). On this, see *DBWE* 9:325n1.

8. *DBWE* 11:235. Although the text cited is reconstructed from student notes, it is likely that the *DCM* citation is Bonhoeffer's own and not a student's addition.

social relation most basic to personhood is the one in which humans exist *coram Deo* as those who are recognized by God.[9] Identifying a corresponding concern for sociality and relationality in Bonhoeffer's theological anthropology is hardly a revolutionary move. Indeed, his concern for the central importance of responsibly being with and for the other undoubtedly plays a key role in the continuing relevance and compelling nature of his theology over the years.

Even so, exploring the theological roots of Bonhoeffer's theology of sociality, especially under the rubric of justification by faith, has been a largely neglected line of inquiry. This is likely due to the fact that almost fifty years after it was first published, Clifford Green's monograph, *Bonhoeffer: A Theology of Sociality*, continues to provide the standard account of sociality's central import in Bonhoeffer's theology. Green masterfully weaves together the social, theological, and biographical, showing how they are intimately intertwined in Bonhoeffer's thought. However, Green's study is constrained by the historical method which he employs. He adopts this method in intentional contradistinction to the numerous, earlier thematic studies of Bonhoeffer which were unable to "concern [themselves] with the question: what are the distinctive marks and developments which characterize Bonhoeffer's theology *as a whole*, within the framework of which a particular theme or subject is to be investigated?"[10] By examining Bonhoeffer's major works in their historical and biographical context, Green believes that he can overcome these weaknesses and identify sociality as the cohering concept in Bonhoeffer's theology.

While this is not the place for an extended critique of Green's seminal work—especially since there remains a great deal of consonance between it and the present study—his chosen method results in two blind spots that are worth pointing out. This is especially the case since the line of inquiry we shall follow in this chapter is located behind those blind spots. First, while Green's historical investigation of the texts does justice to the explicit development and trajectory of Bonhoeffer's theology, it is less well equipped to attend to the implicit, subtextual, and theologically normative assumptions that undergird his arguments.[11] A relevant analogy here might be the case of the *imago Dei*. Many scholars have noted

---

9. On God's recognition as integral to justification, see Gerhard Ebeling, *Luther: An Introduction to His Thought* (London: Collins, 1970), 197–8.

10. Clifford J. Green, *Bonhoeffer: A Theology of Sociality*, Rev. Ed. (Grand Rapids, MI: Eerdmans, 1999), 9.

11. Green is, of course, aware of such theologically normative assumptions. This is evidenced in an editorial footnote he provides for the English, critical edition of *Sanctorum Communio*, where he comments: "For Bonhoeffer the Christian understanding of person at the ontological level is always that of the person in a social and ethical encounter with the other person; this is the Christian basic-relation of I and You, self and other. It presupposes the theological axiom that the human person always exists in relation to an Other, namely God, and that human relations are in some way analogies of this fundamental relation" (*DBWE* 1:50n56). However, even as he gives the theological presuppositions undergirding

that its explicit formulation occurs several times only in the opening chapters of Genesis, yet the vast majority of theologians assume its ongoing significance and import throughout Scripture. Green's approach seems unable to properly accommodate such theologically normative assumptions in his evaluation of Bonhoeffer's theology. The second blind spot is related to the first, and it is Green's assumption that sociality is a sufficiently basic theological category for Bonhoeffer such that it undergirds his entire theology. To prove this point Green cites the preface to *Sanctorum Communio* twice in the first two chapters of his study. Here, Bonhoeffer writes: "The more this investigation has considered the significance of the sociological category for theology, the more clearly has emerged the social intention of all the basic Christian concepts. 'Person,' 'primal state,' 'sin,' and 'revelation' can be fully comprehended only in reference to sociality."[12] Green then sets out to prove that this programmatic statement establishes a trajectory in which sociality is "formative for Bonhoeffer's whole theological development."[13] Yet, is it not equally possible that sociality is a corollary concern and consequent motif of a more basic theological conviction regarding who God is, the being of humanity, and the relation in which they stand? If this is the case, then Bonhoeffer's theology of sociality bears within it formative doctrinal commitments that must be articulated. This is especially the case because if one gives rise to the other, then for the church to learn from Bonhoeffer it needs both.

A key passage from *Sanctorum Communio* will serve as an example of how my line of inquiry is practically distinguished from Green's. It also serves as clear proof that this line of inquiry is warranted. While laying out what he takes to be the Christian concept of person in the second chapter of his doctoral dissertation, Bonhoeffer is actively engaged in a dispute with German idealist philosophy. In opposition to the philosophical anthropology put forth by idealism, Bonhoeffer asserts: "*For Christian philosophy, the human person originates only in relation to the divine; the divine person transcends the human person,* who both resists and is overwhelmed by the divine. . . . The Christian person originates only in the absolute duality of God and humanity; only in experiencing the barrier does the awareness of oneself as ethical person arise."[14] Green rightly acknowledges that this is a "crucial" passage, but the fact that "it disclose[s] the theological basis for [Bonhoeffer's] anthropology" is only a secondary reason for this.[15] His primary concern is to highlight it as "*the first expression of that characteristic social-ethical-historical understanding of transcendence which remains essentially unchanged throughout Bonhoeffer's theological career.*"[16] This primary concern, along with his

---

Bonhoeffer's theology of sociality a nod, he also relegates them to the background of his discussion.
  12. *DBWE* 1:21.
  13. Green, *Bonhoeffer*, 19.
  14. *DBWE* 1:49.
  15. Green, *Bonhoeffer*, 35.
  16. Green, *Bonhoeffer*, 35.

historical approach, allows Green to quickly move past the central importance of the God–human relation in the interest of highlighting Bonhoeffer's near-identification of the divine You with the human You as a social-ethical barrier to the human I.[17] Indeed, Green concludes: "The essence of a person is to will in responsible decision in ethical relationships, and such decision manifests the historicity of human life."[18] However, ascribing such an active definition of human being to Bonhoeffer seems to cut against Bonhoeffer's statement, cited earlier, that human essence is relation to the divine, and in this duality humans are either in active rebellion or passively overwhelmed. It is exactly at this point where our line of inquiry is validated. Indeed, whereas Green continues down the line of sociality, we shall take the road less travelled and consider why, theologically, this duality between God and humanity is the basis for Bonhoeffer's theological anthropology.

Elsewhere in *Sanctorum Communio*, Bonhoeffer again takes aim at the philosophical anthropology of idealism, but this time in terms of "value." Departing from idealism, Bonhoeffer denies the fact that human beings intrinsically bear the highest value within themselves. Instead, he asserts that the concept of value is something that is intelligible only in terms of "the creatureliness of the person."[19] Insofar as the value of a person resides in the fact that she is God's creature, it is necessarily a value-in-relation. Thus, Bonhoeffer draws out the tragic irony of an idealist anthropology, writing: "Every philosophy of value, even where it regards the value of the person as the highest value (Scheler), is in danger of taking away the value of persons as such, as God's creatures, and acknowledging them only insofar as the person is the 'bearer' of objective, impersonal value."[20] In the background here is the classic dispute between justification by faith and justification by works. For idealism, the individual possesses the possibility of highest value within herself and thus the justification of her own existence. However, Bonhoeffer counters this philosophical vision with a theological one, asserting that humans cannot possibly justify their own existence since human value is grounded in one's standing *coram Deo* and is realized in the social sphere.[21] As such, suggesting that the God–human relation is fundamentally shaped by justification is not an empty assertion, but corresponds to the reality that it is in this relation that human meaning and value are created, applied, and upheld by God. This has no other basis than the free grace of God given in the person of Jesus Christ.

Taken on its own, however, the absolute duality between God and the human person might suggest a sort of intense focus on the single individual *a la* Kierkegaard. However, for Bonhoeffer, human persons are creatures who

17. Green, *Bonhoeffer*, 35–6.
18. Green, *Bonhoeffer*, 36.
19. *DBWE* 1:49.
20. *DBWE* 1:49–50.
21. On the fact that "every human You is an image of the divine You" and its implications, see *DBWE* 1:54–5.

are simultaneously structurally open and structurally closed.[22] As Michael Mawson puts it: "Our existence as individuals and social beings was in a sense equiprimordial; God created and intended human persons to be simultaneously distinct from and related to one another."[23] In addition, Bonhoeffer posits that the community—which the individual is inherently open to and in relation to—"*can be interpreted as a collective person with the same structure as the individual person.*"[24] Thus, the personhood of a human being is equally formed by her individuality and her identity with collective persons. Or, as Bonhoeffer puts it: "In God's eyes, community and individual exist in the same moment and rest in one another."[25] In what follows, we shall refer to this dynamic reality as the dialectic of personhood. Ultimately, then, the person *coram Deo* just is the human understood in terms of the dialectic of personhood. Or, put another way, the person *coram Deo* is never merely an individual, but must always be understood as an individual enmeshed in a network of relations, the chief of which is her relationship to God.

In his inaugural lecture at the University of Berlin, Bonhoeffer reiterates his agreement with Luther's assertion that human being is relationally constituted *coram Deo* by the Word of God's address. Indeed, he posits that such a perspective is generally agreed upon by contemporary theology in light of a reorientation to Luther that came about in the early twentieth century.[26] However, despite a basic agreement in this regard, Bonhoeffer asserts that many theologians have ended up interpreting this claim in such a way that locates human possibility at the center of human being.[27] The category of possibility creates a space in which the person can be understood as self-determining, thereby undermining Luther's notion of the basic passivity of the human *coram Deo*.[28] As such, it is closely related to the

---

22. See *DBWE* 1:65–80.

23. Michael Mawson, *Christ Existing as Community: Bonhoeffer's Ecclesiology* (Oxford: Oxford University Press, 2018), 79; cf. *DBWE* 1:78. It is worth noting that Bonhoeffer is speaking here in terms of the primal (i.e., created) state of humanity and qualifies his discussion by grounding its possibility in the eschatological revelation in Christ. Because of this "[t]he doctrine of the primal state is hope projected backward" (*DBWE* 1:60–1).

24. *DBWE* 1:71.

25. *DBWE* 1:80.

26. *DBWE* 10:400. It is likely that he has in mind here both the Luther Renaissance and the emergence of Dialectical Theology.

27. On this front he is especially critical of Holl's religion of conscience, but also identifies Barth's theological anthropology, as well as Gogarten's, as essentially individualistic and thus based in human possibility. See *DBWE* 10:401–3.

28. Cf. *DBWE* 2:116. Drawing on Luther's ordering—in which being created is prior to being, which in turn is prior to acting—Bonhoeffer describes the basic posture of humanity in relation to God in terms of passivity. He draws this concept from a quote by Luther in his *Lectures on Romans*. See *LW* 25:104. Cf. Christiane Tietz on the import of passivity in Bonhoeffer's later theology in "Rechtfertigung Und Heiligung," in *Bonhoeffer Und Luther:*

Lutheran concept of works righteousness.²⁹ In strong opposition to this trend Bonhoeffer asserts that *"the concept of possibility has no place in theology and thus no place in theological anthropology."*³⁰ Or, to state his opposition positively, Bonhoeffer frames his alternative to possibility in the following manner:

> The human being understands himself only by his act-of-relating to God, which only God can establish. The human being sees his own unity grounded in God's word directed toward him, a word whose content is judgment and grace. Here the human being recognizes . . . that his essence is not his own possibilities but rather is determined by the statements, "You are under sin," or "You are under grace."³¹

That Bonhoeffer believes justification is at the very center of theological anthropology is clear here. Far from being self-determined, the human being is what she is only in and through the relationship which is established in God's word of address. Understood in terms of the dialectic of personhood, to be under sin is to be subject to the *cor curvum en se* and participant in the collective person of Adam. Likewise, to be under grace is to be encountered by Christ and be in the collective person of Christ, which Bonhoeffer primarily understands in terms of the church-community. In Christ and the church, the anthropological import of justification is grounded, conditioned, and maintained.³² We shall return to consider this further later. However, Bonhoeffer's invocation of sin and grace as two determinations of human existence *coram Deo* invites us to consider the degree to which he follows Luther in conceiving of human being as fundamentally created, sinful, and reconciled in Christ alone. It is to this that we now turn.

b Creation, Sin, and Reconciliation as a Historical Dialectic

Like Luther, Bonhoeffer's concept of the human person is not an abstract description of a timeless ideal. As such, he seeks to articulate a theological anthropology that takes the historicity of the human being fully into account. He makes this explicit in *Sanctorum Communio*, asserting that "the concepts of person and community, for example, are understood only within an intrinsically broken history, as conveyed in

---

Zentrale Themen Ihrer Theologie, ed. Klaus Grünwaldt, Christiane Tietz, and Udo Hahn (Hannover: Amt der VELKD, 2007), 83–4.
  29. See *DBWE* 10:389.
  30. *DBWE* 10:403.
  31. *DBWE* 10:405.
  32. The lecture concludes with Bonhoeffer's alternative interpretation of theological anthropology in terms of Christology and ecclesiology, respectively (*DBWE* 10:406–8).

the concepts of primal state, sin, and reconciliation."[33] Bonhoeffer is keen to stress that none of these concepts can be isolated from the others. Rather, they must be understood in terms of a "real historical dialectic."[34] The dialectic then entails that theological anthropology must operate in light of humanity's postlapsarian state because the reality of sin is its presupposition and, according to Bonhoeffer, the presupposition of history itself.[35] With all of this, we are firmly in the sphere of Luther's tripartite definition of the human person outlined in Chapter 1. However, the extent to which this historical dialectic informs and shapes the God–human relation, so central to Bonhoeffer's justification-based anthropology, remains to be seen. In what follows, rather than focusing on Bonhoeffer's major works sequentially, we shall proceed thematically, looking at each aspect of the dialectic in turn. Additionally, instead of sequencing the discussion according to the chronology given with the historical dialectic of creation, fall, and reconciliation, we shall begin with sin, followed by reconciliation—giving special attention to the centrality of Luther's *simul iustus et peccator*—before concluding with creation. The reason for this is that the anthropological significance of the *simul* for Bonhoeffer's anthropology is widely recognized. However, creation, as the third aspect of the historical dialectic, is rarely discussed. As such, we shall devote more time to this latter feature.

Historical Dialectic: Sin
Although no aspect of the historical dialectic can be separated from the others, sin features centrally for Bonhoeffer as a universal and total reality for humanity. It is both the break which precludes the possibility of identifying a human ideal in creation and that which is overcome by faith in Christ. In this way it is the historical reality which contradicts any approach to anthropology that seeks to define the human person in terms of an ahistorical, unified essence.[36] As such, Mawson is surely right when he refers to Bonhoeffer's description of the human being as "an account of how God encounters and constitutes human being as person *within the state of sin*."[37]

When Bonhoeffer speaks about the anthropological significance of sin he is careful to distinguish between the epistemic conditions necessary for recognizing

---

33. *DBWE* 1:62. Here, Bonhoeffer is borrowing a concept from Grisebach that involves an implicit critique of idealist philosophy's formal dialectic, which is abstract in nature. On this see 1:62n2.

34. Because of his understanding of the church as the collective person of Christ, this dialectic has both anthropological and ecclesiological implications and the latter are evinced in the structure of the dissertation itself. For a recent and excellent treatment of the import of this dialectic for Bonhoeffer's ecclesiology, see Mawson, *Christ Existing as Community*.

35. See *DBWE* 1:63; cf. 1:44. On the postlapsarian context in which Bonhoeffer locates his dialectical concept of person, see Mawson, *Christ Existing as Community*, 74–6.

36. *DBWE* 1:60.

37. Mawson, *Christ Existing as Community*, 74.

sin and sin as an ontological category. Regarding the former, Bonhoeffer is insistent that one can recognize sin only from within the context of faith.[38] From the start, then, it is evident that a definition of the human person within the historical dialectic of creation, sin, and reconciliation is not a general piece of knowledge which is universally accessible. Rather, it is a specifically theological judgment which becomes intelligible only in Christ and the church-community. On the ontological significance of sin for anthropology, Bonhoeffer maintains Luther's identification of sin as a total reality for humanity, variously stating that "the necessity of sin must be timeless,"[39] sin has the "weight of infinity,"[40] the human being "is sinner in his whole existence,"[41] and that sin must be understood "as a permanent state,"[42] to cite only a few. While Bonhoeffer certainly does not deny the reality of actual sins, the ontological import of sin cannot be ignored.[43] Thus, in a passage on sin from the Bethel confession he writes: "We reject the false doctrine that would see sins only as moral or biological errors or imperfections or ignorance, which human beings could correct by doing better the next time. Our sins brought Christ to the cross, and only through the death of Christ are sins forgiven."[44]

If sin has ontological significance, how is this then made manifest in the being of humanity? In his 1932 essay, "Concerning the Christian Idea of God," Bonhoeffer paints a grim picture: "Man 'in' and 'after' the fall refers everything to himself, puts himself in the center of the world, does violence to reality, makes himself God, and God and the other man his creatures."[45] This is essentially Bonhoeffer's interpretation of Luther's definition of sin in terms of incurvature or the *cur curvum en se*, as he renders it throughout *Act and Being*.[46] By turning in on herself, the person in sin elevates herself as the primary reference point for all reality, thereby denying the relationality which is proper to human being.[47] In *Creation and Fall*, Bonhoeffer

---

38. *DBWE* 2:131; 9:300; 10:405.
39. *DBWE* 9:319.
40. *DBWE* 10:404.
41. *DBWE* 10:473.
42. *DBWE* 12:229.
43. On Bonhoeffer's basic agreement with Luther in identifying sin both as original and as act, see *DBWE* 2:144–7. Kirsten Busch Nielsen suggests that the original, being nature of sin recedes into the background in Bonhoeffer's later work, but even if this is the case, it remains an implicit and important presupposition for him. See "Sünde," in *Bonhoeffer Und Luther: Zentrale Themen Ihrer Theologie*, ed. Klaus Grünwaldt, Christiane Tietz, and Udo Hahn (Hannover: Amt der VELKD, 2007), 116.
44. *DBWE* 12:395. While the Bethel confession was a collaborative effort among a number of members of the Confessing Church, Bonhoeffer penned this particular section along with Hans Fischer. For a specific breakdown of authorship, see 12:374n2.
45. *DBWE* 10:453; cf. 3:115.
46. *DBWE* 2:41, 58, 80, 137.
47. Cf. *DBWE* 3:122–4.

refers to this as being *sicut deus* and asserts that, in being *sicut deus*, the sinner cuts herself off from God and others.[48] The resultant state is one of intense isolation.[49] However, crucially for Bonhoeffer—given the central significance he attributes to sociality—even this isolation is an isolation in solidarity. Sin does not cancel out the reality of the dialectic of personhood, but, rather, entails a collective person marked by infinite fragmentation due to individual sin.[50] As such, sin involves both an individual and a corporate aspect. These are both acknowledged in the anthropological designation "being in Adam," which, according to Bonhoeffer, "is a more pointed ontological, and a more biblically based (1 Cor. 15:22; cf. 15:45; Rom. 5:12-14), designation for *esse peccator*."[51] The fact that being in Adam is an ontological designation which encompasses all of humanity renders two things impossible. First, because the individual always also exists dialectically in the collective person of Adam, the possibility of being made righteous through one's acts is rejected. Second, in much the same way, the individual cannot excuse her acts of sin on the basis of some sort of sinless personal core because her individual being is dialectically bound up with her being in Adam.[52]

Bonhoeffer sums up the resultant picture of humanity in Adam in the following way:

> Here is their limit: human beings cling to themselves, and thus their knowledge of themselves is imprisoned in untruth. To be placed into truth before God means to be dead or to live; neither of these can human beings give themselves. They are conferred on them only by the encounter with Christ in *contritio passiva* and faith. Only when Christ has broken through the solitude of human beings will they know themselves placed into truth.[53]

Sin is not a possibility in relation to God which human beings can remedy, or from which they can withdraw. Rather, it is an actuality grounded in human being in Adam and affirmed time and again in sinful acts.[54] As such, the solitude of the *cor curvum in se* and the fragmented solidarity of being in Adam endure unless the human person is encountered from the outside, put to death in her activity, and passively resurrected in Christ and the faith community of the church. Insofar

---

48. *DBWE* 3:141-3.

49. *DBWE* 1:108, 149; 3:108; cf. 10:405.

50. *DBWE* 1:121. On God's encounter with humanity in judgment as the basis for Bonhoeffer's understanding of collective persons after the fall, see Mawson, *Christ Existing as Community*, 113-18.

51. *DBWE* 2:136. Cf. *DBWE* 1:110, SC-A. "SC-A" denotes text that Bonhoeffer excised from his dissertation in preparation for publication.

52. *DBWE* 2:146.

53. *DBWE* 2:141.

54. For Bonhoeffer's alternative to the Augustinian account of original sin, see *DBWE* 1:109-18.

as this encounter reconstitutes the human being in faith it is both ontologically decisive and epistemically creative with regard to the conditions necessary for speaking of the human being in sin. For this reason one cannot speak about human being in Adam without already presupposing the reality of human being in Christ. It is to this that we now turn.

Historical Dialectic: Reconciliation
If the entrance of sin into the world through the Fall is the historical event that ensures a fragmented understanding of the human person, then reconciliation is the eschatological event in history which ensures that sin does not have the last word. As such, it holds forth the possibility of a unitive—albeit dialectical—definition of human being. In this way, reconciliation is decisive both epistemically and ontologically.[55] However, although reconciliation in Christ is a recapitulation of creation in important respects, it does not entail the reification of a creaturely ideal for theological anthropology.[56] In other words, sin as a total reality remains anthropologically significant insofar as the broken history which conditions humanity persists.[57] This is due to the eschatological nature of reconciliation. Indeed, reconciliation effects "the new creation of the new human being of the future, which here is an event already occurring in faith, and there perfected for view. . . . It is the new creation of those born from out of the world's confines into the wideness of heaven, becoming what they were or never were, a creature of God, a child."[58] The being of new creation is something that the human has in faith, in Christ, and in the church-community, rather than in themselves or in ideality. In this manner, it too is a total reality. Yet, even though the new being of humanity is, indeed, an established reality in Christ, it does not abolish the humanity of Adam, but, rather, stands over against it as God's final word concerning the being of sin.[59] As such, one exists "in the community of faith as one who bears the old human in me until death."[60]

Despite the fact that Bonhoeffer never explicitly invokes Luther's *simul iustus et peccator* designation for redeemed humanity, it is clearly present in the structure

---

55. Cf. *DBWE* 2:102–3.

56. Regarding new creation as recapitulation, albeit with key differences, see *DBWE* 11:438. On the consonance between Bonhoeffer's soteriology and Irenaeus's assertion that the incarnation is a recapitulation of humanity, see Jens Zimmermann, "Being Human, Becoming Human: Dietrich Bonhoeffer's Christological Humanism," in *Being Human, Becoming Human: Dietrich Bonhoeffer and Social Thought*, ed. Jens Zimmermann and Brian Gregor (Eugene, OR: Pickwick Publications, 2010), 31.

57. See *DBWE* 10:467, where Bonhoeffer suggests that the continuity of humanity is continuity in sin.

58. *DBWE* 2:161.

59. Cf. *DBWE* 1:107.

60. *DBWE* 2:123.

of his theological anthropology.⁶¹ It also follows naturally from the historical dialectic.⁶² Therefore, the possibility of basing a theological anthropology on the redeemed person as such is precluded as ideal and ahistorical because it realizes the eschatological new humanity in a way that does violence to the given reality in which real human beings live, move, and have their being. Instead, the *simul iustus et peccator* nature of being in Christ is utterly dependent on the justificatory Word of God:

> It is in being known by God that human beings know God. But to be known by God means to become a new person. It is the justified and the sinner in one who knows God. It is not because the word of God is in itself "meaning" that it affects the existence of human beings, but because it is *God's* word, the word of the creator, reconciler, and redeemer. . . . Thus human beings, when they understand themselves in faith, are entirely wrenched away from themselves and are directed towards God.⁶³

Thus, on this side of the eschaton, redeemed humanity exists *coram Deo* in the simultaneity of sin and justification.⁶⁴

One might object and suggest that the *simul* is merely of soteriological significance for Bonhoeffer, but he makes it clear that anthropology and soteriology are not mutually exclusive: "We must ask, in other words, whether there is in fact a being of human beings in general that is not already determined in every instance as their 'being-in-Adam' or 'being-in-Christ,' as their being-guilty or being-pardoned, and only as such could lead to an understanding of the being of human beings."⁶⁵ Like Luther, Bonhoeffer rejects the possibility that human being can be described in solely formal or material terms, holding, instead, to the anthropological significance of God as the efficient and final cause. Insofar as

---

61. Hans Richard-Reuter suggests that one of the primary dangers Bonhoeffer sensed in Barth's theology was the dissolution of the *simul* "into the imperceptible supratemporality of a 'heavenly double' who endures before God" ("Editor's Afterword to the German Edition," in *Act and Being: Transcendental Philosophy and Ontology in Systematic Theology*, ed. Wayne Whitson Floyd, Jr., trans. H. Martin Rumscheidt, DBWE [Minneapolis, MN: Fortress Press, 2009], 168–9).

62. Cf. James W. Woelfel, *Bonhoeffer's Theology: Classical and Revolutionary* (Nashville, TN: Abingdon Press, 1970), 77–83. It is notable, however, that in identifying Bonhoeffer's anthropological dialectic, Woelfel ignores Bonhoeffer's tripartite formulation in *Sanctorum Communio* and focuses solely on the *simul*.

63. *DBWE* 2:135.

64. In "Church and Eschatology," an early paper from his student days at the University of Berlin, Bonhoeffer also employs something like the *simul* in order to explain the relationship between the coming kingdom of God and the present church (*DBWE* 9:323).

65. *DBWE* 2:74; cf. Philip G. Ziegler, *Militant Grace: The Apocalyptic Turn and the Future of Christian Theology* (Grand Rapids, MI: Baker Academic, 2018), 178.

this highlights the basic significance of the God–human relationship for human ontology, soteriology must necessarily take on anthropological significance because what else does it deal with, if not the relationship between God and humanity? This is not to say that soteriology and anthropology are identical. Indeed, Bonhoeffer himself recognizes a need for a distinction when he writes: "The human being only 'is' in Adam or [*oder*] in Christ, in unfaith or [*oder*] faith, in Adamic humanity and [*und*] in Christ's community; God only 'is' as the creator, reconciler, and redeemer, and that being as such is personal being."[66] It is subtle, but, of the three pairs, he presents the first two in terms of mutual exclusivity— the decisive eschatological reality which defines a person is either in Adam or in Christ, either in unfaith or faith.[67] This is the soteriological situation. However, the third pair is inclusive—joined by *und* rather than *oder*—and thereby indicates the anthropological simultaneity entailed for those who are in Christ and in faith.

Alongside his emphasis on the *simul*, Bonhoeffer also identifies creatureliness as an aspect of being in Christ. Being a creature is not a convenient way of grounding the *simul* in a more basic ontology that is somehow immune to the disruptions of sin and grace.[68] Instead, it is a third term which stretches back to creation but is only realized in faith. "As those living in Christ, the new human beings know themselves in identity with the old human beings that have passed through death—as God's creatures. That sinners too are still creatures is something that can be expressed only by a believer; as long as this is an insight of sinners, it stays an idea in untruth."[69] Here it is evident that being in Christ is not only still marked by the threefold historical dialectic which interprets the human's relational being, but it also reveals to faith that humanity in Adam remain God's creatures by virtue of God's gracious preservation.[70] In order to more fully flesh this out, we shall now turn to the role that creation plays in the historical dialectic.

Historical Dialectic: Creation
Just as sin and reconciliation are not objects of knowledge that can be known independently of revelation to faith, so too with creation.[71] With this in mind,

---

66. *DBWE* 2:153; *DBW* 2:152.

67. On "unfaith" [*Unglaube*] as characteristic of Bonhoeffer's hamartiology, see Nielsen, "Sünde," 113–14.

68. "The doctrine of the primal state cannot offer us new theological insights. In the logic of theology as a whole it belongs with eschatology." *DBWE* 1:58.

69. *DBWE* 2:151.

70. This latter point is an essential element in the Bethel Confession's section on sin: "We reject the false doctrine that because of sin human beings are no longer God's creatures. For Christ went to the cross for the sake of humankind and there bore witness to God's love for God's fallen creatures" (*DBWE* 12:396). Such an affirmation was necessary in order to undercut any faux-Christian justification of the dehumanizing practices of the Nazi party. See Bethge, *Dietrich Bonhoeffer*, 302.

71. *DBWE* 12:219.

Bonhoeffer begins *Creation and Fall* by defining three epistemic standpoints: beginning, middle, and end. These epistemic standpoints correspond, roughly, to three temporal realities, namely, creation, the present, and consummation. Since "[n]o one can speak of the beginning but the one who was in the beginning,"[72] only God knows the beginning as such. The human situation is decidedly different. While all three historical realities are present to God, the human being exists only in the present and on account of this knows reality only from the middle. Thus, "[w]e do not know of this beginning by stepping out of the middle and becoming a beginning ourselves. Because we could accomplish that only by means of a lie, we would then certainly not be in the beginning but only in the middle that is disguised by a lie.... It is only in the middle that we come to learn about the beginning."[73] Yet, from their standpoint in the middle, humanity has lost the beginning and the end because of sin.[74] This is both an ontological and an epistemological claim— humanity in Adam is ontologically fragmented in such a way that epistemic access to the realities of creation and consummation are impossible.

How then can humanity know about creation and God as the creator?[75] For Bonhoeffer, the answer is, quite simply, the resurrection of Christ: "Only in the middle, as those who live from Christ, do we know about the beginning."[76] Like Luther, Bonhoeffer sees *creatio ex nihilo* and the resurrection as closely analogous events. The implications of this are twofold and expressed well by the Old Testament scholar, Wilhelm Vischer: "The Easter message is the verification of the message of the creation story, and the message of the creation story is the presupposition of the Easter message."[77] Thus, God's act of *creatio ex nihilo* is no less a gospel event than the resurrection of Christ. "It is the gospel, it is Christ, it's the resurrected one, who is being spoken of here. That God is in the beginning and will be in the end, that God exists in freedom over the world and that God makes this known to us—that is compassion, grace, forgiveness, and comfort."[78] For Bonhoeffer, as for Luther, then, Christ's resurrection is the justificatory event in which God affirms his identity as the Creator and attests to the fact that he is the same God who created and justified the world *ex nihilo* in the beginning.

That this is more than a clever analogy is made clear when Bonhoeffer discusses God's preservation of the world. "Creation and preservation are two sides of the same activity of God," and preservation is realized in the fact that God looks at what he has made, calls it good, and continues to hold it in his gaze.[79] This goes

---

72. *DBWE* 3:29.
73. *DBWE* 3:30–31.
74. *DBWE* 3:30.
75. *DBWE* 3:30.
76. *DBWE* 3:62.
77. *DBWE* 3:35n32.
78. *DBWE* 3:36.
79. *DBWE* 3:45.

part and parcel with the justificatory reality of *creatio ex nihilo*.[80] In creation, God's Word summons being out of nothing and "God's looking keeps the world from falling back into nothingness, from complete destruction."[81] The favorable posture which God takes toward the world—affirmed and fully revealed in Christ and the resurrection—is the sole reason that a postlapsarian world exists at all. "God's look sees the world as good, as created—even where it is a fallen world. And because of God's look, with which God embraces God's work and does not let it go, we live. . . . [W]hat it means [that God's work is good] is that the world lives wholly before God, that it lives from God and toward God and that God is its Lord."[82] Even though creation "is upheld not for its own sake but because of God's look," this does not negate the fact that "the work that is upheld is still God's good work."[83] While it is clear that Bonhoeffer is speaking cosmically here, rather than specifically anthropologically, humanity is certainly included in the created order which God justifies in *creatio ex nihilo* and continues to preserve in spite of sin.[84]

The fact that God is free for the world in creation and in the resurrection has significant implications for Bonhoeffer's account of the *imago Dei*. "To say that in humankind God creates the image of God on earth means that humankind is like the Creator in that it is free."[85] However, for Bonhoeffer, freedom is not a substance or an essence that one can locate in the person and objectify. Rather, "it is a relation and nothing else. To be more precise, freedom is a relation between two persons. Being free means 'being-free-for-the-other,' because I am bound to the other. Only by being in relation with the other am I free."[86] At the heart of this assertion is the fundamentally Christological locus of his account of the *imago Dei*. In faith, one only knows about the image of God by looking at Christ, who is the fullness of that

---

80. Cf. Ebeling, *Luther*, 197–8.

81. *DBWE* 3:45.

82. *DBWE* 3:45. This is not to say that prelapsarian preservation of creation is the same as postlapsarian preservation, since the former is an affirmation of goodness, while the latter is an affirmation of hope. See 3:47.

83. *DBWE* 3:47. On the ecological implications of Bonhoeffer's affirmation of the created world in Christ, see Steven C. van den Heuvel, *Bonhoeffer's Christocentric Theology and Fundamental Debates in Environmental Ethics* (Eugene, OR: Pickwick Publications, 2017).

84. This serves to mitigate concerns such as Colin Gunton's, when he writes: "The justification of the sinner, then is only a part to what is meant by the justice of God, which is concerned more broadly in terms of the transformation of the whole created order, as the outcome — as we shall see — of God's loyalty to creation." *The Actuality of Atonement: A Study of Metaphor, Rationality and the Christian Tradition* (Edinburgh: T&T Clark, 1988), 103. Indeed, God's loyalty to creation and his justification of the sinner are not two distinct things, but, rather, two sides of the same coin that is God's justificatory posture toward the world.

85. *DBWE* 3:62.

86. *DBWE* 3:63.

image.⁸⁷ Since Christ's life, death, and resurrection are marked by being-free-for-humanity, being-free-for-the-other also stands at the center of humanity's being the *imago Dei*. From this, Bonhoeffer coins the *analogia relationis*: "The likeness, the analogia, of humankind to God is not analogia entis but *analogia relationis*. What this means, however, is, firstly, that the relation too is not a human potential or possibility or a structure of human existence; instead it is a given relation, a relation in which human beings are set, justitia passiva!"⁸⁸ The image, which is central to theological anthropology, is fundamentally a relational, justificatory reality in which God holds humanity.

In all of this it is clear that, for Bonhoeffer, while creatureliness is a substantial aspect of human personhood, it is not something that one can access from the middle, apart from revelation. If this were possible then one would again risk a form of anthropological idealism, but this time on the side creation, rather than redemption. Instead, it is only in faith—because one knows Christ—that one knows about the beginning and the end. As such, creatureliness becomes meaningful for theological anthropology only from the perspective of one who is reconciled. But, here, creatureliness truly becomes meaningful since reconciliation is a recapitulation of creation, and not merely at the level of cosmology.⁸⁹ Bonhoeffer demonstrates this subtly when describing God's relation to the human person as creature in *Act and Being*: "In the idea of the creature, however, the personal-being of God and revelation manifests itself as creative-being and lordly being over my human personal being. And the second of these is the more encompassing of the two latter designations."⁹⁰ Both as creator and as lord, God's identity is recapitulated and affirmed in the reconciliation effected through the crucifixion and resurrection of Christ. In the beginning, God not only creates and grounds human being but is also lord over that being. Likewise, in reconciliation the being of the new human is found only in Christ who is simultaneously lord of her existence.⁹¹ As such, creatureliness is not merely a redemptive reality but is genuinely informed by the beginning. Thus, Bonhoeffer writes: "Even though I am able through faith alone to know myself as God's creature, I know, nonetheless, that I have been created by God in my entirety, as an I and as humanity, and that I have been placed into nature and history. I know, therefore, that these factors, too, have to do with creatureliness."⁹²

So, if humanity is epistemically dependent on reconciliation for knowledge about creation, and reconciliation is the ontological affirmation and recapitulation of creation, then does this entail that creation's role in the historical dialectic

---

87. 2 Cor 4:4; Col 1:15.
88. *DBWE* 3:65; cf. Jüngel, "Humanity in Correspondence to God," 135–6.
89. Cf. *DBWE* 8:229–31.
90. *DBWE* 2:151–2.
91. See Luther: "Search for yourself only in Christ and not in yourself, and you shall find yourself for ever in him." *LW* 42:106, cited in *DBWE* 2:139; cf. 11:295.
92. *DBWE* 2:152.

is merely formal, rather than substantial? Within Bonhoeffer's theological anthropology there is a degree of ambiguity here. On the one hand, Bonhoeffer clearly thinks of humanity's relation to God primarily in terms of sin and reconciliation.[93] One might suppose that in this schema creation is either collapsed into the "in Christ" of the new humanity or plays a merely negative function as the backdrop against which the dire effects of sin are understood.[94] The problem is that these assumptions are based on the presupposition that human ontology is essentially atomistic and a-relational, which is a presupposition foreign to Bonhoeffer's thought. If the relational aspects of Bonhoeffer's thought are filtered out then it certainly does seem as if theology poses an anthropological binary— between sin and redemption—since creatureliness is, at best, a consequence of reconciliation and, at worst, an inaccessible, prelapsarian reality. However, if one accords relationality the theological centrality that Bonhoeffer does, then the anthropological significance of creation is derived not from creation itself, but from the relationship established between God and humanity in creation. Viewed in this way, creation is an essential aspect of Bonhoeffer's dialectic because it is here where God affirms the world and the human being as creature. If it is removed or minimized in the dialectic, then the world and humanity come untethered from God and are subsumed in sin.[95] Likewise, reconciliation ceases to be reaffirmation—a second *creatio ex nihilo*—and risks becoming redemption *from* creaturely reality, which, thought of in this way, is really nothing more than sinful reality.

As such, it is essential that theological anthropology takes the historical dialectic seriously, recognizing humanity *coram Deo* within the framework of creation, sin, and reconciliation as those who are affirmed, judged, and made new in Christ alone. For Bonhoeffer, creation is not merely essential for theological anthropology. It is also of great import for theology more broadly because it "forces [theology's] methodological clarification."[96] Furthermore, "it renders concrete and vivid the real course of things from unity through break to unity."[97] If theology does not take this movement seriously then it is doomed to faulty understandings of both God and humanity.[98] However, Bonhoeffer recognizes that a genuine human ontology is possible only in light of the fullness of who God reveals himself to be in Christ—namely, "the Creator, the Holy, and the Merciful."[99] Thus, we see reflected in God's relation to humanity the three aspects of the historical dialectic

---

93. *DBWE* 2:151.
94. See *DBWE* 1:62.
95. Cf. Martin Westerholm, "Creation and the Appropriation of Modernity," *International Journal of Systematic Theology* 18, no. 2 (2016): 225.
96. *DBWE* 1:62.
97. *DBWE* 1:62.
98. Cf. Michael P. DeJonge, *Bonhoeffer on Resistance: The Word Against the Wheel* (Oxford: Oxford University Press, 2018), 30–6.
99. *DBWE* 12:256.

in which the human being exists: creature (God as Creator), sinner (God as Holy), and made new in Christ (God as Merciful).

III Christ, the Address

Before drawing this chapter to a close we need to say a bit more about the role that ecclesiology and Christology play in Bonhoeffer's justification-based account of the human person. The centrality of Christ and the church has certainly been evident in the preceding discussion. However, the main focus was to highlight the way in which Bonhoeffer's concern for justification is expressed in his emphasis on relationality and the historical dialectic in his theological anthropology. In what follows, we shall focus on Christ and the church as the theological realities which both entail and make possible Bonhoeffer's articulation of what it means to be human. This is to say that Bonhoeffer does not interpret ecclesiology and Christology through an anthropological lens, but, instead, presents an understanding of human being that is essentially undergirded by Christ and the church. Thus, the import Bonhoeffer accords Christology and ecclesiology in his anthropology is reflective of the fact that, for him, justification is essentially related to Christology and is realized only in the context of the church.[100]

In Bonhoeffer's inaugural lecture, he asserts that an understanding of the human person "emerges only from a still *point of unity [Einheitspunkt]*."[101] Thus, what is required for genuine anthropological knowledge is the ontological criteria of unity. Generally, however, this point of unity is identified either within the person or in reference to the limits which circumscribe her. Bonhoeffer rejects both approaches because both define human being in terms of possibility.[102] Instead he argues that unity should be understood in terms of continuity and address.[103] Here, we shall discuss the person of Christ as the address before going on to discuss the church as the continuity. Describing the central importance of God's address in the person of Christ for establishing the person in unity, Bonhoeffer writes: "They see their existence to be founded solely by the word of the person of Christ. They live in God's sight and in no other way. *Being is being in Christ, for here alone is unity and wholeness of life.*"[104] What this means is that justified being—living solely by the Word of Christ in God's sight—is being in Christ, is unified being. Thus, in the context of recent debates concerning forensic and effective interpretations of

---

100. *DBWE* 11:310; cf. 11:221–2.
101. *DBWE* 10:389; *DBW* 10:358.
102. Even though beginning the anthropological endeavor from the perspective of human limits seems to allow for a genuine encounter from the outside, Bonhoeffer goes on to show that even limits collapse into possibilities insofar as they remain posited by the self and are not given in revelation. See *DBWE* 10:399.
103. *DBWE* 10:390.
104. *DBWE* 2:134. Emphasis added. Cf. 10:400; 3:166.

justification, one might say that Christ, as the word of God's address, forensically encounters human beings, providing an extrinsic point of unity via participation in his person.[105]

What, then, are we to make of the historical dialectic of creation, fall, and reconciliation in light of the fact that it seems to imply the inherent fragmentation of the human person? Here, it is necessary to recognize that, in faith, the historical dialectic is a dialectical unity rather than three isolated and fragmented parts. "The unity of the I 'is' 'only in faith.'"[106] In other words, eschatological unity—made possible by and in Christ—is a reality that, in faith, takes history seriously, rather than relativizing it.[107] Such is the nature of reconciliation when it is effected by the God who becomes incarnate in history. Bonhoeffer further demonstrates the compatibility of unity in Christ with the historical dialectic when he writes that "[t]he human being sees his own unity grounded in God's word directed toward him, a word whose content is judgment and grace."[108] Christ, as the Word of God, is both the unity and center of human existence, and because of this "he is the judgment and the justification."[109] Thus, Christ does not unify human being in some sort of ideal way. Rather, he does so both as the historical God-man who takes humanity's judgment upon himself and as the singular human in whom the new humanity is synoptically seen as restored to community with God.[110] In this manner, Christ stands at the boundary of human existence and in humanity's place.[111] As such, human unity in Christ must be understood in the light of historical affirmation, as opposed to historical negation. This is because Christ is not only the word of God's address that encounters human being from the outside and reconstitutes it, but he is also the word of God's address through whom humanity is created, judged, and reconciled. Therefore, in Christ, humanity's relationship to God is both restored to unity in justification and described in terms of the historical dialectic of creation, fall, and reconciliation.[112]

---

105. *DBWE* 2:128.

106. *DBWE* 2:121.

107. Regarding the fact that Adam is only replaced by Christ eschatologically, in hope, see *DBWE* 1:124.

108. *DBWE* 10:405.

109. *DBWE* 12:325.

110. *DBWE* 1:157; cf. *DBWE* 12:327.

111. *DBWE* 12:324; cf. *DBWE* 1:147, SC-A.

112. Cf. Bonhoeffer's assertion that the limited human, whose limits are given to her by God in faith, is the justified human (*DBWE* 10:466–7). Put in the terms of this study: *coram Deo*, humanity is limited as creature, sinner, and reconciled by grace alone. Justification by faith is the dialectical unity of these relational limits, established in Christ and joyfully acknowledged in faith.

IV Church, the Continuity

So, if unity is established in Christ as the word of God's address, how can this extrinsic unity in Christ achieve any continuity of being in humanity? In other words, how is this unity in Christ not simply a legal fiction that has no ontological purchase on the being of the human person? Herein lies the import of the church for Bonhoeffer's justification-based account of the human person. "The unity of the historical I 'in faith' means unity in the community of faith, the historical community of faith that I believe to be the community of faith in Christ."[113] Unity requires not only address but also continuity, and this continuity is realized in Christ existing as the community of faith.

In Bonhoeffer's early theology, two key points emerge concerning the church that are relevant here. First, as the presence of the person of Christ in the world, the church is the locus of Christ's faith-creating encounter with humanity. Second, the church is the collective person of Christ which, in the dialectic of personhood, is decisive for new human being in Christ. What this means is that the church is the context in which the continuity of being in Christ is truly established in reality. Thus, Bonhoeffer writes that "continuity does not lie in human beings, but rather it is guaranteed suprapersonally through a community of persons."[114] However, because he defines the person in terms of the dialectic of personhood, locating continuity of being in the collective does not make it any less ontologically decisive for the individual human being. The new human really is *in* Christ because "'[t]o be in Christ' is synonymous with 'to be in the church-community.'"[115] As such, the church is both the sphere in which humanity is encountered from the outside by the forensic word of God's address and the continuity of the new being in Christ in which humanity participates by grace through faith.[116]

The significance of this for theological anthropology cannot be overestimated. In the church one comes to understand that Christ is both the word of God's address which justifies and the continuity of justified being. Only in this way can that which is extrinsic to humanity also be understood as ontologically constitutive. Justified existence *coram Deo* entails both encounter and incorporation, and the church is the basis on which these two realities are held together and mutually affirmed. As such, the church offers a solution to the dispute between forensic and effective interpretations of justification. Indeed, in the church the forensic is suspended in the effective in such a way that you cannot have one without the other. Bonhoeffer articulates this beautifully when discussing the centrality of preaching to the *sanctorum communio*: "The church is 'Christ existing as church-community';

---

113. *DBWE* 2:121.
114. *DBWE* 2:114.
115. *DBWE* 1:140; cf. 1:165.
116. Cf. Hans Pfeifer, "The Forms of Justification: On the Question of the Structure in Dietrich Bonhoeffer's Theology," in *A Bonhoeffer Legacy: Essays in Understanding*, ed. A. J. Klassen (Grand Rapids, MI: Eerdmans, 1981), 28–9.

Christ's presence consists in the word of justification. But since Christ's church-community is present where he is, the word of justification implies the reality of the church-community, that is, it demands an assembly of the faithful."[117] Where Christ—the forensic word of justification—encounters humanity, there the church is truly present, ensuring the effective continuity of the new human being in Christ. Thus, the personal presence of Christ in the church-community establishes a point of unity from which to interpret the human person. This unity is achieved only through the justifying address of Christ and continuity in his body, the church, which sets human being *coram Deo* as creature, sinner, and graciously reconciled.

V Conclusion

We began this chapter by identifying some potential blindspots in Clifford Green's seminal study of Bonhoeffer's theology of sociality. By considering whether more basic theological commitments undergird Bonhoeffer's emphasis on sociality, we opened up space in which to inquire after the extent to which Bonhoeffer takes after Luther in allowing justification to shape his anthropology. While Luther's more straightforward articulation of justification's import for theological anthropology serves as a backdrop against which to interpret Bonhoeffer's less unified theological understanding of the human person, we have seen that Bonhoeffer elaborates on Luther's account in important ways. Setting himself over against German idealist philosophy and a variety of theological accounts which sought to ground human being in human potential, the counterproposal Bonhoeffer sketches identifies the *coram Deo* relationship as ontologically decisive. Here he gives priority to God's freedom and grace in establishing humanity in creation, preserving them in sin, and reestablishing them in reconciliation. However, Bonhoeffer also recognizes that, by making the justificatory, God–human relation anthropologically determinative, real problems are introduced concerning the implications of God's act for human being. It is here that the dialectic of personhood and Christ existing

---

117. *DBWE* 1:231–2. On the centrality of the formulation "Christ existing as church-community" in Bonhoeffer's ecclesiology, see Mawson, *Christ Existing as Community*, 138–43. While this formulation seems to hint at a total identification between Christ and the church, Joachim von Soosten is surely correct when he writes: "This inseparable connection between ecclesiology and Christology . . . can be pressed by Bonhoeffer to the point where the two become indistinguishable. It must be noted, however, that through this close connection both Bonhoeffer and Luther seek to establish the Christological foundation of the concept of the church. In the unity between Christ and the church the relation of the former to the latter is therefore not reversible" ("Editor's Afterword to the German Edition," in *Sanctorum Communio: A Theological Study of the Sociology of the Church*, ed. Clifford J. Green, trans. Reinhard Krauss and Nancy Lukens [Minneapolis, MN: Fortress Press, 2009], 294). Cf. *DBWE* 11:302, where Bonhoeffer stresses that "*Christ also stands over against the church-community.*

as church-community create a space in which human being can be understood by faith as both *in relation to* the person of Christ as the external word of God's address and *in* Christ existing as church-community. In this manner, one can understand the ontologically fundamental justificatory relation between God and humanity as both a forensic encounter and effectively transformative. Thus, Bonhoeffer elaborates on Luther by acknowledging the complexity of a justification-based anthropology, and in doing so provides a more fully fleshed out model.

Characteristic of Bonhoeffer in all of this is his concern for history and concrete reality. As such, his anthropological thought seeks to do justice to the historical dialectic in which humans do not simply exist *coram* Deo as such, but, rather, as those who are created, sinful, and reconciled by grace in Christ alone. Although reconciled faith serves as a necessary epistemic criterion for recognizing the realities of creation and sin, this does not negate each aspect's distinct, ontological import. While Bonhoeffer's work tends to focus on the simultaneity of sin and reconciliation, we have shown that his thinking evinces a real concern for creatureliness as a third reality that must be considered alongside of them. Here, Bonhoeffer's historical dialectic is analogous to Luther's threefold *simul*. However, by following Bonhoeffer's impulses regarding creation as affirmation, the worldliness of reconciliation is inflected in new and important ways for the discussion to follow.

In conclusion, then, it is evident that although Bonhoeffer complexifies and elaborates on Luther's justificatory account, they are aligned on the basics: the human being is one whose existence is grounded extrinsically *coram Deo*, and this existence is marked by the real historical dialectic of creation, sin, and reconciliation by grace alone. By locating human being solely in its Christ-established relationship to God, Bonhoeffer is self-aware enough to realize that he is setting serious epistemic limits on the anthropological endeavor. He acknowledges that even in the act of reflecting on the self and human being there is an ironic turning away from Christ who is himself the locus of human being. Here, the threat of slipping into a mode of theological anthropology that draws on human possibility looms large. However, for Bonhoeffer, the church is the necessary check which balances theology's tendency to get lost in reflection and in doing so turning away from Christ and faith.[118] Thus, he concludes his inaugural lecture on theological anthropology in the following manner:

> To the extent that this attempt represents a piece of genuine theological thought, it escapes the charge that it too derives from reflection and does not offer any genuine self-understanding, if this is acknowledged without qualification, and only if this theological undertaking is itself incorporated into the reality of the church in which Christ is present. Ultimately, only as the thinking of the church does theological thought remain the only form of thought that does not rationalize reality through the category of possibility. Therefore, every individual

---

118. *DBWE* 10:407.

theological problem not only points back to the reality of the church of Christ, but theological thought in its entirety also recognizes itself as something that belongs solely to the church.[119]

We must keep in mind Bonhoeffer's emphasis on theology's humility in its beholdenness to the church-community as we turn now to the social implications of Bonhoeffer's justification-based anthropology, especially as they emerge in relation to his debate with German idealism.

---

119. *DBWE* 10:407–8.

Chapter 3

JUSTIFICATION AGAINST *WELTANSCHAUUNG*

BONHOEFFER'S EVALUATION OF COMPETING ANTHROPOLOGIES

I Introduction

According to Jean Bethke Elshtain, one of Dietrich Bonhoeffer's great strengths was his sensitivity to the fact that, in the sphere of public discourse, "[s]ooner or later the anthropological questions are going to come up. Sooner or later a debate must occur concerning the adequacy of contrasting anthropologies."[1] For Elshtain, theology's ability to resist de-humanizing philosophical, political, and social ideologies depends on the way in which it answers the question: What does it mean to be human? Thus, she continues: "Bonhoeffer never forgot that it is only through foregrounding the anthropological question . . . that theology can prevent its assimilation into some variant of an ideology external to itself, can forestall its sublimation [*sic*] within some political doctrine or plan or scheme, whether Bolshevism, or fascism, or even liberalism."[2] Her implicit assumptions here are that ideologies yield accounts of the human that are antithetical to the Christian theological account, and that Bonhoeffer's prioritization of the latter was instrumental in his opposition to the former. Yet, it is clear that prioritizing the anthropological question is not sufficient in and of itself. Indeed, there is no monolithic "theological anthropology." There are, rather, a variety of theological accounts of what it means to be human, each drawing on and prioritizing different tools and resources from Scripture, experience, and tradition that, in turn, shape their method and conclusions.[3] Thus, when it comes to resisting dehumanizing

---

1. Jean Bethke Elshtain, "Bonhoeffer on Modernity: 'Sic et Non,'" *Journal of Religious Ethics* 29, no. 3 (2001): 349–50.

2. Elshtain, "Bonhoeffer on Modernity," 350.

3. Elshtain, "Bonhoeffer on Modernity," 350, suggests that the *imago Dei* is at the heart of Bonhoeffer's anthropological concerns. However, insofar as Bonhoeffer's account of the *imago Dei* in *Creation and Fall* is relational (see *Creation and Fall: A Theological Exposition of Genesis 1–3*, ed. John W. De Gruchy, trans. Douglas S. Bax, DBWE [Minneapolis, MN: Fortress Press, 1997], 65), his starting point for thinking about what it means to be human

ideologies, the nature of one's answer to the anthropological question is just as important as foregrounding the question itself.

As we saw in the previous chapter, the doctrine of justification by faith plays an important role in structuring Bonhoeffer's answer to the anthropological question. It follows, then, that it should also play a central role in Bonhoeffer's evaluation of problematic visions of what it means to be a human. In the present chapter, we shall consider two such instances in his early academic theology. The first is his consistent polemic against German idealism along anthropological lines. Here, we shall consider Kant's anthropology as a particularly apt example of what Bonhoeffer was protesting. The second pertains to the anthropological provenance of his concerns with the concept of *Weltanschauung*, which are expressed against the backdrop of the rising tide of National Socialism. I will argue that in both cases Bonhoeffer is concerned with the way in which anthropology gets indexed to a certain ideal or value, which then, in turn, yields a teleology that is achievable on the basis of humanity's rational prowess. As an alternative, Bonhoeffer's justification-based anthropology is indexed to the person of Christ and therefore posits a telos that is available only by grace to faith. Thus, it is by answering the anthropological question in precisely this manner that Bonhoeffer is attuned to the dehumanizing implications of certain philosophical systems and ideologies.

II Bonhoeffer against Idealism

When it comes to careful, textual analysis of philosophical sources, Bonhoeffer is hardly exemplary.[4] With respect to his polemic against German idealism, Reinhold Seeberg's comment on his 1927 dissertation, *Sanctorum Communio*, is illuminating in this regard: "Characteristic of the position of the author is his strong emphasis on the principles of Christian ethics, which always serve as the starting point. From here he struggles in various ways against the worldview [*Weltanschauung*] of 'idealism.'"[5] Indeed, historically speaking, idealism itself is not a monolithic *Weltanschauung*, but is better understood as a proliferation of *Weltanschauungen* post-Kant, culminating in Hegel's attempt at a synthesis.[6]

---

is better characterized by human standing *coram Deo*. Indeed, as we saw in the previous chapter, Bonhoeffer's anthropological thinking starts here and works outward.

4. See Eberhard Bethge, *Dietrich Bonhoeffer: A Biography*, ed. Victoria Barnett, Rev. Ed. (Minneapolis, MN: Fortress Press, 2000), 133.

5. Dietrich Bonhoeffer, *The Young Bonhoeffer: 1918–1927*, ed. Paul Duane Matheny, Clifford J. Green, and Marshall D. Johnson, trans. Mary C. Nebelsick and Douglas W. Stott, DBWE (Minneapolis, MN: Fortress Press, 2003), 176.

6. For a brief account of this progression, see Emil L. Fackenheim, "Holocaust and *Weltanschauung*: Philosophical Reflections on Why They Did It," in *The God Within: Kant, Schelling, and Historicity*, ed. John Burbidge (Toronto: University of Toronto Press, 1996), 183–4.

So, insofar as Bonhoeffer takes issue with idealism as a philosophical system, he is concerned with certain features and positions that he takes to be generally consistent among idealist philosophers.[7] Thus, the *Weltanschauung* of idealism with which Bonhoeffer wrestles throughout his early academic theology does not neatly reflect the position of any one philosophical thinker, and even when he does have the work of a specific philosopher in mind, he does not always make this explicit.

However, few would dispute that Kant's philosophy substantively informed what Bonhoeffer took to be idealism's *Weltanschauung*.[8] Despite Bonhoeffer's less than meticulous citation practices, it is clear that he was familiar with a number of Kant's writings early on in his academic work, including two of the three texts that will feature most centrally in the following account: *Religion Within the Boundaries of Mere Reason* and "Idea for a Universal History from a Cosmopolitan Point of View."[9] While it is impossible to establish the precise role that these texts

---

7. It is also clear that his reading of idealism was heavily informed by secondary literature. For instance, his reading of Hegel was filtered through Seeberg (Bethge, *Dietrich Bonhoeffer*, 70) and Hinrich Knittermeyer's work was foundational to his reading of Kant (Hans-Richard Reuter, "Editor's Afterword to the German Edition," in *Act and Being: Transcendental Philosophy and Ontology in Systematic Theology*, ed. Wayne Whitson Floyd, Jr., trans. H. Martin Rumscheidt [Minneapolis, MN: Fortress Press, 2009], 165).

8. Of course, the extent to which Kant is properly understood as an idealist philosopher is hardly a matter of scholarly consensus. Indeed, Bonhoeffer makes the distinction between Kant's transcendentalism and German idealism in *Act and Being*. However, he often groups Kant in with Hegel and the idealists (see, for example, *DBWE* 1:193–8), and does so because he sees Kant as "the first in a long line that progresses up to Hegel" (*DBWE* 1:23). Hegel's philosophy is similarly foundational, but has received markedly more attention in Bonhoeffer scholarship. See, for example, Jorg Rädes, "Bonhoeffer and Hegel from *Sanctorum Communio* to the Hegel Seminar with Some Perspectives for the Later Works" (PhD Thesis, Chapter Draft, University of St Andrews, 1988); Charles Marsh, "Human Community and Divine Presence: Dietrich Bonhoeffer's Theological Critique of Hegel," *Scottish Journal of Theology* 45, no. 4 (1992): 427–48; Jacob Holm, "G.W.F. Hegel's Impact on Dietrich Bonhoeffer's Early Theology," *Studia Theologica* 56, no. 1 (2002): 64–75; David S. Robinson, *Christ and Revelatory Community in Bonhoeffer's Reception of Hegel* (Tübingen: Mohr Siebeck, 2018). Ultimately, it seems reasonable to assume that, regardless of their otherwise significant differences, the common features which constitute idealism's *Weltanschauung* in Bonhoeffer's mind can be detected in both Kant and Hegel. For a basic overview of Bonhoeffer's interaction with Kant and Hegel, see Wayne Whitson Floyd, "Encounter with an Other: Immanuel Kant and G. W. F. Hegel in the Theology of Dietrich Bonhoeffer," in *Bonhoeffer's Intellectual Formation: Theology and Philosophy in His Thought*, ed. Peter Frick (Tübingen: Mohr Siebeck, 2008), 83–119.

9. Bonhoeffer cites both in *Sanctorum Communio*. See, for example, *DBWE* 1:22, 43. The third text is *Anthropology from a Pragmatic Point of View*, which he did not read thoroughly prior to his imprisonment (*DBWE* 8:98). On Bonhoeffer's early introduction to and interest

played in eliciting and informing his critique of idealism, it will become quite clear that there is a remarkable resonance between Kant's anthropology and the idealist conception of human being that Bonhoeffer sought to theologically problematize. As such, Kant's philosophy is a particularly helpful, concrete example of what Bonhoeffer was protesting under the heading of idealism in his early academic theology. With this in mind, in what follows, I will briefly outline the key aspects of Kant's thinking about what it means to be human, which will then provide a sort of lens through which to evaluate the anthropological contours of Bonhoeffer's polemic against idealism.

a Outlining Kant's Anthropology

When discussing the relationship between philosophy and theology it is worthwhile to note that the birth of Kant's transcendental idealism coincided, roughly, with the formation of the modern research university. As such, Terry Pinkard notes that Kant's philosophy was ascendant around the same time that "'philosophy' actually took over from theology, law, and medicine as the anchor and the heart of the [collegiate] enterprise."[10] Running parallel to these developments was the establishment of anthropology as a new field of academic study. In much the same way as philosophy was supplanting theology in the context of the wider university, anthropology was "a product of the larger Enlightenment effort to emancipate the study of human nature from theologically based inquiries."[11] Thus, when Kant asserts on multiple occasions that "what is the human being?" is the fundamental question that undergirds all of philosophy, he is not only signaling the anthropological import of his own philosophical work, but he is also suggesting that philosophy as such is equipped to address this question.[12] This commitment to the philosophical centrality of anthropology marks Kant as both the progenitor of German idealism and the one responsible for the central import of the human subject in idealist philosophy.

Louden notes that, in a certain sense, "reflection on human nature is the most pervasive and persistent theme in all of Kant's writing, and as a result it is not

in Kant, see Bethge, *Dietrich Bonhoeffer*, 55, 73. It is interesting to note that even though Bonhoeffer took a seminar on Kant's *Critique of Pure Reason* with Karl Groos at Tübingen, in his dissertation he explicitly engages only with texts that are not a part of Kant's critical philosophy proper.

10. Terry Pinkard, "Idealism," in *The Oxford Handbook of German Philosophy in the Nineteenth Century*, ed. Michael N. Forster and Kristin Gjesdal (Oxford: Oxford University Press, 2015), 234.

11. Robert B. Louden, *Kant's Human Being: Essays on His Theory of Human Nature* (Oxford: Oxford University Press, 2011), 78.

12. Louden, *Kant's Human Being*, xvii.

exaggeration to say that *all* of his works are relevant to this question."[13] However, in his self-consciously anthropological work Kant devotes himself to what he calls "pragmatic anthropology." In the preface to *Anthropology from a Pragmatic Point of View*, Kant describes his method in contradistinction to physiological anthropology: "Physiological knowledge of the human being concerns the investigation of what *nature* makes of the human being; pragmatic, the investigation of what *he* as a free-acting being makes of himself, or can and should make of himself."[14] In this way Kant makes it clear that his definition of human being is, or attempts to be, unconditioned by the material world. Yet, even as it is unconditioned by the material world, it is fundamentally empirical and based on observation. Accordingly, it is also not conditioned by the transcendental.[15] As such, Kant's method also serves to delimit his subject matter, since, by bracketing out the biological-material and the supersensible, he narrow's the scope of philosophical anthropology to, as Louden puts it, "the phenomenal effects of human freedom in the empirical world, not their allegedly non-empirical origins."[16] Furthermore, Kant's desire to define human being in terms of what she makes of herself in her freedom is aimed at universals rather than particulars. This is reflected in the preamble to his 1775–6 *Friedländer* lectures on anthropology: "[A]nthropology is not a description of human beings, but of human nature. Thus we consider the knowledge of human beings in regard to their nature. Knowledge of humanity is at the same time my knowledge. Thus a natural knowledge must lie at the basis, in accordance with which we can judge what is basic to every human being."[17]

While Kant's anthropology is multivalent and hardly static over the course of his life, we shall focus here on four key aspects that emerge in his pragmatic anthropology and are particularly relevant to the present line of inquiry:

---

13. Louden, *Kant's Human Being*, xviii. Although this assertion may sound odd to those familiar primarily with Kant's three critiques, it is consonant with recent studies which "indicate that Kant's philosophical development was far more unified, and, in terms of its stages, involved deeper continuities than previously recognized" (Schönfeld, Martin and Thompson, Michael, "Kant's Philosophical Development," *The Stanford Encyclopedia of Philosophy* (Winter 2019 Edition), Edward N. Zalta (ed.), URL = https://plato.stanford.edu/archives/win2019/entries/kant-development/, accessed March 23, 2020). It is also worth noting here Bonhoeffer's own explicit identification anthropology as "the meaning of epistemology" (*DBWE* 2:30).

14. Immanuel Kant, "Anthropology from a Pragmatic Point of View," in *Anthropology, History, and Education*, ed. Günter Zöller and Robert B. Louden, trans. Robert B. Louden (Cambridge/New York: Cambridge University Press, 2007), 231.

15. Louden, *Kant's Human Being*, 81.

16. Louden, *Kant's Human Being*, 81.

17. Immanuel Kant, "Lecture of the Winter Semester 1775–1776 Based on the Transcriptions Friedländer 3.3 (Ms 400), Friedländer 2 (Ms 399) and Prieger," in *Lectures on Anthropology*, ed. Allen W. Wood, trans. G. Felicitas Munzel (Cambridge: Cambridge University Press, 2015), 48–9.

unsociable sociability, cosmopolitanism, teleology, and morality.[18] It is important to note, however, that morality is not merely an aspect of Kant's anthropology; it is also the organizing principle in relation to which unsociable sociability, cosmopolitanism, and teleology are defined. This is, then, consistent with an important line of interpretation, beginning with Hegel, that understands Kant's philosophical system as a moral *Weltanschauung*.[19] Thus, insofar as morality is the organizing principle of his *Weltanschauung*, we will see in what follows that this shapes his account of what it means to be human in distinctive ways.

Within Kant's anthropological thought, there is a significant tension between the cosmopolitan aim of human nature and the unsociable sociability that is necessary to realize this aim. What Kant means by unsociable sociability is the distinctly human "propensity to enter into society, which, however, is combined with a thoroughgoing resistance that constantly threatens to break up society."[20] In the background here, Kant is critiquing the original, pre-critical state of humanity: "an arcadian pastoral life of perfect concord, contentment and mutual love."[21] The problem with such a primal state is that, by nonreflectively living in a peaceful state, humanity neglects its freedom and self-determination toward moral ends. Thus, in opposition to the concord which humanity wills for itself, nature wills discord.[22] Unsociability, then, creates the conditions according to which "the rude natural predisposition to make moral distinctions" is transformed "into determinate practical principles and hence transform[s] *pathologically* compelled agreement to form a society finally into a *moral* whole."[23] On the one hand, Kant certainly intends nothing more by this than a description of the progression of nature in the context of history. Yet, on the other hand, by making this unsociability a necessary

---

18. For a good overview of the numerous and sometimes conflicting aspects of Kant's anthropology, see Louden, *Kant's Human Being*, xix–xxvi.

19. See G. W. F. Hegel, *Phenomenology of Spirit*, trans. A.V. Miller (Oxford: Oxford University Press, 1977), 366–75; Kenneth R. Westphal, "Hegel's Critique of Kant's Moral Worldview," *Philosophical Topics* 19, no. 2 (1991): 133–76; Richard Kroner, *Kant's Weltanschauung*, trans. John E. Smith (Chicago: University of Chicago Press, 1956); Fackenheim, "Holocaust and *Weltanschauung*," 183.

20. Immanuel Kant, "Idea for a Universal History with a Cosmopolitan Aim," in *Anthropology, History, and Education*, ed. Günter Zöller and Robert B. Louden, trans. Allen W. Wood (Cambridge/New York: Cambridge University Press, 2007), 111.

21. Kant, "Idea for a Universal History with a Cosmopolitan Aim," 111–12. Elsewhere Kant racializes this state in his disturbing comment on the subhuman nature of Tahitians. See Immanuel Kant, "Review of J.G. Herder's *Ideas for the Philosophy of the History of Humanity* Parts 1 and 2," in *Anthropology, History, and Education*, ed. Günter Zöller and Robert B. Louden, trans. Allen W. Wood (Cambridge/New York: Cambridge University Press, 2007), 142.

22. Kant, "Idea for a Universal History with a Cosmopolitan Aim," 112; Kant, "Anthropology from a Pragmatic Point of View," 417.

23. Kant, "Idea for a Universal History with a Cosmopolitan Aim," 111.

stop on life's way toward its moral telos, it is evident that Kant is offering more than a merely descriptive, phenomenological account. Indeed, the prescriptive necessity of unsociability is further affirmed by the theological justification Kant gives for its purposiveness when he says that it "betray[s] the ordering of a wise creator."[24]

That this unsociable sociability is proper to humanity is also affirmed by their "pragmatic predisposition," which Kant defines as an ability "to use other human beings skillfully for [one's] purposes."[25] Of course, the way in which human beings "use" others is related to and conditioned by their "moral predisposition," which is humanity's ability "to treat [themselves] and others according to the principle of freedom under laws."[26] In order for humanity to rise above its pre-critical, almost subhuman existence, they must enter into a state of unsociable sociability. Here, they cultivate their rationality and moral freedom in a social context, while, at the same time, seeking to use others unsociably toward their own ends. It is in this tension that all the powers of the human being are activated and genuine movement takes place, in accordance with a moral teleology, toward humanity's cosmopolitan aim.[27]

The cosmopolitanism at which Kant's anthropology aims is notoriously difficult to define. Even as the manner in which Kant writes about it is obviously sociopolitical, details pertaining to the political structure he envisions are scant.[28] However, it is also clear that for Kant, the political structure is not an end in itself. Rather, the "externally perfect state constitution" is the only means by which the hidden plan of nature "can fully develop all its predispositions in humanity."[29] As such, in the context of a "universal cosmopolitan condition" the state enables and makes possible humanity's full realization of its rationality, morality, and freedom, or what Kant frequently calls "talents."[30] Yet, Kant defines cosmopolitanism as a regulative, rather than a constitutive principle. In other words, it is not a guaranteed outcome, but is something hoped for, contingent on the exercise of

---

24. Kant, "Idea for a Universal History with a Cosmopolitan Aim," 112.

25. Kant, "Anthropology from a Pragmatic Point of View," 417. Cf. Louden, *Kant's Human Being*, 82.

26. Kant, "Anthropology from a Pragmatic Point of View," 417.

27. Kant, "Idea for a Universal History with a Cosmopolitan Aim," 111. To be clear, this does not negate the force of the categorical imperative in its various formulations. In general, Kant's account of unsociable sociability seems to be descriptive, while the categorical imperative is obviously prescriptive. However, an unresolved tension does persist insofar as it does seem that the first step on the road to being sociable according to the categorical imperative is the inevitably unsociable activation and development of one's rational and moral capacities.

28. See Louden, *Kant's Human Being*, 89.

29. Kant, "Idea for a Universal History with a Cosmopolitan Aim," 116.

30. Kant, "Idea for a Universal History with a Cosmopolitan Aim," 118.

human freedom.³¹ Thus, Kant writes: "[Human beings] feel destined by nature to [develop], through mutual compulsion under laws that come from themselves, into a *cosmopolitan society* (*cosmopolitismus*) that is constantly threatened by disunion but generally progresses toward a coalition."³²

This leads naturally to Kant's teleological understanding of the human person. Of the nine propositions he lays out in "Idea for Universal History with a Cosmopolitan Aim," eight deal substantially with the aim, purpose, or end of humanity. Yet, it is important to note that Kant begins the essay by delineating between the aim of humanity and the aim of nature. The former, ironically, is too erratic to establish a historical trajectory that is anthropologically useful.³³ Thus, Kant looks to the aim of nature as the teleological context in which to interpret the human being. Within this framework, the aim of nature acts as Kant's interpretation of the history of humanity, undergirding it and lending it coherence. Louden sums this up well when he writes: "The cosmopolitan conception of human nature is in effect a teleological moral map, a practical guide by means of which human beings are to orient themselves in both the present and the future."³⁴ In other words, when Kant speaks of the movement from non-reflective, pastoral life to sociability to unsociability to a gradual realization of cosmopolitanism, he is giving his anthropology a narrative context—and this context is governed by a cosmopolitan telos in which autonomous reason freely chooses morality according to the law.³⁵ However, even with this telos in place, Kant is careful to maintain human freedom in relation to it. In other words, it is up to human beings to freely will the cosmopolitan end toward which nature directs them.³⁶

What then is the nature of Kant's anthropological teleology? Well, it is cosmopolitan, but cosmopolitan human nature is defined in terms of reason, autonomy, and morality. Indeed, for Kant, the anthropological sphere is the arena

---

31. Louden, *Kant's Human Being*, 89.
32. Kant, "Anthropology from a Pragmatic Point of View," 427.
33. Kant, "Idea for a Universal History with a Cosmopolitan Aim," 109.
34. Louden, *Kant's Human Being*, 90.
35. Cf. Kant, "Idea for a Universal History with a Cosmopolitan Aim," 109, where Kant writes that the goal of a human being's predispositions "is the use of his reason." It is essential that the individual lays claim to her telos by the use of her reason alone, independent of instinct and any external influence (Kant, "Idea for a Universal History with a Cosmopolitan Aim," 110). Furthermore, it is necessary to keep in mind that Kant envisions this progress toward cosmopolitanism as happening over innumerable generations ("Anthropology From a Pragmatic Point of View," 419).
36. Kant, "Idea for a Universal History with a Cosmopolitan Aim," 110–11. Here we encounter a potential contradiction in Kant's thought. On the one hand, nature wills that the human being *determine* herself, but on the other hand, nature is *determining* humanity for this very freedom. For a good discussion of this tension and a potential resolution, see Louden, *Kant's Human Being*, 87.

in which morality moves out of the abstract and is fully realized.[37] Thus, morality and anthropology are mutually interpreting concepts. "The sum total of pragmatic anthropology, in respect to the vocation of the human being and the characteristic of his formation, is the following. The human being is destined by his reason to live in a society with human beings and in it to *cultivate* himself, to *civilize* himself, and to *moralize* himself by means of the arts and sciences."[38] Insofar as pragmatic anthropology pertains to what a human makes of herself, it is about how the human exercises her reason, freely willing the morally good. The telos for humanity is, as Louden puts it, the creation of a "moral realm, a realm in which each human being as a rational being is viewed as 'a lawgiving member of the universal kingdom of ends.'"[39]

In *Religion Within the Boundaries of Mere Reason*, Kant offers his account of Christ's role in the realization of humanity's moral telos. There he asserts that it is a universal human duty to elevate oneself to the ideal of moral perfection in Christ.[40] This universal duty exists in tension with his commitment to the reality of radical evil. As such, he says of the human pursuing goodness: "Whatever his state in the acquisition of a good disposition, and, indeed, however steadfastly a human being may have persevered in such a disposition in a life conduct conformable to it, *he nevertheless started from evil*, and this is a debt which is impossible for him to wipe out."[41] However, radical evil, for Kant, is not an *a priori* necessity, but is, rather, a consequence of the free choice of rational human beings whose self-determined maxims are perverted.[42] Corresponding to their role in radical evil, reason and freedom also serve as the condition of the possibility of fulfilling the universal human duty of moral conformation to Christ. In other words, autonomous reason is both the downfall of humanity and its salvation.

Although in some ways Kant describes Christ as the prototype of humanity in traditionally Christian terms, it is clear that, as the telos of humanity, Christ

---

37. See Kant, "Lecture of the Winter Semester 1775–1776 Based on the Transcriptions Friedländer 3.3 (Ms 400), Friedländer 2 (Ms 399) and Prieger," 49.

38. Kant, "Anthropology from a Pragmatic Point of View," 420.

39. Robert B. Louden, "General Introduction," in *Anthropology, History, and Education*, ed. Günter Zöller and Robert B. Louden (Cambridge: Cambridge University Press, 2007), 1–2.

40. Immanuel Kant, *Religion Within the Boundaries of Mere Reason and Other Writings*, ed. and trans. Allen W. Wood and George Di Giovanni (Cambridge: Cambridge University Press, 1998), 80.

41. Kant, *Religion Within the Boundaries*, 88.

42. Kant, *Religion Within the Boundaries*, 78. On the challenge of interpreting Kant's doctrine of radical evil which arises from the tension between the empirical and the universal in his thought, see Patrick R. Frierson, *Freedom and Anthropology in Kant's Moral Philosophy* (Cambridge/New York: Cambridge University Press, 2003), 34–8.

is primarily a moral exemplar, and movement toward that telos is rooted in autonomous reason.[43] To illustrate this, it is worth quoting Kant at length:

> There is no need, therefore, of any example from experience to make the idea of a human being morally pleasing to God a model to us; the idea is present as model already in our reason.—If anyone, in order to accept for imitation a human being as such an example of conformity to that idea, asks for more than what he sees, i.e. more than a course of life entirely blameless and as meritorious as indeed one may ever wish; and if, in addition, he also asks for miracles as credentials, to be brought about either through that human being or on his behalf—he who asks for this thereby confesses to his own moral *unbelief*, to a lack of faith in virtue which no faith based on miracles (and thus only historical) can remedy, for only faith in the practical validity of the idea that lies in our reason has moral worth.[44]

In short, the moral telos of humanity is already present to and within the human being. As such, Christ serves as the instantiation of the moral telos which *affirms* its possibility, while autonomous reason alone remains the *condition* of its possibility. "And the required prototype always resides only in reason, since outer experience yields no example adequate to the idea; as outer, it does not disclose the inwardness of the disposition but only allows inference to it, though not with strict certainty."[45] Ultimately, then, "the idea of the moral good in its absolute purity" lies in our "original predisposition" and Christ assures humans that it is both possible and their duty to freely choose their maxims according to reason in a manner that aligns with this moral good.[46]

Before turning to consider how Bonhoeffer problematizes idealism along the same lines as those we have just sketched in Kant's thought, it is worth noting that to do so is not to unfairly hold Kant's philosophy to an alien theological standard. Indeed, Christopher Insole has rightly noted that Kant's articulation of the Christian religion in terms of mere reason is not intended as a subversion of historical Christian doctrine, but, rather, as its translation.[47] The editors of

---

43. "'In him God loved the world,' and only in him and through the adoption of his dispositions can we hope to 'become children of God'" (Kant, *Religion Within the Boundaries*, 80). Yet, even here Kant equates being in Christ with an adoption of his dispositions.

44. Kant, *Religion Within the Boundaries*, 81.

45. Kant, *Religion Within the Boundaries*, 81-2. It is fascinating that, for Kant, Christ is the prototype for both humanity and their telos, who exists outside of the human being. Kant, then, does not deny Christ's externality, but, rather, relativizes the need for salvific encounter by already locating the potential for reconciliation and transformation within the individual.

46. Kant, *Religion Within the Boundaries*, 98.

47. Christopher J. Insole, *The Intolerable God: Kant's Theological Journey* (Grand Rapids: Eerdmans, 2016), 14. However, accepting this view does not necessarily entail

the Cambridge edition of *Religion Within the Boundaries of Mere Reason* also clearly share this view since if one looks up "justification" in the index she will find the page numbers for the section referenced previously. Indeed, although it does not come through quite so clearly in the English translation, the German word most commonly associated with justification, *Rechtfertigung* and its cognate, *Gerechtigkeit*—variously translated as "righteousness" or "justice" in the Cambridge edition—are invoked repeatedly. This speaks to the translation of historical doctrine which Kant is engaging in because, as noted earlier, Kant is concerned not with the alien righteousness of the person of Christ by which one is justified, but, rather, with the righteousness which is personified in the idea of Christ, validated by autonomous reason, and incorporated into the maxims freely chosen by the individual. Thus, in the following outline of how justification shapes Bonhoeffer's alternative to the anthropology yielded by idealism's *Weltanschauung*, it is important to bear in mind that, at least when it comes to Kant, what it means to be human comports with and is validated by his construal of justification in terms of mere reason.

b Bonhoeffer's Justification-based Anthropology Against Idealism

Insofar as Bonhoeffer's anthropology seeks to locate human being firmly within the realm of history, there is for him, as for Kant, an essential connection between history and anthropology.[48] However, unlike Kant, Bonhoeffer follows Luther in his apocalyptic-theological understanding of history. Oswald Bayer sums up Luther's view in the following way:

> Luther's apocalyptic understanding of creation and history bars the door to him, so that he cannot search for a way to explain history from a comprehensive historical-philosophical perspective, particularly as such a view is expressed in the modern concept of progress. The rupture between the old and the new world, which occurs in what happened on the cross of Christ and which marks

---

affirmation of Insole's later claim that although "[t]he translation certainly puts Kant in a strained relationship with traditional Christianity . . . it is still a type of theology, in that it makes claims about God and our relation to God" (52–3). In fact, according to some of Kant's closest contemporaries, he was entirely uninterested in theology, did not believe in an afterlife, and rejected the idea of a personal God (Manfred Kuehn, *Kant: A Biography* [Cambridge: Cambridge University Press, 2001], 2–3).

48. While Bonhoeffer thinks of history theologically (see his claim that history must be understood in relation to the state of sin and death in *DBWE* 1:62) and Kant thinks of it philosophically, their attention to the connection between anthropology and history distinguishes them from those who conceive of anthropology as the study of human being's timeless structures. For an extended theological treatment of the relation between anthropology and history, see Wolfhart Pannenberg, *Anthropology in Theological Perspective*, trans. Matthew J. O'Connell (Philadelphia, PA: The Westminster Press, 1985), 485–532.

each one biographically in baptism, ruptures metaphysical concepts of an overall unity as well as historical-theological thinking that one can achieve perfection.[49]

Like Luther, Bonhoeffer is deeply suspicious of the comprehensive claims of philosophy in relation to history and anthropology, as well as notions of self-enabled progress toward perfection.[50]

Indeed, Bonhoeffer's theological critique of philosophy is deeply indebted to Luther. In Luther's *Disputation Concerning Man*, he asserts that philosophical anthropology has access to only the formal and material causes of humanity, and even then not infallibly. The efficient and final causes of human being remain entirely inaccessible to unaided reason.[51] This construal parallels Bonhoeffer's discussion, in *Creation and Fall*, of the situatedness of humanity in relation to the beginning and the aim of their existence.[52] He writes: "Humankind no longer lives in the beginning; instead it has lost the beginning. Now it finds itself in the middle, knowing neither the end nor the beginning, and yet knowing that it is in the middle."[53] In the middle, humanity, from a philosophical perspective, is able to engage in anthropology only in a descriptive mode, taking the material and form of human being as its subject matter. The beginning and the end are known only in revelation, and as such, are the domain of theology rather than philosophy. As a result, only theological anthropology can provide an adequate definition of what it means to be human. However, Bonhoeffer recognizes that, because of sin, this ideal delimiting of philosophy in relation to theology is impossible to maintain. "Humankind knows itself to be totally deprived of its own self-determination, because it comes from the beginning and is moving toward the end without knowing what that means. This makes it hate the beginning and rise up in pride against it."[54] For Bonhoeffer, when philosophy grasps after the efficient and final cause of humanity, as is the case in Kant, it is nothing less than a claim to self-determination. Such self-determination is predicated on the expansion of human

---

49. Oswald Bayer, *Martin Luther's Theology: A Contemporary Interpretation*, trans. Thomas H. Trapp (Grand Rapids: Eerdmans, 2008), 9. Cf. Christoph Schwöbel, "Human Being as Relational Being: Twelve Theses for a Christian Anthropology," in *Persons, Divine and Human: King's College Essays in Theological Anthropology*, ed. Christoph Schwöbel and Colin E. Gunton (Edinburgh: T&T Clark, 1999), 169.

50. Cf. Peter Frick, "Bonhoeffer and Philosophy," in *Understanding Bonhoeffer* (Tübingen: Mohr Siebeck, 2017), 181.

51. Martin Luther, "The Disputation Concerning Man," in *Luther's Works: Career of the Reformer IV*, ed. and trans. Lewis Spitz, vol. 34 (Philadelphia, PA: Fortress Press, 1960), 137–8.

52. Floyd suggests that *Creation and Fall* can be read as a sort of "parable" for what Bonhoeffer took to be the "promise and failure of idealism" ("Encounter with an Other," 108).

53. *DBWE* 3:28.

54. *DBWE* 3:28.

reason beyond the limits imposed upon it by both finitude and the noetic effects of sin.[55]

Bonhoeffer sharpens his critique of philosophy in his inaugural lecture on theological anthropology. Indeed, he begins by describing philosophy as human activity par excellence.[56] He goes on to equate philosophy as a human work with "the concretization of a possibility."[57] In other words, philosophy is the realization of a possibility already embedded within human being. One might suggest, however, that philosophy is capable of identifying the limits of human being, and as such, its own limits. Accordingly, philosophy is capable of imposing certain limits on human possibility. By way of a response, it must be acknowledged that Bonhoeffer does allow for a genuinely Christian philosophy: "*Per se*, a philosophy can concede no room for revelation unless it knows revelation and confesses itself to be Christian philosophy in full recognition that the place it wanted to usurp *is* already occupied by another—namely, by Christ."[58] However, philosophy does not get there by discerning its own limits, because, insofar as those limits are self-imposed, philosophy has already transgressed them in order to identify them.[59] In other words, even these limits are haveable and graspable by the human person, based on her possibilities. Thus, regarding philosophical thought, Bonhoeffer acknowledges that "the human being essentially has no boundaries within himself; he is infinite within himself. To that extent, idealism is correct."[60] The boundlessness of thought places the person at the center of her own world as its master.[61] Nothing can stand in the way of reason.

In "Concerning the Christian Idea of God," an article Bonhoeffer published in 1932 during his year abroad in New York City, he contrasts the Christian conception of God as person with idealism's definition of person.[62]

> Idealism defines personality as the subjective realization of objective spirit—that is, of absolute spirit. Each personality is constituted by the same spirit, which is, in the last analysis, reason. Each personality is personality as far as it participates in reason. Thus each one knows the other. Personality is no secret and, therefore,

---

55. Cf. Bonhoeffer's critique of Hegel: "The Hegelian question how are we to make a beginning in philosophy can therefore be answered only by the bold and violent action of enthroning reason in the place of God" (*DBWE* 3:27).
56. *DBWE* 10:391.
57. *DBWE* 10:391.
58. *DBWE* 2:76–8.
59. *DBWE* 10:399.
60. *DBWE* 10:399.
61. Cf. *DBWE* 10:353.
62. Although Bonhoeffer uses "personality" in the text, rather than "person," this is merely a conformation to the conventions of American English at the time. See *DBWE* 10:455n28.

another personality is no real limit for me because, in the last analysis, I have at my disposal the spirit of reason, as does also the other person.[63]

On this account, idealism enthrones reason as that which transcends social boundaries and makes possible universal definitions of what it means to be human. In other words, reason as absolute spirit sweeps aside particularity while elevating the authority of universals. Over against the priority idealism places on reason, the Christian concept of person involves both transcendence and genuine freedom. "God as the absolutely free personality is, therefore, absolutely transcendent."[64] As such, what it means to be human cannot be found in the universal, sovereignty of reason, but can only be received from God in the person of Jesus Christ.

There is also, for Bonhoeffer, a correlation between person and history. Since idealism defines personhood abstractly with little regard for concrete reality, its interpretation of history is more concerned with ideas than it is with facts or events. "History becomes 'symbol,' transparent to the eternal spirit. . . . The earnestness of ontological consideration is weakened through reinterpretation in axiological judgments."[65] Consequently, revelation is separated from history and the truths it conveys are relegated to the realm of abstract ideas, ripe for reason's picking. This brings us to the crux of Bonhoeffer's critique of an idealist conception of personhood and history. By reducing history to the material husk which houses the spiritual kernel, idealism fails to "take seriously the ontological category in history. Which means that it does not take history seriously."[66] Bonhoeffer recognizes that this reduction of history to abstract ideas, which can be commanded and accessed by reason, has serious implications in the anthropological realm, especially regarding "the interpretation of the other man, of the neighbor, that is, of present history."[67]

In contrast, the Christian concept of history is necessarily ontological since history cannot be absorbed into the self as an idea. It is the theater of decision where humanity encounters that which stands over against it.[68] From this follows a definition of history as the existence of humanity *coram Deo*. To be clear, Bonhoeffer is primarily interested here in preserving the integrity of historical revelation in the person of Christ from the abstracting influence of German idealism. Yet, preservation of history and personhood in revelation has profound anthropological implications, since, for Bonhoeffer, anthropology receives its shape and structure from revelation in Christ.[69] Thus, it is telling that Bonhoeffer

---

63. *DBWE* 10:455.
64. *DBWE* 10:455.
65. *DBWE* 10:457.
66. *DBWE* 10:457–8.
67. *DBWE* 10:458.
68. *DBWE* 10:458.
69. On Christ as the *Einheitspunkt* (point of unity) from which to interpret the human, see *DBWE* 10:389.

concludes his article by identifying justification as the proof and doctrinal affirmation of God's freedom which grounds history and personhood.[70]

So, we have seen that Bonhoeffer directly opposes the idealist tendency to enthrone reason along with its corresponding conception of history and the human person. But what then of its moral teleology? Perhaps the clearest articulation of Bonhoeffer's critique of idealism on this front is found in some of his earliest theological writing, specifically his 1926 essay, "Church and Eschatology (or Church and the Kingdom of God)." Here, Bonhoeffer identifies and critiques the way in which idealism engages in "the secularization of the concept of the kingdom of God," identifying Kant as particularly representative of this sort of move.[71] By replacing the kingdom of God with "the general concept of rational spirit," idealism makes the kingdom visible, which ties its realization to human works and renders the church irrelevant.[72] In this way, idealism presents the kingdom of God as nothing more than the moral telos of humanity. "Through gradual progress evil is removed from the earth. All of humankind will find itself united in the kingdom of God. The history of the world is at the same time the history of the kingdom of God. The church will merge into the world of morality."[73] Insofar, as cosmopolitan culture and the state are central aspects of idealism's realization of this telos, the church gradually dissolves into the sociopolitical realm as history progresses. Bonhoeffer rebuts this theologically and empirically. Theologically, the incarnation militates against human realization of the kingdom of God in history. "For the Christian faith, idealism's framework shatters especially upon the thought that God became human: the necessity of sin must be timeless, not something that would eventually disappear."[74] Empirically, Bonhoeffer points to the way in which so-called advanced, Western societies often fall prey to rampant "moral disintegration" and "the unhappy course of innumerable grand undertakings."[75] Thus, in opposition to a sociopolitical and moral conception of the kingdom which can be realized in history, Bonhoeffer asserts that "the empirical church is the sole signpost pointing beyond this world toward the kingdom of God."[76] In other words, the telos of history and humanity—the kingdom of God—is discovered and encountered only in the church's proclamation of the word and administration of the sacraments because that is where Christ *is*.[77] Up to this

---

70. *DBWE* 10:461.
71. *DBWE* 9:318.
72. *DBWE* 9:319.
73. *DBWE* 9:319.
74. *DBWE* 9:319. By "timeless" here Bonhoeffer does not mean that sin is an eternal reality, but, rather, that it will not be fully done away with until the end of history in the eschaton.
75. *DBWE* 9:319.
76. *DBWE* 9:320.
77. For an excellent discussion of Bonhoeffer and the Lutheran "is," see Michael P. DeJonge, *Bonhoeffer's Reception of Luther* (Oxford: Oxford University Press, 2017), 67–75.

point, I have identified some central aspects of Kant's anthropology and seen that Bonhoeffer critiques idealism exactly in relation to these aspects—namely, its rational, moral, and teleological understanding of history, revelation, and the person. Now, we shall consider how Bonhoeffer's justification-based anthropology serves as the basis from which he launches his critical evaluation. In *Sanctorum Communio*, Bonhoeffer identifies two basic deficiencies in idealist anthropology: "In the last analysis the reason why idealist philosophy fails to understand the concept of person is that it has no *voluntaristic* concept of God, nor a profound concept of sin."[78] We shall take each one of these in turn in relation to Bonhoeffer's justification-based anthropology.

By defining humanity *coram Deo*, Bonhoeffer sees anthropology as beginning with God and God's freedom in creation. This freedom forms the ground for God's justifying work in *creatio ex nihilo*, preservation in the midst of sin, and reconciliation. Furthermore, for Bonhoeffer, Christ is the word of God's freedom through whom he creates, preserves, and reconciles. In contrast, idealism either turns Christ into an abstract, moral exemplar or posits the necessity of God entering into history.[79] Both cases describe the necessary mechanisms of reason in the world. On account of this necessity, reason abolishes the first principle of all properly Christian theology—namely, that God freely became human.[80] Idealism, then, posits that God's revelation can be known independently of God. Based on this epistemic judgment, an ontology of human being emerges in which the human is fundamentally autonomous and rational. However, due to his substantial understanding of God's freedom for humanity in Christ, Bonhoeffer arrives at a very different definition of human being. Rather than asserting that humans are free for self-determination, he holds that humans are truly free only when, through justification by faith, they are determined by and in relation to God.[81] Justification, as an anthropological category, necessitates heteronomy in the anthropological sphere because the human person exists only in encounter with an other. Christianity is not the perfect, religious embodiment of rational autonomy, as Kant would have it, but, rather, depends on heteronomous encounter between God and humanity in creation, preservation, and reconciliation. Thus, human ontology is fundamentally marked by relationality, faith, and heteronomous encounter, rather than rationality and autonomy.

Moreover, because God enters into history as a human in the person of Jesus Christ, theological anthropology must refrain from ahistorical interpretations of what it means to be human. The issue of ahistoricity plagues idealist anthropology because it fails to recognize sin as the fundamental disruption that it is. Idealism fails to take sin seriously as an irrational break in which human beings sever their relationship with God, thereby denying their source and meaning. Instead, idealism

---

78. *DBWE* 1:48.
79. Cf. *DBWE* 12:317, 337.
80. *DBWE* 12:338.
81. Cf. *DBWE* 1:49.

rationalizes sin as unsociable sociability—a necessary stage in the development of reason toward its moral telos. Interpreted against the backdrop of Bonhoeffer's real historical dialectic—in which the human being is simultaneously creature, sinner, and reconciled in Christ alone—idealism's rationalizing of sin is actually evidence that its anthropology only takes into account the human *as sinner*.[82] In other words, idealism is able to rationalize sin because it has accorded humanity a final cause which is contingent on human self-realization, rather than on Jesus Christ. Creation, sin, and reconciliation are all contained within human being and are epistemically accessible to it. As such, there is no real, historical dialectic in which disruption is possible. Instead, there is only smooth progression from one phase to another. Thus, Bonhoeffer writes:

> The fundamental difference between our position and that of idealism is this knowledge of the inner history of the concept of person in the move from the primal state [creation] to sin—in other words, the weight that we give to sin as having real and qualitative character when connected to history. *For idealism, origin and telos remain in unbroken connection and are brought to synthesis in the concept of "essence."* Nothing in between—sin, on the one hand, and Christ on the other—can essentially break this eternal, necessary connection. <<Hegel also seems to me to be no exception here.>> Such a view of history as an unbroken straight line basically eliminates everything specifically Christian. In this view, neither sin nor redemption alters the essence of history.[83]

For Bonhoeffer the human being is properly understood only according to the historical dialectic, but such an understanding is inaccessible to reason as such. Rather, proper understanding of what it means to be human is available only in faith. Here, sin's disruption becomes serious because only in faith can a person recognize that she is cut off from her origin and in need of a second disruption to remedy this. As such, humanity's telos is not something that can be seized rationally and morally. Instead, it can only be given by grace in the person of Jesus Christ. "Since death as the wages of sin (Rom. 6:23) first constitutes *history*, so *life that abides in love* breaks the continuity of the historical process—not empirically, but objectively."[84]

Finally, in his concept of the church, Bonhoeffer challenges and provides a theological alternative to Kant's cosmopolitanism.[85] Christ exists within the church not as an ideal, moral exemplar, as Kant would have it, but, rather, as a person—as the justifying image of God. The telos of humanity is not something

---

82. On the real historical dialectic, see *DBWE* 1:62.

83. *DBWE* 1:59–60, SC-A. "SC-A" denotes text that Bonhoeffer excised from his dissertation in preparation for publication, while "<<>>" indicates footnotes to that text.

84. *DBWE* 1:146.

85. Cf. Robert Vosloo, "Body and Health in the Light of the Theology of Dietrich Bonhoeffer," *Religion & Theology* 13, no. 1 (2006): 27.

that the state can accomplish, nor is it a moral ideal to which Christ beckons. Rather, it is simply the person of Christ who encounters humanity in and through the church, reconstituting them in his body through Word and sacrament.[86] This insight is summed up well by Christoph Schwöbel when he writes: "The place where this dialectic between the imperfectability of humanity by its own efforts and the promise of perfection in communion with the triune God is constantly exercised and enacted is the church as the community of faith."[87]

Thus, insofar as Bonhoeffer takes issue with the *Weltanschauung* of idealism in his early academic theology, it is clear that one important reason he does so is the sort of vision it casts for what it means to be human. Our brief survey of Kant's anthropology provided a lens through which to identify the key aspects of idealism's construal of human being—namely, autonomous reason and a moral teleology aimed at a cosmopolitan utopia. We then saw that not only does Bonhoeffer critique idealism precisely along these lines, but that in doing so his reasoning also reflects the contours of his justification-based anthropology. In the next section, we shall see that Bonhoeffer's problematization of the anthropology yielded by idealism's *Weltanschauung* is, in fact, paralleled by the manner in which he questions the philosophical concept of *Weltanschauung* more broadly in the midst of National Socialism's ascendancy.

III Bonhoeffer against Weltanschauung

It is common in Bonhoeffer scholarship to identify 1933 as a pivotal year in his life—one in which his time in the academy, for all intents and purposes, came to an end. In subsequent years, his life and work came to be marked by his resistance to the rising tide of National Socialism, especially his fierce involvement in *Kirchenkampf*.[88] Indeed, there is little room to question whether Bonhoeffer's best friend and biographer, Eberhard Bethge, was correct when he wrote: "The political turning point on 30 January 1933 would force Bonhoeffer's life onto a different course. It did not require a reorientation of his personal convictions or theology, but it became increasingly clear that academic discussion must give way to

---

86. For a concrete example of what Bonhoeffer was up against on this front, see the way in which Pastor Friedrich Peter, at the Theological Conference of the Provisional Bureau for Ecumenical Youth Work, separates faith from the church and links it more essentially to the nation-state (*DBWE* 11:354).

87. Schwöbel, "Human Being as Relational Being," 169.

88. Bonhoeffer's resistance can be further divided into three phases. For a brief sketch of these phases, see Michael P. DeJonge, *Bonhoeffer on Resistance: The Word Against the Wheel* (Oxford: Oxford University Press, 2018), 9, where he draws on the more detailed framework sketched by Florian Schmitz in *"Nachfolge": Zur Theologie Dietrich Bonhoeffers* (Göttingen: Vandenhoeck & Ruprecht, 2013), 299–402.

action."[89] Here, even as he identifies a shift in the nature of Bonhoeffer's theological work—from academic preoccupations to thinking and acting in relation to the challenges facing the Confessing Church—which coincided with the swearing in of Hitler as the chancellor of Germany, Bethge also points to a basic continuity in his theological impulses.[90]

One such continuity lies in Bonhoeffer's theologically motivated resistance to *Weltanschauung* thinking. While his active opposition to the dehumanizing implications of the National Socialist *Weltanschauung* is common knowledge, little attention has been given to his criticisms of *Weltanschauung* as a philosophical concept prior to 1933. In what follows, I will draw on the work of Emil Fackenheim in order to offer a definition of *Weltanschauung*, as well as a brief overview of its historical development. I will then consider Bonhoeffer's critique of *weltanschauliche* thinking, making the case that at the heart of his contention is the manner in which *Weltanschauungen* undermine justification's decisive import for what it means to be human.

When it comes to defining *Weltanschauung*, Emil Fackenheim begins by disambiguating the concept as it was understood in nineteenth- and early twentieth-century Germany from the way one might define its typical English translation—"worldview"—today.[91] Indeed, rather than identifying the interpretive framework within which a given person imbues experience and ideas with meaning, *Weltanschauung* was something hard won and worthy of admiration. This is because it is not something a person just has by virtue of being human, but must be comprised of three things in order to earn such respect. First, it must be cosmic in scope. Fackenheim distinguishes here between mere ideologies and *Weltanschauungen*, asserting that the former do not aspire to transcend and

---

89. Bethge, *Dietrich Bonhoeffer*, 258.

90. Although the question of continuity in his theological development was an important one in early Bonhoeffer scholarship, most now follow Bethge in stressing continuity. See, for example, DeJonge, *Bonhoeffer's Reception of Luther*, 5–6; Clifford J. Green, *Bonhoeffer: A Theology of Sociality*, Rev. Ed. (Grand Rapids, MI: Eerdmans, 1999), 7–13; Stephen Plant, *Bonhoeffer* (London: Continuum, 2004), xi.

91. To this point, I have only used the German term, rather than its most common English translation, "worldview." This is primarily to distinguish the present argument from adjacent discussions taking place, predominantly in American evangelical circles, concerning the theological validity of worldview thinking (however that might be defined). See, for example, James K. A. Smith, *Desiring the Kingdom: Worship, Worldview, and Cultural Formation* (Grand Rapids, MI: Baker Academic, 2009), 31–2; N. T. Wright, *Paul and the Faithfulness of God*, Christian Origins and the Question of God (Minneapolis, MN: Fortress Press, 2013), 27–36; Samuel V. Adams, *The Reality of God and Historical Method: Apocalyptic Theology in Conversation with N. T. Wright* (Downers Grove, IL: IVP Academic, 2015), 207–13. The goal here is not to pass judgment on the usefulness of worldview thinking for Christian theological method, but, rather, to consider, along with Bonhoeffer, the correlation between *Weltanschauungen* and problematic anthropologies.

redefine history, but the latter do.⁹² In other words, mere ideologies may serve as a driving force in the present and, as such, shape the future, but ideological groups do not *necessarily* aspire to cosmic significance, claiming to provide frameworks within which one should interpret not only the present and future, but also the past.⁹³ *Weltanschauungen*, on the other hand, do.⁹⁴ The other two features they must possess are "internal coherence or *Geschlossenheit*, and a sincere commitment on the part of its devotees."⁹⁵ Conspicuously missing from the required features of a *Weltanschauung* is the consideration of whether its truth or rationality can be verified with reference to something external. Indeed, its cosmic scope means that it encapsulates, reorganizes, and redefines categories of rationality and truth in relation to its *Geschlossenheit*.

The concept of *Weltanschauung* was first developed by Kant and accrued cultural weight in its subsequent elaboration by German idealist philosophers such as Fichte, Schelling, and Hegel.⁹⁶ Thus, Fackenheim writes: "The greatest German age began when Kant—*der Alleszermalmer* [the all-crusher]—having smashed metaphysics, placed moral duty into the vacated place, thus giving it cosmic significance."⁹⁷ However, insofar as Kant's system was divided within itself—between realism and idealism—a choice had to be made in order to make it coherent.⁹⁸ Thus, it already presented the possibility of two *Weltanschauungen* and opened the door to many more. According to Fackenheim, the ensuing proliferation of *Weltanschauungen* was initially restricted by the generally humane nature of German culture during the so-called golden age. Those that were developed "were supported by philosophical argument, as subtle as it was honest, for their *coherence*; they also all culminated in the noblest of human experiences affirming their *truth*—respectively, moral freedom, religious devoutness, and the aesthetic creativity by which truth is wedded to beauty."⁹⁹ Yet, this humane restriction could not last forever. Even though the failure of Hegel's synthesis to

---

92. Fackenheim, "Holocaust and *Weltanschauung*," 181. This is not to deny, however, that *Weltanschauungen* might provide fertile ground for ideology production.

93. Cf. Angela A. Aidala, "Worldviews, Ideologies and Social Experimentation: Clarification and Replication of 'The Consciousness Reformation,'" *Journal for the Scientific Study of Religion* 23, no. 1 (1984): 48.

94. Citing a German encyclopedia article from 1931, Fackenheim suggests that at the motivational crux of a *Weltanschauung* is the need to discover "a firm, unified framework for life that transcends the achievement of the senses, of thought, of the sciences—to find it with the help of other powers" (182).

95. Fackenheim, "Holocaust and *Weltanschauung*," 182.

96. Eilert Herms, "*Weltanschauung* (Worldview)," in *Religion Past and Present*, ed. Hans Dieter Betz et al. (Leiden: Brill, 2012), 448.

97. Fackenheim, "Holocaust and *Weltanschauung*," 183.

98. See Fichte's critique of Kant along these lines in J. G. Fichte, *Science of Knowledge*, ed. and trans. Peter Heath and John Lachs (New York: Meredith Corporation, 1970), 12–16.

99. Fackenheim, "Holocaust and *Weltanschauung*," 184.

solve the problem of the glut of *Weltanschauungen* should have once and for all undermined their claim to respect and status, it did not. As such, *Weltanschauung* proved to be a powerful philosophical and political tool that could be as easily utilized by the villain as by the hero.

This, then, is the background against which Bonhoeffer's criticism of *Weltanschauung* must be understood. The cultural capital accrued over the years by *Weltanschauung* as a philosophical concept transformed it into a powerful sociopolitical tool, one that National Socialism wielded to great effect in post-World War I Germany. Bonhoeffer was sensitive to this and proved to be quite prescient in expressing his concerns regarding the powerful sway *Weltanschauungen* held over German culture. In an illuminating passage from a November 1931 sermon on Luke 12:35-40, Bonhoeffer writes:

> We find ourselves in an age of worldviews [*Weltanschauugen*]. Seldom—maybe never—has a period in history been so filled, moved, and divided by worldviews [*Weltanschaulich*] as ours. How one dresses, what one eats, how one exercises have already become a question of worldview [*Weltanschauung*]. And seldom has one been as committed, as doctrinaire, as intolerant in matters of worldview [*Weltanschaulich*] as today.... And it is doubtless one single great theme around which all our thinking in the matter of worldview [*Weltanschauliches*] revolves. And that is the human being of the future.... The human being should not be driven into ruin. He should hold his own. The powers of reality should not crush him underfoot and enslave him. He should remain master of the world, master of the future. And because that is what people want, that is why they are working so feverishly to shape a new human being [*Neugestaltung*].[100]

In the process of describing the influence of *Weltanschuungen* in Germany at the time, Bonhoeffer asserts that their appeal is tied to concern for securing particular visions of "the human being of the future." However, he does not have in mind benign interest in preserving the species. Rather, as Bonhoeffer sees it, *Weltanschauung* is the means by which social, political, and religious entities "shape a new human being" that is capable of mastering the world and the future.[101] Over against *Weltanschauung* and human ideals, Bonhoeffer asserts that the person of God in Christ secures a future for humanity "through grace alone, through God's incomprehensible mercy."[102]

The gracious, justifying person of Christ, then, emerges in Bonhoeffer's early theology as his alternative to the various *Weltanschauungen* that compete for one's allegiance and their attendant anthropological visions that malform one's

---

100. Dietrich Bonhoeffer, *Ecumenical, Academic, and Pastoral Work: 1931–1932*, ed. Mark S. Brocker and Michael B. Lukens, trans. Douglas W. Stott et al., DBWE (Minneapolis, MN: Fortress Press, 2012), 410–11.
101. Cf. Bonhoeffer, *Ecumenical, Academic, and Pastoral Work*, 410n13.
102. Bonhoeffer, *Ecumenical, Academic, and Pastoral Work*, 415.

social imagination. The result is a radical alternative to and basis from which to critique instances in which Christianity has fallen prey to religious and political *Weltanschauungen*. In another sermon on Col. 3:1-4 from June 1932, Bonhoeffer asserts that hidden behind both tendencies is "our irrepressible craving for freedom and our own will—to do in the name of God what *we* want, in the name of the Christian worldview [*Christlichen Weltanschauung*] to play off one nationality against another and stir them up to conflict with one another."[103] With the rising tide of nationalism clearly in view here, Bonhoeffer identifies *Weltanschauung* as the means by which Christians leverage religion in order to lay claim to a vision for the future that is inevitably stamped with their political hopes and aspirations. In this manner they exchange God's gracious determination and justification in the person of Christ for self-determination and self-justification. There is, then, a sense in which, for Bonhoeffer, the security offered by wedding Christianity and *Weltanschauung* is inimical to the peace of Christ and his present and coming kingdom. Thus, "peace can never consist in reconciling the gospel with religious worldviews [*Weltanschauungen*],"[104] and "[n]o one can pray for the kingdom who imagines himself in bold utopias, in dreams and hopes of the kingdom, who lives his worldview [*Weltanschauung*], who knows thousands of programs and prescriptions with which to heal the world."[105]

It should be evident, then, that the academic provenance of his early theological work had real relevance for and was in continuity with his later active opposition to National Socialism. Nowhere is this more clear than in a key passage from his *Ethics* manuscript, "Natural Life." There he writes:

> The thesis that killing innocent sick life is permissible for the benefit of the healthy has its roots not in fundamental social, economic, or hygienic reasons, but in worldview [*weltanschauliche*]. A superhuman [*übermenschliche*] attempt is proposed in order to liberate the human community from seemingly meaningless sickness. A battle is fought against fate or, as we can also say, against the essence of the fallen world. One supposes that with rational means one can create a new, healthy humanity.[106]

---

103. Bonhoeffer, *Ecumenical, Academic, and Pastoral Work*, 455.
104. Dietrich Bonhoeffer, *Berlin: 1932–1933*, ed. Larry L. Rasmussen, Isabel Best, and David Higgins, DBWE (Minneapolis, MN: Fortress Press, 2009), 261.
105. Bonhoeffer, *Berlin: 1932–1933*, 289. Translation altered.
106. Dietrich Bonhoeffer, *Ethics*, ed. Clifford J. Green, trans. Reinhard Krauss, Charles C. West, and Douglas W. Stott, DBWE (Minneapolis, MN: Fortress Press, 2005), 196. Bonhoeffer's word choice is particularly notable since, elsewhere in *Ethik*, he opts for the more general "*Ideologie*" when critiquing problematic conceptions of reality. National Socialism is almost certainly the implied and primary referent in his disdain for ideology, but his pointed use of "*Weltanschauung*" here in "Natural Life" suggests that he intends not only a critique of the particular *Weltanschauung* of National Socialism, but also *Weltanschauung* more broadly as a philosophical concept.

What Bonhoeffer is getting at here, historically, is the manner in which National Socialism's *Weltanschauung* gave birth to a deeply flawed anthropology according to which the lives of the sick and socially unacceptable should be extinguished in order to guarantee the future health of a superior human race. Theologically, he has in mind the way in which *Weltanschauung* creates the illusion that humanity justifies itself, overcoming its fallenness by "rational means" and securing a future of its own making. In other words, *Weltanschauung* provides the conceptual framework within which humanity is empowered to fix itself in a manner attuned to the imminent telos at which the *Weltanschauung* is aimed and around which it is organized.

From this brief survey of Bonhoeffer's thinking over against *Weltanschauung* we have seen that, regarding the substance of his critique, Bonhoeffer understood *weltanschauliche* thinking as a means to organize world and self-understanding in a way that aligns with the aspirations, beliefs, and hopes of an individual or group, be they religious, political, or otherwise. Theologically, this means that *Weltanschauung* is hermetically sealed off from considerations of the disruptive nature of sin and gracious personal encounter with God in Christ, wherein the nature of the world and what it means to be human are revealed to faith. To borrow language that Bonhoeffer would develop only later in his *Ethics*, *Weltanschauung* establishes a human understanding of self and reality over against the *Christuswirklichkeit* [Christ-reality]. We shall consider the relationship between justification, the *Christuswirklichkeit*, and ethics in more depth in chapter 6.

IV Conclusion

Reflecting on the relationship between the *Weltanschauung* of National Socialism and the concept's roots in idealist philosophy, Fackenheim writes that "[a] wide gulf still exists . . . between the darkest period in German history and the brightest."[107] However, in acknowledging this gulf he is not denying a connection between the two. To the contrary, Fackenheim effectively suggests that the *Weltanschauung* of National Socialism was formally consonant with and dependent on the concept's genetic roots in Germany's golden age.[108] While the content—the *Geschlossenheit*—of National Socialism's *Weltanschauung* differed markedly from that of Kant, Fichte, or Schelling, the form popularized by idealism and enshrined in German

---

107. Fackenheim, "Holocaust and *Weltanschauung*," 184.

108. To argue for formal consonance and genetic dependence is not, however, to argue for historical causation. For a nuanced discussion of the methodological challenges related to drawing connections between enlightenment ideals and Nazi ideology, see Berel Lang, *Act and Idea in the Nazi Genocide* (Syracuse: Syracuse University Press, 2003), 165–70. Cf. Michael Mack, *German Idealism and the Jew: The Inner Anti-Semitism of Philosophy and German Jewish Responses* (Chicago: The University of Chicago Press, 2003), 4.

culture became the vehicle in which the Nazis' aspirations and hatred cohered to lay claim to cosmic significance and national ascendancy.[109]

If Fackenheim is correct about this connection, then he holds forth a new way of thinking about how Bonhoeffer's critical interactions with German idealism in his early theology are related to his active resistance later in life, one in which both are understood as instances in which he was sensitive to how *Weltanschauungen* yield distorted understandings and valuations of human being. At its root, this distortion is the result of indexing humanity to a central organizing concept, idea, or principle, rather than to God in the person of Jesus Christ. Insofar as the possibility of unfolding this *Geschlossenheit* toward its telos is imminent to the person, sin and grace as disruptive and determinative realities for human existence are ignored. As such, for Bonhoeffer, *weltanschauliche* evaluations of reality inevitably displace the central significance of human being *coram Deo* and abstract human existence from the historical dialectic of creation, sin, and reconciliation. In this manner, the decisive import of the justificatory person of Christ for what it means to be human is undermined.

At the start of this chapter we considered Elshtain's claim that Bonhoeffer's sensitivity to the anthropological question enabled him to resist dehumanizing ideologies. However, more important than this was how Bonhoeffer answered the question himself. To illustrate this we considered the manner in which he problematized the anthropological implications of idealism's *Weltanschauung* and *Weltanschauung* more broadly as a culturally influential philosophical concept. Ultimately, Bonhoeffer's affirmation of the decisive import of God's gracious justification of humanity in the person of Jesus Christ for anthropology provided

---

109. On Hitler and the mechanics of the National Socialist *Weltanschauung*, see Eberhard Jäckel, *Hitler's World View: A Blueprint for Power*, trans. Herbert Arnold (Cambridge, MA: Harvard University Press, 1981). Jäckel comes to the conclusion that the heart of the national socialist *Weltanschauung* can be traced to the fact that Hitler's philosophy of history—that "history is the peoples' life struggle for living space" (103)—enabled him to synthesize his foreign policy (national expansion) with his anti-Semitism. This conclusion is based on a complex interplay between the struggle for land that Hitler believed was essential to history and his conviction that the Jewish people essentially lacked the will and ability to establish a territorial state. Since the Jews possess a will to self-preservation like all other peoples, they must go about in securing themselves in a way that is unnatural because it detached from such a territorial state. This leads Hitler to the conclusion that "if the Jews neither had nor could have any soil of their own, then they had to live on the 'productive forces' of their host nations, then they were parasites" (104). Their goal, then, was to erode nations from within, relativizing the natural, God-given struggle for soil and diluting national identity. Thus, for Hitler, the Jews posed a universal threat to all nations, and, as a result, opposition to them was incumbent on all humankind. What this all means for Hitler's *Weltanschauung* is that its *Geschlossenheit* was a dual responsibility to "annihilate the Jews, thus restoring the meaning of history, and within the thus restored, nature intended struggle for existence, he at the same time had to conquer new living space for the German people" (106).

him with theological criteria for measuring the adequacy of the various definitions of human being on offer by the *Weltanschauungen* of his day. While his rejection of idealist philosophy along these lines was theoretical and academic in nature, it is clear that his justification-based anthropology was not merely relevant in the abstract. Rather, it shaped how he thought about real human beings and provided a critical theological basis from which to evaluate the dehumanizing impact of *Weltanschauung* on real human beings when wielded by National Socialism. As such, the manner in which justification informed Bonhoeffer's thinking about what it means to be human cannot be divorced from the role it played in forming his convictions regarding what it means to act humanly. In other words, for Bonhoeffer, justification is decisive not only for anthropology, but also for ethics, as we shall see in the following chapters.

Chapter 4

FROM ANTHROPOLOGY TO ETHICS

A PAULINE CASE FOR CONTINUITY IN BONHOEFFER

I Introduction

After considering Bonhoeffer's early, academic theology in the first three chapters we have seen that the human being is, fundamentally, one who exists relationally *coram Deo*. This relational ontology is structured by the historical dialectic—a threefold simultaneity in which humanity is at once created, sinful, and reconciled in Christ alone. Although this points to a fundamentally fragmented existence, Christ binds humanity to himself in the incarnation in such a way that unity is made possible through participative encounter with and in Christ and the church by faith. As such, the person who *is* justified does not cease to be marked by the historical dialectic, but she knows her standing *coram Deo* to be extrinsically sourced and unified in the mediatorial person of Christ.

As we transition and turn our attention to how, for Bonhoeffer, justification not only shapes what it means to be human but also what it means to act humanly, we must pause to consider whether, insofar as both are inflected by the logic of justification, Bonhoeffer's ethics of discipleship unfold naturally from his early anthropology. In other words, does the doctrine of justification provide a lens through which to understand the continuity between Bonhoeffer's anthropology and ethics? And does the continuity lie in conceptual correspondence or development? One way to go about answering these questions—and the approach we shall take here—involves two steps. The first is to evaluate Bonhoeffer's justification-based anthropology in relation to a relevantly similar account in order to see if the latter provides us with particularly useful ways of conceptualizing the way in which humanity's relational being *coram Deo* and the historical dialectic can be extended into the ethical sphere. The second step, then, is to consider whether the ethics of discipleship that emerge in Bonhoeffer's later theology extend his early anthropology in a like manner.

Our focus in this chapter shall be on the first step. We have already seen that there are deep resonances between Bonhoeffer and Luther when it comes to how justification inflects their understanding of what it means to be human. In the variety of places where Bonhoeffer mentions the theological genealogy within and in relation to which he understands himself, the only other figure who is mentioned each time is the Apostle Paul.¹ Pauline theology is then, it would seem, a natural place to turn when it comes to considering what the ethical valences of Bonhoeffer's justification-based anthropology might be.² As such, in what follows, we shall evaluate Bonhoeffer's account of what it means to be human in light of recent scholarship relating to justification and anthropology in Paul. In doing so, our primary aim will be to see how Pauline theology might help us conceptualize the continuity between how justification inflects Bonhoeffer's anthropology, on the one hand, and his ethics of discipleship, on the other. However, it is also worth noting at this point that this evaluation will suggestively gesture toward the Pauline provenance of Bonhoeffer's justification-based anthropology.³

The chapter will unfold in two parts which correspond to the relational being of humanity *coram Deo* and the historical dialectical structure of human existence, respectively. In the first part, we shall see that Bonhoeffer's understanding of human

---

1. See, for example, *DBWE* 10:460; 11:229; 12:304. It is hardly a stretch to suggest that his ambition was not simply to maintain fidelity with Luther, but, perhaps even more fundamentally, to remain faithful to Paul. In other words, he was implicitly committed to the Reformation principle of *semper reformanda*. See Wolf Krötke, "Dietrich Bonhoeffer and Martin Luther," in *Bonhoeffer's Intellectual Formation: Theology and Philosophy in His Thought*, ed. Peter Frick (Tübingen: Mohr Siebeck, 2008), 56; cf. Eberhard Jüngel, "The World as Possibility and Actuality: The Ontology of the Doctrine of Justification," in *Theological Essays*, trans. John Webster (Edinburgh: T&T Clark, 1989), 104.

2. Brigitte Kahl has suggested that Bonhoeffer's stance on justification "is much more influenced by his Paulinism than his Lutheranism" ("Justification, Ethics, and the 'Other': Paul, Luther, and Bonhoeffer in Trialogue," in *Luther, Bonhoeffer, and Public Ethics: Re-Forming the Church of the Future*, ed. Michael P. DeJonge and Clifford J. Green [Lanham, MD: Lexington Books/Fortress Academic, 2018], 63). It is doubtful whether Bonhoeffer's reading of Paul can be helpfully separated out from his reading of Luther in the clear-cut way that Kahl suggests. Indeed, time and again throughout Bonhoeffer's works Paul and Luther are held together as consonant thinkers. However, Kahl does point to the relevance of the line of questioning we are pursuing here—namely, that reading Bonhoeffer in service of the *ecclesia semper reformanda* requires tying him back to Paul just as much as, if not more than, we tie him back to Luther (69–70).

3. Given the sea change in Pauline studies since Bonhoeffer's death, the degree to which his theology of justification comports with many of the more recent insights into Paul's thinking on this front is really quite incredible. However, in at least one problematic respect, Bonhoeffer remains patently Lutheran in his reading of justification—namely, his conviction that justification is primarily about correcting a faulty soteriology typified in Judaism. Indeed, this exists in tension with his proper appreciation for the reconciliatory aspect of justification. For an even-handed evaluation of how of this plays out in his essay, "The Church and the Jewish Question," see Andreas Pangritz, "Bonhoeffer and the Jews," in *The Oxford Handbook of Dietrich Bonhoeffer*, ed. Michael Mawson and Philip G. Ziegler (Oxford: Oxford University Press, 2019), 93–7.

ontology in fundamentally relational terms is consonant with Paul's participatory anthropology. It gains ethical traction when the participation that defines human being is understood as participation in the living Christ. The second part will then consider the Pauline provenance of the historical dialectic. Here, we shall see that Bonhoeffer's view that humans exist *coram Deo* as those who are simultaneously creatures, sinners, and reconciled in Christ alone also comports with Pauline theology. However, we shall see that insofar as Paul conceives of the historical dialectic in embodied terms he draws it into the ethical sphere in a manner that does not directly correspond to Bonhoeffer's account. As such, Paul shows us that one important way in which the ethical implications of the historical dialectic can be envisaged is by developing it in embodied terms. In the end, with the help of recent Pauline scholarship, we shall see that embodiment and participation in the living Christ serve as helpful ways of conceptualizing how justification might inflect Bonhoeffer's ethics in a manner that is in continuity with his anthropology. It will be the task of the next two chapters to show how these themes surface in *Discipleship* and *Ethics*.

II Relational Ontology and Participation

Susan Grove Eastman has recently suggested that Paul "displays a functional understanding of human beings as relationally constituted agents who are both embodied and embedded in their world."[4] She fleshes this out textually by comparing Gal. 2:19-20 and Rom. 7:15-18, 20: "Taken together, [the two texts] suggest a pattern of talking about persons in which the self is never on its own but always socially and cosmically constructed in relationship to external realities that operate internally as well."[5] Core to Eastman's reading of Paul's anthropology, then, is the idea that, for Paul, the social-relational sphere precedes individuated personhood and serves as the context in which it arises.[6] Indeed, Paul's account of the person is relational and "participatory all the way down."[7] Bonhoeffer's theological anthropology, then, corresponds quite closely to Eastman's interpretation of Paul methodologically and structurally. Methodologically, like Paul, Bonhoeffer is unconcerned to put forth a precisely formulated theological anthropology.[8] Instead, he speaks of humanity functionally—at times almost

---

4. Susan Grove Eastman, *Paul and the Person: Reframing Paul's Anthropology* (Grand Rapids, MI: Eerdmans, 2017), 2.
5. Eastman, *Paul and the Person*, 8.
6. Cf. James D. G. Dunn, *The Theology of Paul the Apostle* (Edinburgh: T&T Clark, 1998), 53, 344.
7. Eastman, *Paul and the Person*, 9.
8. Although Clifford Green claims that *Act and Being* is, fundamentally, a work of theological anthropology, the fact remains that it is neither systematically so, nor was it Bonhoeffer's intent to produce such a work. Rather, its prominent anthropological concerns

phenomenologically—by interpreting what it means to be human within the soteriological contours of the biblical-theological narrative and in relation to concrete human existence.

Structurally, for Bonhoeffer, humanity is constituted relationally in a twofold manner. To borrow Eastman's language, the person is defined by both cosmic and social-relational frameworks. This is not to say that Bonhoeffer would have signed on for Ernst Käsemann's assertion that "anthropology is cosmology *in concreto*," as Eastman does.[9] However, insofar as Bonhoeffer believes that human being is formed by the tripartite narrative of creation, fall, and reconciliation, the *coram Deo* relationship which grounds this narrative is certainly cosmic in scope. In other words, the historical dialectic, which Bonhoeffer outlines in *Sanctorum Communio*, reflects the cosmic context of anthropology.[10] Meanwhile, Bonhoeffer virtually echoes Eastman verbatim when it comes to the constitutive import of human sociality, writing: "[T]he person comes into being only when embedded in sociality."[11] Thus, Käsemann's description of the relational import of justification applies to Bonhoeffer as well: "The justification of the sinner is the only path on which God's creature remains before and under God and at the same time part of mankind, so that while he is in this world of ours he is also beneath the open heavens."[12] Justification, then, provides the framework within which the constitutive implications of humanity's standing *coram Deo* and *coram hominibus* can be held and thought together.[13] That is, the specific sort of being *coram Deo* which justification narrates in the anthropological sphere is not abstracted from concrete existence but, rather, has definite implications in the ethical sphere.

---

should be seen as a basic expression of Bonhoeffer's fundamentally Lutheran understanding of the task of theology. See Clifford J. Green, *Bonhoeffer: A Theology of Sociality*, Rev. Ed. (Grand Rapids, MI: Eerdmans, 1999), 68–70.

9. Ernst Käsemann, "On Paul's Anthropology," in *Perspectives on Paul* (London: SCM Press, 1971), 27; Eastman, *Paul and the Person*, 91. See also Ernst Käsemann, *Commentary on Romans*, trans. G.W. Bromiley (London: SCM Press, 1980), 33, 150. For a helpful discussion of Käsemann's articulation of Paul's theological anthropology, see, Ziegler, *Militant Grace*, 56–67.

10. *DBWE* 1:62.

11. *DBWE* 1:78.

12. Ernst Käsemann, "Justification and Salvation History," in *Perspectives on Paul* (London: SCM Press, 1971), 74; cf. Bert Jan Lietaert Peerbolte, "A New Perspective on Justification: Recent Developments in the Study of Paul," *Zeitschrift Für Dialektische Theologie* Supplement Series 6 (2014): 148–9.

13. A key difference between Bonhoeffer and Eastman that deserves more exploration is the latter's assertion that relationality is prior to individuality. Bonhoeffer, on the other hand, refuses to ease the tension between the individual and corporate. However, for the purposes of this chapter it is sufficient to note their fundamental agreement that individual and relational realities are interrelated and, therefore, must be held together. See *DBWE* 1:80; Eastman, *Paul and the Person*, 13.

However, it is important for both Paul and Bonhoeffer that relationality is not a generic theological concept. Rather, Eastman asserts that "Paul constitutes all humanity... as Adam's heirs and as those for whom Christ died; there is no innate or individual criterion by which some might be included and others excluded from this capacious embrace."[14] Humanity, theologically understood, is defined in relation to Adam and Christ.[15] This is exactly the typology that Bonhoeffer puts forth in the second half of *Act and Being*. For Bonhoeffer, these are the two basic relational realities that define, shape, and enfold all of humanity. To be in—which is, at the same time, in relation to—Adam "means to be in untruth, in culpable perversion of the will, that is, of human essence. It means to be turned inward into one's self, *cor curvum in se*. Human beings have torn themselves loose from community with God and, therefore, also from that with other human beings, and now they stand alone, that is, in untruth."[16] In contrast, to be in Christ is to be turned outward and set in relation to God through Christ's mediatorial person.[17] John Barclay affirms Bonhoeffer's intuitions when he writes:

> Crucial to Paul's theology is that this new life is not in the first place an anthropological phenomenon: it is experienced by human beings only inasmuch as they share in, and draw from, a life whose source lies outside of themselves, the life of the risen Christ. Their identity is recentered, since their life is now wholly dependent on the life of Another, the One who is risen from the dead.[18]

However, it is not as if being in Adam and being in Christ are equally weighted. Insofar as Christ participates in God's act of creation and created reality is constituted through him, he stands on both sides of the Fall.[19] This Christological

---

14. Eastman, *Paul and the Person*, 13–14; cf. Ziegler, *Militant Grace*, 58.

15. See how Leander Keck (*Romans* [Nashville: Abingdon Press, 2005], 145) speaks of participation in the condition of Adam or the condition of Christ, in relation to Rom 5:12–21. Cf. Susan Grove Eastman, "Apocalypse and Incarnation: The Participatory Logic of Paul's Gospel," in *Apocalyptic and the Future of Theology: With and Beyond J. Louis Martyn*, ed. Joshua B. Davis and Douglas Harink (Eugene, OR: Cascade Books, 2012), 174.

16. *DBWE* 2:137.

17. *DBWE* 2:150–51.

18. John M. G. Barclay, "Under Grace: The Christ-Gift and the Construction of a Christian *Habitus*," in *Apocalyptic Paul: Cosmos and Anthropos in Romans 5–8*, ed. Beverly Roberts Gaventa (Waco, TX: Baylor University Press, 2013), 65. Barclay does not here intend "anthropological" as an adjective in the way we have been using it. Rather, by "anthropological" he means that which has its impulse or impetus in the human sphere. This goes back to and reflects its usage in relation to the pivstiV Cristou debate in Richard B. Hays, *The Faith of Jesus Christ: The Narrative Substructure of Galatians 3:1–4:11*, 2nd ed (Grand Rapids/Dearborn, MI: Eerdmans/Dove Booksellers, 2002), 277.

19. On Paul's extension of God's covenant with Israel back to creation, see Ernst Käsemann, "Justification and Freedom," in *On Being a Disciple of the Crucified Nazarene*:

bracketing of human existence is thus the defining mark of humanity. Thus, being in Adam, as the relational expression of sinfulness, is a break in the anthropologically basic relationship with God in Christ, rather than a separate and equal alternative. Reconciliation in Christ, then, is the recapitulation and affirmation of both created reality and God's justifying posture toward humanity. To this end, Eastman writes: "[F]or Paul, regardless of personal beliefs or 'self-understandings,' the person always and already exists in the presence of another; personhood is constituted in the self-donation of Christ for all humanity. It is grounded in gift, regardless of criteria."[20] In this way, the justificatory relationship which grounds humanity is a product of, and exists only in, the gracious gift of Christ's self.[21] Put another way, it is in the gift of Christ that humanity comes to know the measure of itself, namely its justification. "The Pauline doctrine of justification is entirely and solely Christology, a Christology, indeed, won from Jesus' cross and hence an offensive Christology. Its point is the *ecce homo* presented so that we, confronted with the Nazarene, learn how little our illusions about ourselves and the world can stand up to its reality."[22] What this means is that, for Paul, Christ is not simply an exemplar to be imitated, but, rather, the one who creates, confronts, and reconstitutes humanity in himself.[23] Thus, Paul's anthropology is fundamentally shaped by the conviction that what it means to be human is grounded and given in the person of Christ.

What this means, then, is that human being is inherently extrinsic and grounded in the person of Christ. Indeed, one of the key contributions of Luther—and the Reformers in general—to Pauline exegesis is his emphasis on the extrinsic nature of justified human existence.[24] According to Barclay: "Believers are to consider themselves 'dead to sin and alive to God,' in both respects like Christ ([Rom]6:10) and in Christ (6:11). They present themselves 'as those alive from the dead' (6:13) because they draw upon a reality extrinsic to themselves, true of them because it is true first of all of Christ."[25] Bonhoeffer offers a similar reading in the notes from his lectures on theological anthropology at the University of Berlin: "If he wants to

Unpublished Lectures and Sermons, ed. Rudolf Landau and Wolfgang Kraus, trans. Roy A. Harrisville (Grand Rapids, MI: Eerdmans, 2010), 56.

20. Eastman, *Paul and the Person*, 14.

21. To this end, Jonathan Linebaugh suggests that we retain Luther's subjective genitive rendering of the pivstiV Cristou, but understand it as an anthropological negation. See "The Christo-Centrism of Faith in Christ: Martin Luther's Reading of Galatians 2.16, 19–20," *New Testament Studies* 59, no. 4 (2013): 541.

22. Käsemann, "Justification and Salvation History," 73. This reflects Bonhoeffer's concern in his 1933 Christology lectures to prioritize Christ's person rather than—although never at the expense of—his works. See *DBWE* 12:308–10.

23. Cf. *DBWE* 12:301–3.

24. "Only outside of the self and in Christ can the believer receive new life" (Chester, *Reading Paul with the Reformers*, 191). Cf. *LW* 26:170, 387.

25. John M. G. Barclay, *Paul and the Gift* (Grand Rapids, MI: Eerdmans, 2015), 501.

know himself, the person of the Reformation looks beyond himself."[26] Later in the lectures Bonhoeffer draws on this historical observation in order to offer his own systematic theological assessment of human ontology: "One's own being, which encompasses the creatureliness and ontological structure, is a being *from* God. . . . Because he has his being from God, the human being understands himself not through himself but through God."[27]

While knowledge of humanity's extrinsic existence is contingent on faith in Christ, Bonhoeffer takes it to be a universal anthropological principle because he assumes that the Christological dynamics of soteriology also point to basic and important anthropological realities. Eastman, without referring to Bonhoeffer, affirms his theological intuition on this front while discussing Paul's multivalent use of *sōma*. She notes that it can be used to name a "suprahuman power," a physical body, or a corporate body. This "suggests that embodied human existence is always embedded in, and qualified by, supracorporeal forces, whether those be merely human social realities or cosmic powers."[28] In other words, insofar as relationality precedes individuality, human identity is grounded and shaped by extrinsic forces. Eastman dialogues with a variety of philosophical and psychological perspectives in order to support this claim. However, her primary criteria for making such an assertion is theological. While innumerable external, and often conflicting, forces determine one's relational matrix, Paul ultimately consolidates them in a way consistent with the alternatives of being in Adam or being in Christ discussed previously.[29] In other words, human existence is extrinsically grounded and determined in terms of lordship—either Christ is Lord or sin reigns through Adam. Anthropology, then, is fundamentally shaped by "who is really and actually our lord."[30]

What we have seen, then, is that Bonhoeffer's justification-based anthropology is consistent with a Pauline conception of what it means to be human insofar as it is relationally grounded, Christologically focused, and extrinsically sourced. However, these descriptions of human being take on ethical valences when one take into account the fact that it is the *risen and living* Christ in whom humanity is reconstituted and reconciled.[31] Indeed, for Paul, participation in the resurrected

---

26. *DBWE* 12:217.
27. *DBWE* 12:219.
28. Eastman, *Paul and the Person*, 91.
29. Cf. Ziegler, *Militant Grace*, 58.
30. Käsemann, "Justification and Freedom," 58.
31. Although Bonhoeffer's construal of being in Christ in his early theology is participatory in many respects, he is primarily concerned with how this determines human being, whereas, as we shall see, in his later theology his focus turns to how being bound to the living Christ determines what it means to act humanly. This, however, should not be taken as a cut-and-dried distinction, since clear exceptions exist. See, for example, his description of Christian love in *DBWE* 1:165–92. However, here his account is limited to the conduct of Christians *within the church*. This ecclesiological focus in Bonhoeffer's early

Christ is determinative for Christian ethics precisely because it locates human being extrinsically in the Son of God who is alive and at work in the world by his Spirit.[32] Reconciliation with God in Christ does not reestablish human beings *coram Deo* before once again handing over the reins to them. Rather, it transfers humanity out from under the lordship of sin in the flesh and places them under the lordship of Christ, in whom and through whom they live, move, and have their being. As the Lord who creates, preserves, and reconciles, Christ is both determinative for what it means to be human and for what it means to act humanly. The result is that "the believers' new mode of existence—their new allegiances, dispositions, emotions, and *actions*—is attributable to the miraculous life of Christ himself."[33] However, as we shall see in the next section, for Paul, participation in the living Christ is not an abstract state of affairs that is only tangentially related to Christian ethics.[34] Rather, it is determinative for embodied human existence.

III *The Historical Dialectic and Embodiment*

We shall now turn to the threefold, historical dialectic of creation, sin, and redemption that narrates and structures the being of humanity *coram Deo*. Here, however, we shall take a different tack because even as some recent and influential Pauline scholarship serves to affirm this dimension of Bonhoeffer's anthropology, it also develops it in a way that is ethically relevant by construing justification in embodied terms.

That Bonhoeffer's account can be developed in this respect is not to suggest that his early theology neglects or disparages concerns pertaining to the body and embodiment. To the contrary, Bonhoeffer includes a fairly detailed theological defense of the body in *Creation and Fall*.[35] In his theological exegesis of Gen. 2:7,

---

theology leads Javier Garcia to suggest that it "complements his later turn to the world, because it solidifies their mutual eschatological relation" (Javier A. Garcia, *Recovering the Ecumenical Bonhoeffer: Thinking After the Tradition* [Lanham, MD: Lexington Books/Fortress Academic, 2019], 135). On this account, participation in Christ and church in Bonhoeffer's early theology is in continuity with his later emphasis on participation in the living Christ and the *Christuswirklichkeit*.

32. Barclay, *Paul and the Gift*, 500; cf. Grant Macaskill, *Living in Union with Christ: Paul's Gospel and Christian Moral Identity* (Grand Rapids, MI: Baker Academic, 2019), 128-9.

33. Barclay, *Paul and the Gift*, 501. Emphasis added.

34. For a book-length treatment of this topic, see Macaskill, *Living in Union with Christ*.

35. That there is continuity in Bonhoeffer's defense of the body's significance throughout his theology can be seen in his earlier thought in *Sanctorum Communio* (*DBWE* 1:285-7) and his essay, "The Essence of Christianity" (10:355-6), as well as in his later work in *Ethics* (6:185-96). Although not specifically reflecting on embodiment, Brian Brock has recently suggested that, in *Creation and Fall*, Bonhoeffer is exploring "the thematic unity of the same constellation of doctrinal themes we see set out by Paul" with regard to a doctrine

he highlights the connection between the body and the earth from which it is taken, going so far as to paraphrase Sirach 40:1 in order to suggest that the earth is the body's mother.[36] Equally important is the fact that humanity is formed from the earth before the ground is cursed. The body, then, is not simply good, it is also a necessary prerequisite for the system of relationships which define human being. "For in their bodily nature human beings are related to the earth and to other bodies; they are there for others and are dependent on others. In their bodily existence human beings find their brothers and sisters and find the earth."[37] Furthermore, it is as embodied beings that humans are free in and for relationship with God.[38] Here, Bonhoeffer makes a distinction between other creatures and humanity, noting that while everything is created by God's word, only humanity is imbued with and created by his spirit. The spirit is not only that which animates and inhabits human being, but it "is what constitutes its essential being."[39] Through the bearing of God's spirit, the human body glorifies God. This creational reality is, then, what grounds human worth and God's reconciling work in Christ.[40] It is "why where the original body in its created being has been destroyed, God enters it anew in Jesus Christ.... Because Adam is created as body, Adam is also redeemed as body [and God comes to Adam as body], in Christ and in the sacrament."[41]

Thus, Bonhoeffer's concern for the body demonstrates his awareness that embodiment is essential for relationality. The relational matrix that it sets human beings in is not merely interpersonal, but is also cosmic in scope, thereby setting humanity in relationship to both God and the earth. Furthermore, Bonhoeffer identifies the body, in its pre-fall state, as inhabited by an extrinsic power, namely the spirit of God. There is, then, a high degree of consonance between Bonhoeffer's theological account of bodily life and that ascribed to Paul by recent New Testament scholarship. As we move forward, this consonance will become clear even as we consider how such scholarship helpfully suggests a way in which the historical dialectic might be developed in a more ethically substantive way—namely, by identifying the body as its locus.

For James Dunn, Paul's concern for embodied human existence is directly related to the relational nature of his anthropology. Indeed, Dunn offers a definition of Paul's theology that sounds a lot like Luther when he writes:

Paul's theology is relational. That is to say, he was not concerned with God in himself or humankind in itself.... As the opening of his exposition of the

---

of creation. See Brian Brock, "On Becoming Creatures: Being Called to Presence in a Distracted World," *International Journal of Systematic Theology* 18, no. 4 (2016): 437.

36. *DBWE* 3:76.
37. *DBWE* 3:79.
38. *DBWE* 3:78.
39. *DBWE* 3:79.
40. Cf. Brock, "On Becoming Creatures," 450.
41. *DBWE* 3:79.

gospel in Rom. 1.16ff. clearly shows, his concern was rather with humankind in relation to God, with men and women in their relationships with each other, and subsequently with Christ as God's response to the human plight.[42]

He goes on to suggest that this relational and soteriological context is essential to understanding Paul's anthropology. According to Dunn, the fact that humans are embedded in these relational matrices presupposes the existence of a particular body, or, in Paul's terms, the *sōma*. *Sōma*, however, denotes more than a physical body, and can be conceptually construed in reference to embodiment. By understanding Paul's use of *sōma* in terms of embodiment, it becomes clear that "*sōma* is a relational concept."[43] The body, then, is the means by which the human being is shaped by and, in turn, shapes the world. However, *sōma* also clearly has corporate connotations for Paul, the most obvious evidence being his description of the church as the body of Christ.[44] *Sōma* and its implied social relations can be inflected in three different ways when Paul talks about it. First, he speaks of the body as the means by which "the person participates in creation and functions as part of creation."[45] This is not to say that Paul posits some sort of ideal, knowable, pre-Adamic body. Indeed, his references to *sōma* frequently involve acknowledgment of the body's frailty and corruptibility. Yet, even as the body is corrupted by sin and death, it remains the case that embodiment is an anthropological reality that God intended in the beginning. This is ultimately affirmed in the resurrection of the dead (1 Cor. 15:35-49). Dunn suggests that "God's act in raising from the dead, the climax of his salvation, is of a piece with his act in creating: 'he who gives life to the dead' is 'he who calls things that have no existence into existence' (Rom. 4.17)."[46] For Dunn, this points to an "integration of creation and salvation (Col. 1.15-20; v. 20—'all things' reconciled to God)."[47] We have already mentioned the second and third way in which *sōma* is inflected for Paul—namely, in relation to its corruption and weakness on account of sin (e.g., 1 Cor. 15:42-44) and in relation to the spiritual, incorruptible body promised in the resurrection (e.g., 1 Cor. 15:50). Thus, it would seem that, for Paul, the *sōma* is something of an anthropological constant. Embodiment as a good, creational reality is not negated by sin but, rather, is attested to and affirmed in Paul's emphasis on the resurrection from the dead.[48]

---

42. Dunn, *The Theology of Paul the Apostle*, 53.
43. Dunn, *The Theology of Paul the Apostle*, 56.
44. Rom 12:5; 1 Cor 6:15; 12:12, 27; Eph 4:12; 5:23; Col 1:24.
45. Dunn, *The Theology of Paul the Apostle*, 61.
46. Dunn, 40; cf. Barclay, *Paul and the Gift*, 461, on redemption as creation *ex nihilo* in Romans. See also 2 Macc. 7:28 for one of the oldest references to *creatio ex nihilo*. My thanks to Alan Torrance for drawing my attention to this passage.
47. Dunn, *The Theology of Paul the Apostle*, 40.
48. See Barclay, "Under Grace," 68.

So, Dunn affirms *sōma* as an anthropological constant in creation, sin, and redemption, for Paul, even though it is inflected differently in relation to each. He also notes its importance for grounding the embedded and relational nature of humanity. However, while he is careful to stress the particularity of the body and the specific environment in which it is set, he only obliquely touches on the way that embodiment embeds humanity within a cosmic history.[49] As such, he fails to stress the fact that, insofar as *sōma* is both an individual and a corporate reality, humans are set in relation to both their particular environment and the wider cosmic history of God's dealings with humanity and the world. In other words, because individual bodies participate in and are shaped by corporate bodies they not only have their own discrete histories, but also share in the histories of the corporate bodies of which they are a part.

N. T. Wright, although ambivalent about relational understandings of soteriology and anthropology, is helpful in drawing out this cosmic, contextualizing scope.[50] Like Dunn, Wright suggests that *sōma* "*denotes* the entire human being and *connotes* the public, visible and tangible physical presence in, and in relation to, the world."[51] He also stresses that the body is corrupted unto death, not because of inherent deficiencies, but on account of its subjection to sin.[52] However, he moves beyond Dunn in his treatment of Paul's anthropology when he suggests that "the normal 'sin/salvation' scheme usually fails to spot the connection with the larger cosmic plot."[53] To make humanity the focus in this way obscures God's wider, cosmic purpose "that through *humankind* (Adam and Eve), God would reflect his image and glory into the *world*."[54] Rather than focusing on the sin and salvation of individuals in their specific environments and histories, Wright wants to speak of a cosmic history in which God in Christ rescues humanity for the purpose of his glory.[55] As such, individual salvation is a consequence of what happens on a

---

49. Dunn, *The Theology of Paul the Apostle*, 56. Dunn certainly touches on the importance of this cosmic history elsewhere in relation to Paul's theology. However, he neglects it as a central, shaping feature of Paul's anthropology.

50. For Wright on relational frameworks and his worry that they circumvent the centrality of covenant, see *Paul and the Faithfulness of God*, Christian Origins and the Question of God (Minneapolis, MN: Fortress Press, 2013), 490–4, 928.

51. Wright, *Paul and the Faithfulness of God*, 491.

52. Wright, however, does not think of subjection to sin in terms of lordship, as does the AIP. Rather, he takes sin to be "a human propensity and action" rather than an external force or power. See Wright, *Paul and the Faithfulness of God*, 491–2.

53. Wright, *Paul and the Faithfulness of God*, 494.

54. Wright, *Paul and the Faithfulness of God*, 487.

55. Here, Wright is intent to focus on the story of Israel as the locus of the rescue mission, rather than the person of Christ. We must and should affirm his desire to emphasize the import of Israel's story. However, it seems that he inverts the order of priority here. In other words, rather than being an instantiation of Israel's story, Israel is an instantiation of Christ's story, which begins with creation (cf. Col 1:15–20), is affirmed in the face of sin by the initial

cosmic and corporate level. Put another way, Christ's justification of the individual cannot be separated from his justification of humanity and the cosmos.

Here, then, we are very close to Käsemann's assertion, noted earlier, that anthropology is a projection of cosmology. Anthropology is shaped by the cosmic history of God's creation, preservation, and redemption of the world in Christ.[56] To an even greater degree than Dunn and Wright, Käsemann seizes upon *sōma*—which he discusses using the language of corporeality—as a basic presupposition of Paul's anthropology and soteriology.[57] Indeed, he asserts: "The coherence of Pauline soteriology is destroyed once we modify in the slightest degree the fact that for Paul all God's ways with his creation begin and end in corporeality."[58] Soteriology is tied to anthropology via embodiment because Paul "always assigns to the body the reality of creatureliness, the reality of the fall, of redemption, of the resurrection from the dead, with all of which the appropriate functions are associated."[59] Corporeality, then, tethers humanity to their particular environment, but it *also* subjects them to the cosmic history and soteriological realities which narrate God's relationship with humanity and the world. We might say, then, that how a person relates to her particular environment is dependent on corporeality, and the nature of corporeality is determined by who a person's lord is. Käsemann sums this up in the following way: "[T]here is no such thing as man without his particular and respective world. But world means more than the mere sphere of living in, let us say, co-humanity. The world is always a sphere of sovereignty whether under the insignia of creation, the insignia of sin, or the insignia of the redemption which can be experienced today as that which is still to come."[60] Although Käsemann does not use this terminology, we might think here, again, primarily in terms of two collective persons—namely, being in Adam or being-in-Christ. However, the collective person does not consolidate the body under any one insignia: creation, sin, or redemption.

How then does Paul suggest we understand the manner in which the body is at one and the same time created, sinful, and reconciled? Barclay, by providing an alternative rendering of Luther's *simul* in relation to Rom. 7:7-25, is helpful here. Like Werner Kümmel and many others following him, Barclay asserts that the *simul iustus et peccator* cannot be exegetically sourced from this passage because

promise (Gen 3:15), climaxes in the incarnation (Col 1:20), and is consummated in the eschaton (1 Cor 15:20-28).

56. See Käsemann, "On Paul's Anthropology," 12.

57. As an enduring theme in his theology, see his doctoral thesis, published in 1933 (*Leib und Leib Christi: Eine Untersuchung zur paulinischen Begrifflichkeit* [Tübingen: J. C. B. Mohr, 1933]), and his 1985 lecture, "Corporeality in Paul," in *On Being a Disciple of the Crucified Nazarene: Unpublished Lectures and Sermons*, ed. Rudolf Landau and Wolfgang Kraus, trans. Roy A. Harrisville (Grand Rapids, MI: Eerdmans, 2010), 38–51.

58. Käsemann, "On Paul's Anthropology," 18.

59. Käsemann, 19; cf. Käsemann, "Justification and Freedom," 57.

60. Käsemann, "On Paul's Anthropology," 28.

Paul is speaking of fleshly, pre-Christian life.[61] However, there is clearly a dynamic of simultaneity at play in Paul's "I, but not-I" language. As such, Barclay suggests an alternative: "The believer is here described as both mortal and eternally alive, *simul mortuus et vivens*."[62] Insofar as the body is mortal it exists unto death, but insofar as it is alive, it is alive unto Christ and the new creation. As such, the body can, indeed, be simultaneously sinful and reconciled. But where, then, is the created goodness of the body in this formula? Although it is not explicit, it is strongly implied in the fact that the body which is subject to sin and death is also the body which is reconciled. The very fact that, despite the dishonor and corruption caused by sin, the body will be resurrected is a recapitulation and reaffirmation of its created goodness.

This gives rise to a troubling question: Has the body become the anthropological source of continuity and unity, insofar as it simultaneously sets the human being in relation to creation, sin, and reconciliation? Surely this would be problematic, since Bonhoeffer insists that the unity of the historical dialectic is sourced extrinsically in Christ alone, and the continuity of human being is grounded in Christ's body, the church.[63] However, this is to suppose that there is a distinction between the body and spirit. Insofar as Paul, when using *sōma* to refer to human beings, intends the whole person, both body and spirit are fragmented when sin enters the world. In the body of sin the created goodness of the body and its corruption are at odds. Similarly, in the believer, the frailty of the body persists even as the resurrection is promised as God's definitive word concerning humanity.[64] As such, the whole person, including the body, is subject to the historical dialectic which structures one's relationship to God. Thus, we can conclude, along with Käsemann: "It is only God who gives continuity, the God who, as creator, does not abandon his creatures, not even after the fall and far less under the token of promise and grace. In the whole of history, continuity only results from the divine faithfulness; and hence it manifests itself in miracle."[65]

---

61. Barclay, *Paul and the Gift*, 501–2. For Luther's strident defense of Paul's Christian life as the provenance of this passage, see *LW* 25:338–43. This is not to suggest that there is no exegetical basis for the *simul*, but simply to argue against Rom 7:7–25 as that ground.

62. Barclay, *Paul and the Gift*, 502.

63. *DBWE* 10:405; 2:114. So too, Käsemann, "On Paul's Anthropology," 27. See our discussion of this in Chapter 2.

64. For Bonhoeffer's thoughts on the spiritual nature of the resurrected body, see *DBWE* 1:286.

65. Käsemann, "On Paul's Anthropology," 9. For more on the issue of continuity and discontinuity in Paul's life and the life of the Christian, see Eastman, *Paul and the Person*, 102, 155–60; *Recovering Paul's Mother Tongue: Language and Theology in Galatians* (Grand Rapids, MI: Eerdmans, 2007), 33–43, 184–9; John M. G. Barclay, "Paul's Story: Theology as Testimony," in *Narrative Dynamics in Paul: A Critical Assessment*, ed. Bruce W. Longenecker (Louisville, KY: Westminster John Knox Press, 2002), 142–4.

How, then, does all of this comport with and point to a possible development of Bonhoeffer's understanding of the historical dialectic in relation to the framework of his justification-based anthropology? It would appear that Bonhoeffer is simply following Paul in stressing the created goodness of the body, its central role in grounding human relationality at an interpersonal, corporate, and cosmic level, and its subjection to external powers. However, Bonhoeffer never grounds his "real, historical dialectic" of creation, sin, and reconciliation in that which is most obviously real and historical about humanity—namely, the body. When embodiment is taken into account, the relationship between soteriology and anthropology comes into sharper focus because the body is the anthropological reality onto which Paul maps his soteriology. Human beings are not only created, they are created, embodied, and embedded. Humans are not only sinful, their bodies are frail, corrupted, marked by dishonor, and destined for death. Believers are not only reconciled with God, they participate in Christ's resurrected body and are sealed by the Holy Spirit unto the redemption of their own bodies. In other words, the justificatory relationship between God and humanity which the historical dialectic narrates presupposes the anthropological centrality of the body. Insofar as justification has everything to do with human standing *coram Deo*, it has everything to do with the body, and as such, has necessarily social implications.

We might say then that when the historical dialectic is extended into the ethical sphere, the manner in which it inflects embodied human existence must be interpreted in relation to participation in the body of the living Christ. In other words, Christian ethics, insofar as it is indexed to the doctrine of justification, should be understood in terms of the embodied participation of the believer—as creature, sinner, and one who is reconciled—in the incarnate, crucified, and risen Christ. How one acts as a Christian is then determined by how Christ relates the believer to herself and to others.[66] In Christ the incarnate one, the goodness and particularity of bodily life in this world is affirmed and the believer is set free to advocate for this goodness on behalf of those around her. In Christ the crucified one, the Christian dies to and repents of her own active participation in sin, even as she boldly names the sin she sees in the world and suffers alongside those who are victimized by it. In Christ the risen one, the believer realizes and enacts her reconciliation with God through Word and sacrament in the communion of saints, while also participating in the church's mission to bear witness to Christ's reconciliation *of* the world *in* the world. Embodied participation in the living Christ, then, orients the believer toward a world that is created, preserved, and reconciled in Christ alone as one who bears witness to that reconciliation in word and deed.

IV Conclusion

In this chapter, we have endeavored to evaluate Bonhoeffer's justification-based anthropology in light of and in relation to a Pauline account of what it means to be

---

66. Cf. *DBWE* 12:306–307.

human. The primary reason for doing so was in order to see if Paul's theology sheds light on how Bonhoeffer's commitment to humanity's relational being before God and its historical dialectical structure might be extended into the ethical sphere. What we saw in this respect was that, for Paul, humanity's relational ontology is participatory in nature. For Christians, this means participation in the living Christ who not only draws people into himself but also into his mission in the world. We then saw that Paul understands justification in terms of corporality and, as such, renders the historical dialectic in thoroughly bodily terms. Insofar as the historical dialectic structures human being *coram Deo*, both the God-relation and the believer's participation in the living Christ who maintains that relation must be understood in terms of embodiment. As such, embodied participation in the living Christ emerged as a plausibly Pauline way of conceiving how justification might inflect Bonhoeffer's ethics of discipleship in a manner that is in continuity with his early anthropology. Indeed, as we turn to *Discipleship* in Chapter 5 and *Ethics* in Chapter 6, we shall see that this theme is central to how Bonhoeffer conceives of what it means to act humanly.

Chapter 5

JUSTIFICATION AND WITNESS-BEARING

DISCIPLESHIP AS EMBODIED PARTICIPATION IN CHRIST

I Introduction

In the first three chapters we identified some key ways in which the doctrine of justification shaped Bonhoeffer's understanding of what it means to be human in his early, academic theology. This culminated when we made explicit the social import of this way of evaluating human being by arguing that justification shaped his anthropology in a manner that alerted him to the dehumanizing implications of *Weltanschauungen*. Then, in the previous chapter, we considered how recent developments and deliverances in the realm of Pauline theology might help us to conceptualize how justification inflects Bonhoeffer's ethics of discipleship in a manner that is in continuity with his anthropology. There we saw that Paul's understanding of participation in the living Christ naturally corresponds to and extends Bonhoeffer's relational ontology into the ethical sphere. However, while the historical dialectic is evident in Paul's thinking about what it means to be human, he develops it in embodied terms, thereby signaling its ethical import in a way that is not immediately evident in Bonhoeffer's early thought.

In this chapter, we shall turn our sights to the development of Bonhoeffer's theology of discipleship at Finkenwalde. Particularly, we shall see that, when seeking to mobilize the Confessing Church in its following after Christ, Bonhoeffer again turns to the doctrine of justification by faith, this time drawing on its participatory and embodied valences in a way that is ethically substantive, oriented toward reconciliation in Christ, and consistent with Pauline theology. Indeed, it will become clear that when it comes to articulating the social orientation entailed by justification, Bonhoeffer saw fertile ground in these themes.

The goal of this chapter, then, is to show that, insofar as both his early anthropology and his theology of discipleship are held together by and interpreted in light of the doctrine of justification, the latter moves us in the direction of realizing a holistic picture of the doctrine's social implications. Toward this goal, the chapter will unfold in four parts. First, we shall provide some historical and biographical context from the writings surrounding Bonhoeffer's work on *Discipleship*. We shall see that it is not Bonhoeffer's focus on justification *as a doctrine* that yields his emphasis on participation, embodiment, and reconciliation in discipleship, but, rather, his focus on Scripture as witness to the living Christ. The next two sections will look at the way participation and embodiment, respectively, inform his theology of discipleship. In a way that is consistent with Bonhoeffer's early theology, we shall see that Christology and ecclesiology are of central importance to his unfolding of these themes within the framework of discipleship. Finally, we shall conclude by considering reconciliation and the social aim of discipleship. Here, it will become evident that Bonhoeffer falls short of rendering the church's relation to the world in a way that yields a concrete vision for the relationship between discipleship and reconciliation in the social sphere. This, in turn, will point us forward to Chapter 6, in which we shall turn to Bonhoeffer's *Ethics* as a necessary supplement to *Discipleship*. The resultant picture of the social implications of the doctrine of justification by faith will then be brought to bear on the challenge of white supremacy in Chapter 7. In doing so, we shall see how justification can serve the church by way of critique while also contributing to a constructive way forward.

II Contextualizing Discipleship *in the Finkenwalde Period*

Within Bonhoeffer's wider body of work, *Discipleship* is generally thought of alongside *Life Together*, both because of their shared roots in the Finkenwalde period and because they are his two most popular books. *Discipleship* can also be linked backward to Bonhoeffer's earlier theology.[1] Indeed, an implicit argument of this study is that Bonhoeffer's early theology and his theology of discipleship are linked, at least in part, by a common concern for how justification shapes what it means to be human and live *coram Deo*. Furthermore, *Discipleship* is often and justifiably linked to *Ethics*.[2] The themes of the former's final chapter, "The Image of Christ," are especially resonant with the latter's chapter manuscript entitled "Ethics

---

1. Joseph McGarry, "Bridging the Gap: Dietrich Bonhoeffer's Early Theology and Its Influence on Discipleship," *Bonhoeffer Legacy: Australasian Journal of Bonhoeffer Studies* 2, no. 1 (2014): 13–31.

2. On this connection, see, for example, Martin Kuske and Ilse Tödt, "Editor's Afterword to the German Edition," in *Discipleship*, ed. Geffrey B. Kelly and John D. Godsey, trans. Barbara Green and Reinhard Krauss (Minneapolis, MN: Fortress Press, 2001), 305–7; Jennifer M. McBride, *The Church for the World: A Theology of Public Witness* (Oxford: Oxford University Press, 2012), 87–118; Philip G. Ziegler, "'Completely Within God's Doing': Soteriology as Meta-Ethics in the Theology of Dietrich Bonhoeffer," in *Christ, Church, and World: New Studies in Bonhoeffer's Theology and Ethics*, ed. Michael Mawson and Philip G. Ziegler (London: Bloomsbury T&T Clark, 2016), 11; Kirsten Busch Nielsen, "Community Turned Inside Out: Dietrich Bonhoeffer's Concept of the Church and of Humanity Reconsidered," in *Being Human, Becoming Human: Dietrich Bonhoeffer and Social Thought*, ed. Jens Zimmermann and Brian Gregor (Eugene, OR: Pickwick Publications, 2010), 207;

as Formation."³ Finally, Bonhoeffer's retrospective evaluation of *Discipleship* in *Letters and Papers from Prison* looms large over its scholarly reception. There, in a letter to Eberhard Bethge, penned the day after the failed assassination attempt on Hitler in which Bonhoeffer was involved, he writes: "I thought I myself could learn to have faith by trying to live something like a saintly life. I suppose I wrote *Discipleship* at the end of this path. Today I clearly see the dangers of that book, though I still stand by it."⁴ Stephen Plant is surely correct when he warns: "Too much can be read into this passing comment (and indeed has been)."⁵

However, Plant is also surely correct when he suggests that Bonhoeffer had begun "to see considerable danger in speaking as if there was either a metaphorical or physical space that is 'Church' in relation to an entirely separate space that is 'world.'"⁶ If the church-community is "a sealed train passing through enemy territory," then there is no space for concrete action in and for the world as the body of Christ.⁷ What Bonhoeffer came to see later was that his "turn toward the ultimate, for the sake of the penultimate" could not be the final word on discipleship, but had to involve a second step: a decisive turn back toward and into the penultimate for the sake of the ultimate.⁸ The fact that a second step was needed post-Finkenwalde was hardly something that caught Bonhoeffer off-guard. When describing the purpose of the House of Brethren—a communal house for Confessing Church pastors who had been educated at Bonhoeffer's preacher's seminary in Finkenwalde—in a 1935 letter to the Council of the Evangelical Church of the Old Prussian Union, Bonhoeffer writes: "The goal is not monastic isolation but rather the most intensive concentration for ministry to the world."⁹ The first step, then, is formation for ministry, while the second step is the enactment of that ministry in and for the world. *Discipleship* clearly bears the marks of "intensive concentration for ministry" but is somewhat lite when it comes to concretely identify how formation for discipleship connects to and serves Christ's mission in the world. Although Bethge, like Bonhoeffer, stands by *Discipleship*, he even-handedly admits that as the book gained popular traction its

---

Ernst Feil, *The Theology of Dietrich Bonhoeffer*, trans. Martin Rumscheidt (Philadelphia, PA: Fortress Press, 1985), 82–6.

3. Geffrey B. Kelly and John D. Godsey, "Editor's Introduction to the English Edition," in *Discipleship*, ed. Geffrey B. Kelly and John D. Godsey, trans. Barbara Green and Reinhard Krauss (Minneapolis, MN: Fortress Press, 2001), 20–21.

4. *DBWE* 8:486.

5. Stephen Plant, *Bonhoeffer* (London: Continuum, 2004), 105.

6. Plant, *Bonhoeffer*, 104–5.

7. *DBWE* 4:260.

8. Eberhard Bethge, *Dietrich Bonhoeffer: A Biography*, ed. Victoria Barnett, Rev. Ed. (Minneapolis, MN: Fortress Press, 2000), 459.

9. *DBWE* 14:96.

"dynamic ghetto began to resemble a ghetto that was cut off and had grown sterile. With familiarity, the costly otherness of grace once again grew 'cheap.'"[10]

Thus, we might say that, in *Discipleship*, Bonhoeffer clearly develops justification's import for discipleship in participatory and embodied terms, employing them in order to describe the formation of disciples within the church. A concrete picture for what reconciliation with Christ in the church means for bearing witness to Christ in the world, however, never fully emerges. Plant illustrates the disconnect well when describing Bonhoeffer's powerful rhetoric in *Discipleship*: "This siren-like quality is the book's strength and its weakness. In the flow of the book's language and approach one feels there can be no other way of understanding Christian faith; but re-enter a context in which faith is foreign and it can be hard to make the book connect."[11] In the next chapter, we shall see how Bonhoeffer's *Ethics* helps to make this connection, rendering reconciliation concrete and enabling us to see the full scope of the social implications of justification in Bonhoeffer's thought.

Christiane Tietz points to the shaping influence of Bonhoeffer's context on the content of *Discipleship* when she writes that it "views the Christians of that era at a fork in the road."[12] Even the title, suggests Ferdinand Schlingensiepen, promises that within its pages Bonhoeffer offers a pointed alternative to the Nazi way of life. According to Schlingensiepen, it is likely that Bonhoeffer, in choosing *Nachfolge* as the title for his book, was consciously reworking the refrain of a Nazi war song: "'Führer, command, we'll follow you [*wir folgen dir*].'" As such, "he was not only using a New Testament concept, but also contrasting it expressly to a term widely used by the Nazis."[13] This context helps to explain the sharpness of Bonhoeffer's rhetoric. However, it also offers an implicit warning along the lines of the previous suggestion—namely, that retrieval of Bonhoeffer's theology of discipleship must guard against uncritical acceptance of some of the dichotomies he presents therein.

What, then, of how *Discipleship* is contextualized within Bonhoeffer's biography? The intervening years between the informal end of his academic career in 1933 and the beginning of his post as the director of a preacher's seminary for the Confessing Church at Finkenwalde were a formative time for him.[14] Specifically, they saw the development and maturation of a fresh commitment to Scripture, the beginning of which we cannot pinpoint exactly, but likely occurred sometime

---

10. Bethge, *Dietrich Bonhoeffer*, 460.

11. Plant, *Bonhoeffer*, 98.

12. Christiane Tietz, *Theologian of Resistance: The Life and Thought of Dietrich Bonhoeffer*, trans. Victoria Barnett (Minneapolis, MN: Fortress Press, 2016), 63.

13. Ferdinand Schlingensiepen, *Dietrich Bonhoeffer, 1906–1945: Martyr, Thinker, Man of Resistance*, trans. Isabel Best (London: T&T Clark, 2010), 206.

14. For the formal end of Bonhoeffer's lectureship at the University of Berlin, see the August–September 1936 letters concerning his termination in *DBWE* 14:231, 246–7, 251. Regarding the key role that Bonhoeffer's work at Finkenwalde played in shaping the manuscript of *Discipleship*, see Bethge *Dietrich Bonhoeffer*, 451.

between 1931 and 1932.¹⁵ In a 1936 letter to his friend, Elizabeth Zinn, Bonhoeffer describes this change:

> For the first time, I came to the Bible. That, too, is an awful thing to say. I had often preached, I had seen a great deal of the church, had spoken and written about it—and yet I was not yet a Christian but rather in an utterly wild and uncontrolled fashion my own master. I do know that at the time I turned the cause of Jesus Christ into an advantage for myself, for my crazy vanity. I pray to God that will never happen again. Nor had I ever prayed, or had done so only very rarely. Despite this isolation, I was quite happy with myself. The Bible, especially the Sermon on the Mount, freed me from all this. Since then everything changed. I have felt this plainly and so have other people around me. That was a great liberation. It became clear to me that the life of a servant of Jesus Christ must belong to the church, and step-by-step it became clearer to me how far it must go. Then came the crisis of 1933. This strengthened me in it.¹⁶

The pivotal role that the Sermon on the Mount played for Bonhoeffer is self-evident, given that he devotes a third of *Discipleship* to its exposition. According to Bethge, "[t]he book clearly owes its conclusive style and momentum to his preoccupation with the Sermon on the Mount that had begun long before 1935." However, "Bonhoeffer's reconsideration and reexamination of its implications with respect to the Pauline writings was a new step."¹⁷ The fact that justification and Pauline themes played a central role in grounding and orienting his theology in this period is evident in another 1936 letter, this time to Karl Barth. In the letter, he speaks of his desire to hammer out his thoughts in relation to Scripture before consulting Barth. At the same time, he confesses that much of his thinking between his sojourn in London and 1936 involved an "ongoing, silent dispute" with Barth in relation to "questions concerning the interpretation of the Sermon on the Mount and the Pauline doctrine of justification and sanctification."¹⁸ A large part of Bonhoeffer's wrestling with the doctrines of justification and sanctification

---

15. Bethge (*Dietrich Bonhoeffer*, 206) refrains from identifying a precise occasion. For a later date, during his time lecturing at the University of Berlin, see Clifford J. Green, *Bonhoeffer: A Theology of Sociality*, Rev. Ed. (Grand Rapids, MI: Eerdmans, 1999), 140. For an earlier date, during his time at the Union Theological Seminary, specifically in conjunction with his time spent in Harlem, see Reggie L. Williams, *Bonhoeffer's Black Jesus: Harlem Renaissance Theology and an Ethic of Resistance* (Waco, TX: Baylor University Press, 2014), 109–10.

16. *DBWE* 14:134.

17. Bethge, *Dietrich Bonhoeffer*, 451.

18. *DBWE* 14:252–3. Barth's response to this letter at the time expressed concerns regarding a possible abandonment of "the original christological and eschatological approach"(*DBWE* 14:267) in the Finkenwalde project and *Discipleship*. However, he later called the early chapters of *Discipleship* "the best that has been written on this subject." See

was due to the ecclesial malaise he saw among German Christians, who were ostensibly devoted to the primacy of the former.[19] Thus, although the Sermon on the Mount is materially and exegetically essential to Bonhoeffer's theology of discipleship, Geffrey Kelly and John Godsey, in their editorial introduction to the critical, English edition of *Discipleship*, are able to state quite plainly: "It is clear that here, as throughout his theology, Bonhoeffer's framework is Luther's doctrine of justification by faith alone."[20]

It is important to underscore, however, that Bonhoeffer's approach to the doctrine of justification during the Finkenwalde period is governed in a way that is distinct from his earlier theology. In a manner congruent with the pivotal change noted earlier in his letter to Zinn, Bonhoeffer looks to the Bible in order to forge the connection between justification and discipleship. Yet, his turn to Scripture is hardly evidence of a form of biblicism.[21] Rather, it is a turn to Scripture *as* witness to the risen and living Christ. This emphasis is most fully fleshed out in his "Lecture on Contemporizing New Testament Texts," given at a meeting for the hierarchy of the Confessing Church in August 1935. Here, Bonhoeffer asserts that contemporizing is not something the Christian does to the New Testament, but, rather, something God does to the Christian by the Holy Spirit through Scripture. Indeed, he goes so far as to suggest that the present is not a "temporal feeling," nor is it the claims of the temporal moment. Rather, it is "solely the Holy Spirit."[22] As such, "the *concretissimum of the Christian message* and textual exposition is not a human act of contemporizing but rather always God, the Holy Spirit."[23] Insofar as the substance of the New Testament is the Word that Christ speaks through the Spirit, attentiveness and obedience to this Word is the means by which scripture draws the Christian into the present.[24] For Bonhoeffer, this is nothing less than the eschatological orientation of the gospel; it is a Word from outside—from the future—which constitutes the present.[25]

The eschatological determination of the present by the Spirit of Christ does not, however, endorse a method of interpreting Scripture that amounts to searching for the eternal kernel within the temporal husk. This is exactly the sort of method that sets the self in a position of authority over the text of scripture. According to this

---

Karl Barth, *Church Dogmatics: The Doctrine of Reconciliation*, ed. G. W. Bromiley and T. F. Torrance, trans. G. W. Bromiley, vol. IV/1 (Peabody, MA: Hendrickson, 2010), 533–4.

19. Kelly and Godsey, "Editor's Introduction to the English Edition," 3.

20. Kelly and Godsey, "Editor's Introduction to the English Edition," 7. The extent to which Bonhoeffer's interpretation of the Sermon on the Mount is shaped by concerns for justification is a promising line of inquiry that we, unfortunately, do not have the time to enter into here.

21. *DBWE* 14:425.
22. *DBWE* 14:417.
23. *DBWE* 14:417.
24. *DBWE* 14:417.
25. *DBWE* 14:418.

method, Bonhoeffer writes: the *"norm of contemporizing resides within us; the Bible is the material to which this norm is applied."*[26] Yet, such a method does not match the substance of Scripture as the Word of Christ. Indeed, the only norm appropriate to this substance is "the word of God itself, and our own circumstances, reason, conscience, and ethnonational [völkisch] experience are the material to which this norm is to be applied."[27] As such, substance and norm are one and the same. The Word of Christ, spoken by the Spirit, both constitutes the substance of Scripture and norms those who hear it. By identifying the two, Bonhoeffer effectively makes the case that all of Scripture is relevant for theology and the formation of those to whom it is proclaimed. Thus, theology's goal is not to identify what in Scripture is relevant for the church, but, rather, to make *"the whole of Holy Scripture audible as a witness to the word of God."*[28]

In this way, Bonhoeffer denies the distinction between historical texts (e.g., the gospels) and doctrinal texts (e.g., the Pauline epistles).[29] For theology, both are of the same substance and value.[30] Both bear witness to Christ and have decisive significance for the human being. "*The common character of the New Testament witness* is that it is Christ who performs this miracle, speaks the parable, issues the commandment, and that through such a miracle, parable, commandment, or teaching Christ is always aiming at one and the same thing, *namely, to bind human beings to himself* as the absolutely unique, historic one."[31] Thus, doctrine can no longer be thought in isolation from Scripture. Instead, it must witness to Christ, recognizing that doctrine is that which Christ speaks first through Scripture.[32] In other words, doctrine that witnesses to Christ is a form of repetition that is made effective only by the Spirit. Furthermore, such witness is not merely cognitive or verbal. Rather, it aims at binding the one who hears to the person of Christ, who became incarnate in history, died, and is risen. As such, Bonhoeffer controversially

---

26. *DBWE* 14:421.

27. *DBWE* 14:421.

28. *DBWE* 14:421. This is not to suggest, however, that God's hiddenness in revelation ceases to be hidden. On this as a key aspect of Bonhoeffer's approach to Scripture, see Michael Mawson, "The Weakness of the Word and the Reality of God: Luther and Bonhoeffer on the Cross of Discipleship," *Studies in Christian Ethics* 31, no. 4 (2018): 458–9.

29. This is especially relevant, given that in *Discipleship* he is explicitly integrating the historical (the Sermon on the Mount) with the doctrinal (justification by faith).

30. Here, we see his methodological basis for drawing together the Sermon on the Mount and the doctrine of justification in his theology of discipleship.

31. *DBWE* 14:424. For how this might apply to Old Testament texts, see Bonhoeffer's Christological approach to the book of Psalms in *DBWE* 5:141–77. On the topic of Bonhoeffer's reading of the Old Testament more generally and how it evolved over time, see Martin Kuske, *The Old Testament as the Book of Christ: An Appraisal of Bonhoeffer's Interpretation*, trans. S. T. Kimbrough (Philadelphia, PA: The Westminster Press, 1976).

32. Cf. Nadine Hamilton, "Dietrich Bonhoeffer and the Necessity of Kenosis for Scriptural Hermeneutics," *Scottish Journal of Theology* 71, no. 4 (2018): 452–3.

asserts that "[o]ne does not correctly interpret a Pauline doctrinal text if one transmits it as a piece of genuine theology[,] as *pura doctrina*."[33] In other words, what makes a doctrine—such as justification—genuinely theological is not the fact that it is the doctrine on which the church stands or falls.[34] Instead, justification's theological import and significance rest solely in the fact that it bears witness to the "crucified, resurrected Lord who calls to discipleship."[35] Bonhoeffer sums up this line of thinking in a notational fragment tacked onto the end of a sentence: "theology as witness!"[36]

This is not to say that Bonhoeffer no longer sees the value of doctrine. Indeed, in the student notes from his "Lecture Section on Ministry" in 1935, he identifies doctrine as the key consideration at play in determining whether a pastor has become unfit for ministry.[37] When it comes to dismissal from ministry "[d]octrine [is] to receive priority. Incorrect doctrine attacks the substance of the church, excludes from the church."[38] Rather, doctrine, as witness to the living Christ, must now be interpreted and expounded as Christ's forming Word which, when spoken by the Holy Spirit, shapes those in faith in particular ways. Thus, the student notes on Bonhoeffer's 1935-6 "Lecture on Catechesis" attribute the following formulation to him: "Christianity is doctrine related to a certain form of existence (speech *and life!*)."[39] Such formation of existence is possible only when doctrine is understood as Christ's Word which comes from the outside. In this way, Bonhoeffer is counterintuitively grounding the efficacy of doctrine in a doctrine—namely, the doctrine of justification by faith. Just before the aforementioned formulation, the notes read: "What makes Christian education and instruction possible is the fact of *iustitia aliena*, which is given in baptism and justification."[40] In other words, the

---

33. *DBWE* 14:425; cf. *DBWE* 4:55. This is, perhaps, already a modification of his assertion in a 1934 letter to his friend, Erwin Sutz, where he favorably advocates for the importance of pure doctrine (*DBWE* 13:217).

34. This phrasing is often misattributed to Luther. On its most likely origin in later Lutheranism, see Alister E. McGrath, Iustitia Dei: *A History of the Christian Doctrine of Justification*, vol. 2 (Cambridge: Cambridge University Press, 1986), 193n3.

35. *DBWE* 14:427. This is important to keep in mind when considering Bonhoeffer's criticisms of doctrine in *Discipleship* (see, for example, *DBWE* 4:47, 50).

36. *DBWE* 14:425.

37. When citing from student notes on Bonhoeffer's lectures from the Finkenwalde period, it is assumed, by virtue of its inclusion in the critical edition of his works, that although the direct wording is not Bonhoeffer's, the idea or concept expressed can accurately be attributed to him.

38. *DBWE* 14:333.

39. *DBWE* 14:540. Crucially, this form of existence is not a generic pursuit of the good, but a bearing witness to the truth of the gospel through proclamation and enactment. Cf. Philip G. Ziegler, "'Not to Abolish, but to Fulfil': The Person of the Preacher and the Claim of the Sermon on the Mount," *Studies in Christian Ethics* 22, no. 3 (2009): 281.

40. *DBWE* 14:539.

alien righteousness received in justification and baptism is what makes doctrine genuinely formative and educational. The righteousness of Christ, which is the believer's in faith, is both the basis for encountering doctrine as a witness to Christ and what makes this encounter necessarily formative. Indeed, its effects are both epistemic and ontological. Any formulation of doctrine that pertains only to speech, on the one hand, or to the ethics of existence, on the other hand, fails to recognize the intimate connection between cognition and formation for action in Scripture's witness to Christ.

What, then, did this mean for Bonhoeffer's thinking, in relation to justification as he was formulating his theology of discipleship? It meant that his understanding of justification was beholden to Scripture in new ways. The result was an articulation of justification as a doctrine that bears witness to Christ and thereby contributes to a particular form of concrete, human existence. This fresh attention to justification in Scripture, especially insofar as it is oriented to the concrete existence of the believer, is borne out in the two lecture courses he gave during the third and fourth sessions at Finkenwalde—"New Life in Paul" and "Concrete Ethics in Paul," respectively. In the student notes for these lectures, Bonhoeffer makes several important moves that set the stage for our discussion of how justification unfolds in *Discipleship*. First, Bonhoeffer frames his understanding of justification in a way that, initially, seems to have little to do with its formative significance for the Christian life. He poses the question: "What is the gift of faith?" To which he offers this answer: "In faith we receive justification = assurance of God's righteousness."[41] This is hardly a revolutionary formulation, but Bonhoeffer unfolds it in an unexpected way. God's righteousness is, in the first place, not an object given to humanity. Rather, it is God's justification of himself on the cross.[42] Justification is centrally about God's justification of himself and only in God's self-justification does humanity find a basis from which it might be justified.[43]

For Bonhoeffer, this way of defining justification has consequences in both the practical and the theological sphere. Bonhoeffer believed that the degradation of justification—not only by the *Deutsche Christen* but also by moderates in the Confessing Church—was a product of turning grace into the principle of justification, rather than its consequence. "In effect, one has God's righteousness by merely possessing the principle. But one does not have to actualize the principle. Simply holding it and defending it against the counterprinciple of good works was sufficient."[44] The result is cheap grace, which justifies sin, but not the sinner.[45] However, by making God's self-justification in Christ's death the locus

---

41. *DBWE* 14:608.

42. On how Bonhoeffer departs from Luther without contradicting him by highlighting God's subjective righteousness alongside of God's objective righteousness, see Michael P. DeJonge, *Bonhoeffer's Reception of Luther* (Oxford: Oxford University Press, 2017), 234–6.

43. *DBWE* 14:609. See also *DBWE* 4:254.

44. Kelly and Godsey, "Editor's Introduction to the English Edition," 11.

45. Cf. *DBWE* 4:44.

of humanity's justification he removes grace from the realm of principle and ties it to participation in Christ's death and resurrected life. In other words, grace is the consequence of Christ's death and resurrection, which humanity comes to participate in by faith. Here, we see that Bonhoeffer's move to accentuate the forensic nature of justification actually creates the space in which participation becomes a central aspect of justification. "In faith in the Christ *outside me*, I have Christ *in me*."[46] As such, participation is not, for Bonhoeffer, a sort of theosis, but, rather, faith-based union with Christ wrought by the Holy Spirit. Thus, justification by faith is the reestablishment of the believer in relation to God's righteousness through union with Christ, in which his death and resurrected life become the believer's own. In this manner, justification witnesses to Christ, the crucified and risen Lord, who binds humanity to himself and calls them to discipleship.

That Bonhoeffer is here drawing on justification in a way that makes participation in Christ central is also evident from the way he begins the aforementioned lecture series. "New Life in Paul" begins with the question: "How do I come to participate in this being in Christ?"[47] Likewise, "Concrete Ethics in Paul" begins with a lecture section "on Acts 2:43–47 and on the Actions of Christians ἐν Χριστῷ."[48] In both cases justification and being in Christ are woven tightly together, with the latter drawing sanctification into the mix. For Bonhoeffer, justification and sanctification are not two separate phases in a linear development. Rather, they are two sides of the same coin.[49] "Placement into the space of the church-community is justification; abiding in this space is sanctification."[50] Bonhoeffer fleshes out this relationship in *Discipleship*, forming an analogy between creation and justification on the one hand, and preservation and sanctification on the other.[51] Justification is the ground of being in Christ, while sanctification is the preservation of that union unto redemption. Ultimately, however, both justification and sanctification have the same substance—namely, community with Christ.[52] In what follows, our focus will remain on justification since a full treatment of Bonhoeffer on

---

46. *DBWE* 14:606.

47. *DBWE* 14:605.

48. *DBWE* 14:718.

49. For a recent argument in the realm of Pauline theology against seeing a cut-and-dried distinction between sanctification and justification, see Stephen J. Chester, *Reading Paul with the Reformers: Reconciling Old and New Perspectives* (Grand Rapids, MI: Eerdmans, 2017), 374–5; cf. John M. G. Barclay, *Paul and the Gift* (Grand Rapids, MI: Eerdmans, 2015), 517–18.

50. *DBWE* 14:724.

51. *DBWE* 4:260.

52. *DBWE* 4:259. Bonhoeffer's construal of the relationship between justification and sanctification also finds an unlikely ally in T. F. Torrance. See his essay, "Justification: Its Radical Nature and Place in Reformed Doctrine and Life," in *Theology in Reconstruction* (London: SCM Press, 1965), 161–2.

sanctification is outside of the scope of this project.[53] Furthermore, Bethge insists that by introducing sanctification Bonhoeffer was not seeking to develop it as a parallel doctrine to justification. Rather, "[h]e believes that justification by faith remains the incontestable presupposition and needs no supplement."[54] According to Bethge, then, sanctification is merely the means by which the costliness of the gift of grace in justification is preserved.[55]

Our focus in the preceding discussion has been to highlight why, and the way in which, Bonhoeffer begins to draw on the doctrine of justification in a different manner during this period. Specifically, we saw that the need to offer a fresh articulation of justification arose against the backdrop of the doctrine's degradation at the hands of the *Deutsche Christen*. This need, then, coincided with Bonhoeffer's decisive turn to Scripture's witness to Christ as the locus for his theology. Thus, we can say that the priority Bonhoeffer attributes to the Holy Spirit's witness to Christ through Scripture provides him with a basis from which to articulate God's justification of the sinner and costly grace over against the justification of sin and cheap grace. As a result, Bonhoeffer begins to explicitly think of justification as a witness to the living Christ who calls humanity to a particular form of life—namely, a life of discipleship. Core to this fresh articulation of justification's import for the Christian life is participation in Christ. This, of course, dovetails nicely with the Pauline emphasis outlined in the previous chapter. In the sections that follow, we shall look more closely at the role of union with Christ in discipleship and how, for Bonhoeffer, it unfolds in embodied terms which are significant for the disciple's vocation as a minister of reconciliation.

III Participation as Discipleship's Content

a Costly Grace in Christ the Mediator

As we turn to consider the way Bonhoeffer locates participation in Christ at the center of his theology of discipleship, it is worthwhile to note the range of language he uses to describe this reality. He writes in different places of "being bound to" (*Bindung*),[56] "participation in" (*Teilhabe*),[57] "communion with" (*Gemeinschaft*),[58]

---

53. For a recent discussion of this topic, see M. J. Knight, "Christ Existing in Ordinary: Dietrich Bonhoeffer and Sanctification," *International Journal of Systematic Theology* 16, no. 4 (2014): 414–35.

54. Eberhard Bethge, "The Challenge of Dietrich Bonhoeffer's Life and Theology," in *World Come of Age: A Symposium on Dietrich Bonhoeffer*, ed. Ronald Gregor Smith (London: Collins, 1967), 57.

55. Bethge, "The Challenge of Dietrich Bonhoeffer's Life and Theology," 57.

56. See, for example, *DBWE* 4:59, 89; *DBW* 4:47, 82.

57. See, for example, *DBWE* 4:120, 285; *DBW* 4:121, 301.

58. See, for example, *DBWE* 4:89, 127; *DBW* 4:83, 129.

and "union with" (*Vereinigung*).[59] In addition, Bonhoeffer also speaks of being "in Christ" in ways that do not employ this technical language. Within the context of Bonhoeffer's wider corpus, each of the aforementioned terms could be shaded differently, particularly *Gemeinschaft*. However, they all broadly refer to the Pauline notion of being "in Christ." As such, "binding," "participation," "communion," and "union" will be used interchangeably in the following discussion.

Bonhoeffer begins the second chapter of *Discipleship* with the call of Levi in Mark 2:14, before asking after the content of discipleship. The short answer to this rhetorical question is: "Follow me, walk behind me! That is all."[60] Indeed, there is no specific content associated with following Christ, insofar as it is not paired with a prescribed program or a systematic framework. Rather, Jesus's call to Levi in Mark 2:14 is a call away from his previous existence and into a new way of being in the world.[61] As such, the content of discipleship is not a new road to travel down among others from which one might choose. Instead, it is a new mode of existence and the whole content of this new existence is "nothing other than being bound to Jesus Christ alone."[62] It is important to emphasize, however, that being bound to Christ is not and cannot be a static reality. Union with Christ is union with a living person who beckons forward to movement and mission in service of the Kingdom of God. As such, discipleship—being bound to Christ—is an inherently active mode of existence.

Understanding discipleship as union with Christ, then, provides a lens through which to read Bonhoeffer's discourse on cheap and costly grace in the first chapter. There he writes that costly grace "is costly, because it calls to discipleship; it is grace, because it calls us to follow *Jesus Christ*."[63] What Bonhoeffer means by this is that grace is costly because it lays holistic claim to the life of the disciple, and it is grace because it invites the disciple to take on Christ's yoke, which is easy and light. Insofar as costly grace entails real discipleship, it also entails a binding to Christ. This implies that costly grace's opposite—cheap grace—is cheap precisely because it does not call one into a new mode of existence marked by participation in Christ. Alongside of and in parallel to the opposed pairing of costly grace and cheap grace, Bonhoeffer also poses the justification of the sinner and the justification of sin as oppositional realities. The resultant picture is one in which the justification of the sinner and costly grace are inseparably tied to discipleship and participation in Christ.[64] Cheap grace allows the church to claim that because it "is in possession

---

59. See, for example, *DBWE* 4:266; *DBW* 4:283.

60. *DBWE* 4:58.

61. Bethge notes in relation to this passage that "when Christ steps up to Levi, his entire real existence is affected" (*DBWE* 4:58n3).

62. *DBWE* 4:58–59.

63. *DBWE* 4:45.

64. Cf. Michael P. DeJonge, *Bonhoeffer on Resistance: The Word Against the Wheel* (Oxford: Oxford University Press, 2018), 117.

of a doctrine of justification, then it is surely a justified church."[65] According to costly grace, however, justification as a doctrine means nothing if it fails to witness to Christ's justifying work in which he binds believers to himself in faith and by the Holy Spirit.

Therefore, union with Christ serves as Bonhoeffer's starting point for unfolding costly grace and the justification of the sinner in the sphere of discipleship. In other words, if costly grace and justification of the sinner reconstitute concrete existence, the mechanism by which they do so is union with Christ. And since union with Christ is a dynamic reality, as noted earlier, it takes on the character of following after, of discipleship. This is not to say, however, that union with Christ and discipleship are human possibilities. Indeed, they remain governed by the logic of justification by faith. "Discipleship is not a human offer. The call alone creates the situation."[66] We might say, then, that Christ's call is carried by the Holy Spirit, creates faith, justifies, binds, and enlists in Christ's mission.

How, then, does being bound to Christ unfold to reveal the character of discipleship? Here, we can distinguish between the immediate relationship established in union with Christ, on the one hand, and mediated relationships, on the other hand.[67] The basis for this distinction is Bonhoeffer's radical interpretation of Christ's mediatorial status, the foundation for which was laid in his 1933 Christology lectures.[68] For Bonhoeffer, Christ mediates not only between God and humanity, but also between believers and the world. Given the widespread implications of this construal it is worth quoting his formulation in detail:

> It is true, there is something which comes between persons called by Christ and the given circumstances of their natural lives. But it is not someone unhappily contemptuous of life; it is not some law of piety. Instead, it is life and the gospel itself; it is Christ himself. In becoming human, he put himself between me and the given circumstances of the world. I cannot go back. He is in the middle. He has deprived those whom he has called of every immediate connection to those given realities. He wants to be the medium; everything should happen only through Him. He stands not only between me and God, he also stands between me and the world, between me and other people and things. *He is the mediator*, not only between God and human persons, but also between person and person, and between person and reality. Because the whole world was created by him and for him (John 1:3; 1 Cor. 8:6; Heb. 1:2), he is the sole mediator in the world.[69]

---

65. *DBWE* 4:53.
66. *DBWE* 4:63.
67. Cf. *DBWE* 5:32.
68. See *DBWE* 12:324–7. It is also picked up again in *Life Together* (*DBWE* 5:43–4).
69. *DBWE* 4:93. Clifford Green takes issue with this construal because of its potentially authoritarian depiction of Jesus. However, his objection is partly based on a mistranslation. Just prior to the aforementioned quote (*DBWE* 4:93; *DBW* 4:88) Bonhoeffer asks what sort of *ärgerliche Macht* comes between human persons and the natural orders of their

Christ's mediation is essentially related to and an outworking of the logic of participation within the context of discipleship. Indeed, thinking back to the conceptualities Bonhoeffer employed in his Christology lectures, being bound to Christ means that Christ both stands in immediate relationship to the single individual as her center and mediates between her and all else as her boundary.[70] Thus, the two types of relationships established in participation are easily identified: the individual's immediate relationship to Christ and all other relationships, which are necessarily mediated.[71] We shall now turn and look at the character of the disciple's immediate relation to Christ.

b The Baptismal Nature of Communion with Christ

As we have seen earlier, being bound to Christ is an important aspect of justification properly construed. This means that, for Bonhoeffer, following after Christ in discipleship is imbued with a justificatory or baptismal logic.[72] Put another way, we might say that the death and resurrection of the individual, sacramentally enacted in baptism, is a once and for all event with ongoing implications for life in Christ. So, for Bonhoeffer, the import of baptism into Christ for human beings can be described in two related ways: either with regard to their personal, salvific status or with regard to their relationships throughout life.[73] On the one hand, a person's salvific status corresponds to the once and for all nature of baptism, which is grounded in the once and for all nature of Christ's death and resurrection. On the other hand, a person's relationships throughout life are shaped by their ongoing participation in the crucified and resurrected Christ. Thus, insofar as baptism binds individuals to Christ, his life, death, and resurrection become determinative

---

lives. Green translates *ärgerliche Macht* as "angry power." However, the critical, English edition of *Discipleship* rightly renders it as "annoying power." The latter translation lacks the authoritarian implications of Green's, and fits better with the context—namely, the hypothetical human resistance to Christ's mediation that Bonhoeffer is voicing. For Green's discussion of the authoritarian Christ of *Discipleship*, see Green, *Bonhoeffer*, 173-9.

70. *DBWE* 12:324-5. There too Bonhoeffer speaks of Christ as mediator. However, it must be pointed out that whereas he speaks of Christ as the center and boundary of history, here he speaks, without using this exact language, of Christ as center and boundary of individual existence.

71. The concept of mediation unfolded here provides a retroactive safeguard against loose interpretations of Bonhoeffer's suggestion in *Santorum Communio* that Christians "ought to become a Christ to the other." *DBWE* 1:183.

72. Bonhoeffer is typically Lutheran in his close association of baptism and justification. On Luther's own evolving identification between the two, see Jonathan Trigg, "Luther on Baptism and Penance," in *The Oxford Handbook of Martin Luther's Theology*, ed. Robert Kolb, Irene Dingel, and Ľubomír Batka (Oxford: Oxford University Press, 2014), 311.

73. *DBWE* 4:235.

of their entire existence. "Participation brings about justification, the cessation of sin, transferal into a new kingdom."[74]

While, in *Discipleship*, Bonhoeffer is decidedly more interested in outlining justification *away from* sin and into a life of following after Christ, this does not come at the expense of the soteriological reality of being pronounced righteous, since both are dependent on being in Christ.[75] This is due to his expanded definition of Christ's righteousness: "[B]ecause that righteousness [which is required by the law] is not only a good deed to be performed, but complete, true, and personal communion with God, Jesus not only *has* righteousness, he *is* righteousness personified."[76] The righteousness of Christ is not some representational package of good works which is given to the human person to cancel out their sin. Rather, Christ simply *is* righteousness and in order for human beings to be righteous they must be bound to him by the Spirit. "He is the disciples' righteousness. In calling his disciples, Jesus granted them participation in himself; he gave them community with him; he let them participate in his own righteousness; he granted them his own righteousness."[77] This, of course, further proves the point from earlier that participation in Christ is centrally important to Bonhoeffer's unfolding of justification in the realm of discipleship. Returning to the baptismal framework identified previously, death to one's old existence and resurrection in Christ, as a once and for all event, is salvific because being in Christ simply is being righteous. "Being baptized into the death of Christ is what brings forgiveness of sins and justification and a complete separation from sin."[78]

What then of the ongoing significance of baptism for life in Christ? While the individual's death and resurrection in Christ is a once and for all event, the new existence which the believer lives is one that is shaped, oriented, and empowered by the crucified and resurrected Christ. Thus, the logic of baptism shapes what it means to be united to Christ in an ongoing manner. And, insofar as it shapes participation in Christ, it also shapes one's relationship to all other aspects of reality. This is because of Bonhoeffer's comprehensive interpretation of Christ's mediation, noted earlier. Bonhoeffer writes: "I am deprived of my immediate relationship to the given realities of the world, since Christ the mediator and Lord has stepped in between me and the world. Those who are baptized no longer belong to the world, no longer serve the world, and are no longer subject to it. They belong to Christ alone, and relate to the world only through Christ."[79] Governed by the logic of baptism, relating to the world through Christ means relating to the world through his life, death, and resurrection.

---

74. *DBWE* 14:475.
75. On justification away from sin, see *DBWE* 4:209; *DBWE* 14:610–11.
76. *DBWE* 4:119.
77. *DBWE* 4:119–20.
78. *DBWE* 4:209.
79. *DBWE* 4:208. Cf. *DBWE* 5:41.

Bonhoeffer, however, overwhelmingly prefers to focus on the implications of participation in Christ's death.[80] "Discipleship as allegiance to the person of Jesus Christ places the follower under the law of Christ, that is, under the cross."[81] Here, we come to one of the central themes of *Discipleship*—namely, bearing one's cross in union with Christ. Indeed, Bethge writes that "the chapter 'Discipleship and the Cross' was a cornerstone of the work from the beginning."[82] However, it is also one of the more fraught aspects of the work. While Bonhoeffer by no means neglects the resurrection altogether, his conception of discipleship is so governed by suffering and the cross that he seems to underemphasize participation in the triumph of the resurrection.[83] On her way to advocating for a deeper emphasis on the resurrection in Christian theology, Marit Trelstad criticizes Bonhoeffer's fixation on the cross, asserting that "[c]hoosing the way of the cross may be an important act of discipleship for those who have the option to choose, but when there is no other option than suffering this message can further oppression."[84] Indeed, one might wonder if Bonhoeffer is instrumentalizing suffering when he writes: "Suffering is distance from God. That is why someone who is in communion with God cannot suffer. . . . Indeed, suffering remains distance from God, but in community with the suffering of Jesus Christ, suffering is overcome by suffering. Communion with God is granted precisely by suffering."[85] It is difficult to escape the sense that Bonhoeffer has slipped into a sort of Christian idealism here that abstracts suffering from the real-world context in which it occurs.

There is certainly an extent to which Bonhoeffer's emphasis on death and suffering risks instrumentalization and fails to fully hold out the promise of the resurrection to those already suffering. However, the resurrection still plays an important, if understated, role in his understanding of discipleship under the cross.[86] This is due to the fact that, for Bonhoeffer, carrying one's cross in discipleship can never be divorced from the fact that this carrying takes place only

---

80. This is superficially demonstrated by the fact that when one looks at "resurrection" in the index to the critical, English edition of *Discipleship*, there is only one page number listed, and it is cross-referenced to "cross."

81. *DBWE* 4:85. For a treatment of the interplay between allegiance, union, and justification in the realm of New Testament studies, see Matthew W. Bates, *Salvation by Allegiance Alone: Rethinking Faith, Works, and the Gospel of Jesus the King* (Grand Rapids, MI: Baker Academic, 2017), 166–8.

82. Bethge, *Dietrich Bonhoeffer*, 450.

83. For a similar criticism of *Discipleship* on exactly this front, see John Webster, "Discipleship and Obedience," *Scottish Bulletin of Evangelical Theology* 24, no. 1 (2006): 8.

84. Marit Trelstad, "The Way of Salvation in Luther's Theology: A Feminist Evaluation," *Dialog: A Journal of Theology* 45, no. 3 (2006): 238.

85. *DBWE* 4:90.

86. Contra Hamish Walker, who suggests the resurrection has merely a "structural significance" in *Discipleship*. See "The Incarnation and Crucifixion in Bonhoeffer's *Cost of Discipleship*," *Scottish Journal of Theology* 21, no. 4 (1968): 407.

in union with the risen Christ. Even though "[d]iscipleship is being bound to the suffering Christ,"[87] Bonhoeffer also notes that "God's love for the people brings the cross and discipleship, but these, in turn, mean life and resurrection."[88] Carrying one's cross and discipleship do not "mean" life and resurrection in the sense that they are the means by which those realities are attained. Rather, they mean that the believer has life and resurrection in Christ, and this is why she can joyfully take up her cross in discipleship. As such, suffering and taking up one's cross can never be the instrumentalized means by which one is made righteous or takes part in the resurrection. The believer takes up her cross in discipleship simply because she lives out of her unity with the resurrected Christ who has taken up his cross, calls her to do likewise, and goes with her under it. Thus, Bonhoeffer concludes that "[t]he acts of the church's first martyrs give witness that Christ transfigures the moment of greatest suffering for his followers through the indescribable certainty of his nearness and communion."[89]

Teased out another way, for Bonhoeffer, union with Christ in discipleship both leads to and prepares for suffering. "The call to follow Jesus, baptism in the name of Jesus Christ, is death and life."[90] Because the call to follow, like baptism, is justificatory in nature it implies a break with one's former life. It is for this reason that Bonhoeffer calls the death of one's old existence in the call to discipleship "[t]he first Christ-suffering that everyone has to experience."[91] Being bound to Christ means participation in his death. This is why, in Mark 8:34, Jesus makes taking up one's cross a stipulation for discipleship. "The cross is suffering with Christ. Indeed, it is Christ-suffering. Only one who is bound to Christ as this occurs in discipleship stands in seriousness under the cross."[92] However, union with Christ prepares believers for suffering as well, and herein lies the logic of resurrection. Christ prepares his disciples for suffering by urging them to deny themselves and know only him, the one they are bound to by the Spirit. "When we know only him, then we also no longer know the pain of our own cross."[93] Knowing only Christ is the means by which the present suffering of discipleship is transformed by the eschatological reality of the resurrection. In other words, being bound to Christ means living from the resurrection while participating in Christ's suffering in a world no longer ruled, but still marked by sin.[94]

---

87. *DBWE* 4:89.
88. *DBWE* 4:197.
89. *DBWE* 4:89.
90. *DBWE* 4:88.
91. *DBWE* 4:87.
92. *DBWE* 4:87.
93. *DBWE* 4:86; cf. Bonhoeffer's discussion of *actus directus* in relation to baptism in *DBWE* 2:157–61.
94. Although Bonhoeffer has little to say about the ascension in *Discipleship*, it is worth briefly noting the light it sheds on the manner in which the disciple's life is sourced from the resurrection even as it shares in Christ's sufferings on earth. To a certain extent Christ's high

Bonhoeffer's great virtue is his ability to unfold the implications of Luther's *theologia crucis* for a life of discipleship.[95] In doing so, he emphasizes the cross and suffering, but he also incorporates the logic of the resurrection through his insistence that communion with Christ transforms suffering.[96] However, insofar as the resurrection remains a subtext in his discussion of discipleship and the cross—and his discussion of baptism, for that matter!—he does not always succeed in holding the eschatological tension inherent in being bound to the one who is both crucified *and* risen. We see this, on the one hand, when he slips and sounds as if he is suggesting that suffering is constitutive of communion with Christ, rather than a consequence of it.[97] In doing so, he neglects the fact that the resurrected Christ stands between the disciple and her suffering. On the other hand, we also see him slacken the eschatological tension when he goes so far as to say that "someone who is in communion with God cannot suffer." Here, the eschatological reality of the resurrection is over-realized to the point that Bonhoeffer is no longer able to call a thing what it is in a manner consistent with the *theologia crucis*.[98] Christ mediates between the disciple and her suffering, but this does not mean that suffering ceases to be suffering. Rather, it means that suffering is cradled by a sure and certain hope. At his best, though, Bonhoeffer integrates the logic of the resurrection into his description of discipleship as participation in Christ's suffering. This is expressed perfectly when he writes: "Bearing the cross does not bring misery and despair. Rather, it provides refreshment and peace for our soul; it is our greatest joy. Here we are no longer laden with self-made laws and burdens, but with the

priestly role at the right hand of the Father is implied in Christ's mediatorial work. Indeed, he makes this explicit later, in 1940, when he pens a meditation on the ascension that fully takes into account Christ's high priestly role (*DBWE* 16:476-481). However, it is clear from a sermon outline on Acts 1:1-11 during the Finkenwalde period that, at the time, Bonhoeffer thought of the ascension primarily in terms of Christ's enthronement and kingship. Yet, if we fully take into account Christ's priestly intercession on behalf of the disciple it is precisely this high priestly work that enables her to live from the resurrection even as she takes up her cross and follows Christ. J. B. Torrance describes the dynamic at play in Christ's intercession as follows: "This is the 'wonderful exchange' . . . by which Christ takes what is ours (our broken lives and unworthy prayers), sanctifies them, offers them without spot or wrinkle to the Father, and gives them back to us, that we might 'feed' upon him in thanksgiving" (*Worship, Community and the Triune God of Grace* [Downers Grove: IVP Academic, 1996], 15). Thus, living out of the resurrection in the suffering and cross-bearing of the present has real power and promise precisely and only because the resurrected Christ has ascended to heaven and intercedes at the right hand of the Father on behalf of humanity.

95. On this, see H. Gaylon Barker, *The Cross of Reality: Luther's Theologia Crucis and Bonhoeffer's Christology* (Minneapolis, MN: Fortress Press, 2015), 303-28.

96. Rachel Muers comes to a similar conclusion in *Keeping God's Silence: Towards a Theological Ethics of Communication* (Malden, MA: Blackwell, 2004), 81-2.

97. *DBWE* 4:90.

98. See *LW* 31:40.

yoke of him who knows us and who himself goes with us under the same yoke."[99] Indeed, bearing the cross, while marked by suffering, cannot be abstracted from the baptismal logic which governs participation in Christ. As such, bearing one's cross means being borne by the resurrected one who has already taken up the cross unto death once and for all.

Thus, we have seen that at the core of Bonhoeffer's theology of discipleship is the reality of participation in Christ. This reality marks the believers' relationship to Jesus as their only unmediated relationship. Just as being bound to Christ is based in the once and for all event of death and resurrection sacramentally enacted in baptism, so too is the ongoing character of one's immediate relation to Christ shaped by a baptismal logic. For Bonhoeffer, because discipleship is carried out in the midst of a sinful world which continues to oppose Christ, following after Christ in his suffering and death is its central feature. With varying degrees of success, he attempts to articulate participation in the suffering Christ in a way that takes seriously the fact that the suffering Christ is "the first-born from the dead" (Col 1:18). Indeed, suffering in discipleship must be understood in a manner that is inflected by the eschatological reality of the resurrection. What we have not yet touched on is how the baptismal logic of participation in Christ informs and orients the disciple toward reconciliation in her mediated relationships. This connection is vitally important to Bonhoeffer's theology of discipleship, even if its articulation remains frustratingly general and abstract. However, we shall first engage with the embodied nature of participation and Bonhoeffer's corresponding concern to highlight the import of the church for discipleship.

IV The Embodied Nature of Discipleship

As we noted in the previous chapter, Bonhoeffer does give some attention to the theological import of the body in *Creation and Fall*. However, *Discipleship* marks his first engagement with the body as a theologically formative reality of the Christian life. Lisa Dahill suggests that in *Discipleship* "he articulates fully for the first time . . . that the intimate and ultimate Other encountered in another's body and being—the One encountering and forming us as persons—is Jesus Christ. In *Discipleship*, Bonhoeffer insists on the necessarily bodily nature of our life with Jesus in discipleship."[100] Indeed, Bonhoeffer's increased attention to the body in *Discipleship* makes good sense, given that one of his primary goals is to unfold

---

99. *DBWE* 4:91.

100. Lisa E. Dahill, "Con-Formation with Jesus Christ: Bonhoeffer, Social Location, and Embodiment," in *Being Human, Becoming Human: Dietrich Bonhoeffer and Social Thought*, ed. Jens Zimmermann and Brian Gregor (Eugene, OR: Pickwick Publications, 2010), 180; cf. Green, *Bonhoeffer*, 195; Jonathan D. Sorum, "The Eschatological Boundary in Dietrich Bonhoeffer's *Nachfolge*" (PhD Thesis, Luther Northwestern Theological Seminary, 1994), 346–55.

the doctrine of justification by faith in a manner that emphasizes its orientation toward action and simple obedience. Theologically, though, his rationale is firmly grounded in the incarnation. Because Christ assumes a body and intercedes for humanity bodily before God, being bound to Christ in discipleship is a necessarily embodied reality.[101] Furthermore, participation in Christ's bodily life, death, and resurrection as that which justifies humanity stands in stark contrast to justification as rote doctrine. Bonhoeffer is emphatic on this point: "A truth, a doctrine, or a religion needs no space of its own. Such entities are bodyless. They do not go beyond being heard, learned, and understood. But the incarnate Son of God needs not only ears or even hearts, he needs actually, living human beings who follow him."[102] Justification as *pura doctrina* or participation as a mystical, inner state are insufficient because they fail to account for the fact that in justification Christ lays claim to the whole person, binding believers bodily to himself in the following after of discipleship.

Bonhoeffer primarily speaks of three types of embodiment in *Discipleship*, so we shall take each in turn. First, he speaks of the body of the disciple: "Even the body of the disciple belongs to Christ and discipleship; our bodies are members of his body."[103] Prospectively, this means that disciples are called to embody their new existence in Christ through an active following after which is marked by the righteousness of him in whom they participate. To demonstrate this, Bonhoeffer juxtaposes humanity's bodily enslavement to sin with their new vocation as disciples: "The fruit of being freed from sin by Christ's death is that those who once surrendered their bodies as instruments of unrighteousness are now able to use them in service of righteousness as instruments of their sanctification."[104] Retrospectively, then, embodied discipleship is impossible apart from real bodily acceptance in Christ, which, again, is grounded in the reality that "God's mercy sends the Son in the flesh, so that in his flesh he may shoulder and carry all of humanity."[105]

Bodily life receives a much fuller treatment in *Ethics*, but Bonhoeffer does not wholly neglect to affirm the goodness of the human body as such in *Discipleship*. Indeed, he provides the following comment on the Lord's Prayer: "Give us this day our daily bread. As long as disciples are on earth, they should not be ashamed of asking their heavenly Father for the things they need for their bodily life. God who created human beings on earth intends to preserve and protect human bodies. God

---

101. *DBWE* 4:127, 217. Cf. the manner in which Jüngel locates embodiment at the heart of the *imago Dei* (Eberhard Jüngel, "Humanity in Correspondence to God: Remarks on the Image of God as a Basic Concept of Theological Anthropology," in *Theological Essays*, trans. John Webster [Edinburgh: T&T Clark, 1989], 136–9).

102. *DBWE* 4:226; cf. Dahill, "Con-Formation with Jesus Christ," 181.

103. *DBWE* 4:127.

104. *DBWE* 4:253.

105. *DBWE* 4:214.

does not intend that God's own creation become disdained."[106] However, insofar as his primary concern is to give an account of discipleship—the content of which is being bound to Christ—he primarily focuses on the body of the disciple as it relates to and is determined by the body of Christ. This is typified when he asserts that the goal of the disciple "is to be shaped into the entire *form* of the *incarnate*, the *crucified*, and the *risen one*."[107]

The body of Christ, then, is both the second and the third type of body that Bonhoeffer takes to be central to discipleship. In keeping with his early, academic theology, "the body of Christ" can refer either to Christ's physical body, the church-community, or both at the same time. It is important to note that even though, for Bonhoeffer, Christ's body and the church-community are intimately connected and associated in his assertion that Christ exists as church-community, they are not identical.[108] One way to put it is that, although the church-community does not exist apart from Christ's body, Christ's physical body does not stand in contingent relation to the church-community. So, on the one hand, Bonhoeffer can write quite straightforwardly that "Christ is the church," while, on the other hand, "categorically rul[ing] out any idea of a mystical fusion between church-community and Christ."[109] This tension between unity and distinction is grounded in the fact that Christ does not simply ascend to the right hand of God, but he also promises to come again.[110] While the disciple awaits the second coming of Christ she participates in his body, knowing in faith that Christ actively cares about and is interceding on behalf of her embodied existence and the right hand of God.

The church-community is also the means by which Christ continues to be bodily present to believers. Bonhoeffer points in this direction when he writes that "those who are baptized are still meant to live, even after the Lord's death and resurrection, in the bodily presence of and community with Jesus."[111] The bodily presence of Christ in the church-community is what allows Bonhoeffer to suggest, echoing Kierkegaard, that "[f]or the first disciples the bodily community

---

106. *DBWE* 4:156. See Robert Vosloo's excellent treatment of the physical body in Bonhoeffer's theology in "Body and Health in the Light of the Theology of Dietrich Bonhoeffer," *Religion & Theology* 13, no. 1 (2006): 23–37.

107. *DBWE* 4:285.

108. "A complete identification between Christ and the church-community cannot be made, since Christ has ascended into heaven and is now with God, and we still await Christ's coming (Eph. 4:8ff.; 1 Thess. 4:16; Phil. 3:20; 1 Cor. 15:23)" (*DBWE* 1:140).

109. *DBWE* 4:219, 220. Although Bonhoeffer rejects mystical fusion, his salvation-historical basis for asserting both unity and differentiation between Christ and church may point to a middle way between John Zizioulas's more mystical model and the scholastic emphasis on differentiation with which Zizioulas takes issue. See John D. Zizioulas, *Communion and Otherness: Further Studies in Personhood and the Church*, ed. Paul McPartlan (London: T&T Clark, 2006), 289–96.

110. *DBWE* 4:220.

111. *DBWE* 4:213.

with Jesus did not mean anything different or anything more than what we have today."[112] Yet, the church-community is not the body of Christ in virtue of its natural structure or on account of the purity of its faith. Rather, it is the body of Christ because the Holy Spirit forms it as a "yes" and "amen" to Christ's promise to be with his disciples always, even to the end of the age (2 Cor. 1:20; Matt. 28:20).[113] In other words, the Holy Spirit, who unites individuals to Christ in faith, also gathers the church-community, making the ascended Christ present to it in such a way that we can really and truly say that participation in the church-community is participation in the body of Christ.[114]

What materializes, then, is a picture of embodiment in which "[t]o be in Christ means to be in the church-community. But if we are in the church-community, then we are also truly and bodily in Jesus Christ. This insight reveals the full richness of meaning contained in the concept of the body of Christ."[115] Being bound to Christ in an embodied manner is made possible in the incarnation and is necessary because the human body, although created and preserved by God, is also enslaved and corrupted by sin. This can only be remedied by participation in Christ's resurrection body.[116] Even as being bodily bound to the resurrected Christ entails the merciful acceptance of individual sinners by God, it also binds those individuals to a new social reality in Christ existing as church-community. "With all our bodily living existence, we belong to him who took on a human body for our sake. In following him, the disciple is inseparably linked to the body of Jesus."[117] And in this new social reality, "the law of vicarious representative action [*Stellvertretung*] is actualized. It is the body given for our benefit, on our behalf. The organizational law of this body is thus that of *service*."[118] Thus, embodied participation in the body of Christ imbues the disciple with a bodily vocation

---

112. *DBWE* 4:213; cf. Søren Kierkegaard's treatment, under his "Johannes Climacus" pseudonym, of "The Situation of the Contemporary Follower" in *Philosophical Fragments*, ed. and trans. Howard V. Hong and Edna H. Hong (Princeton, NJ: Princeton University Press, 1985), 55–71. Regarding the influence of Kierkegaard on Bonhoeffer across his written corpus, see Matthew D. Kirkpatrick, *Attacks on Christendom in a World Come of Age: Kierkegaard, Bonhoeffer, and the Question of "Religionless Christianity"* (Eugene, OR: Pickwick Publications, 2011).

113. Cf. *DBWE* 8:515.

114. *DBWE* 4:221. On the Holy Spirit's role in constituting the church as Christ's body, see Tom Greggs, *Dogmatic Ecclesiology: The Priestly Catholicity of the Church*, vol. 1 (Grand Rapids, MI: Baker Academic, 2019), 88–92; Christopher R. J. Holmes, "The Holy Spirit," in *The Oxford Handbook of Dietrich Bonhoeffer*, ed. Michael Mawson and Philip G. Ziegler (Oxford: Oxford University Press, 2019), 172–4.

115. *DBWE* 4:218.

116. Cf. Barclay, *Paul and the Gift*, 504–5.

117. *DBWE* 4:232.

118. *DBWE* 14:463–64.

empowered by the resurrection and shaped by the cross. As such, it is disposed toward service and reconciliation, and it is to this that we now turn.

V Reconciliation and the Social Aim of Discipleship

As we move to address the form of social life that participation in Christ entails, the first things to consider are Bonhoeffer's weaknesses on this front. We can broadly identify two ways in which his otherwise helpful theology of discipleship may prove problematic. The first way is related to our earlier discussion of the eschatological tension that Bonhoeffer seeks to hold between the cruciform nature of discipleship in a world still beset by sin and the triumph of the resurrection. In Bonhoeffer's discussion of love for one's enemy, he again risks slackening this tension. For example, although *Discipleship* has become popular among those who seek to emphasize Bonhoeffer's pacifistic tendencies,[119] there is something troubling when he asks, "[h]ow does love become unconquerable?" and answers in the following manner: "By never asking what the enemy is doing to it, and only asking what Jesus has done. Loving one's enemies leads disciples to the way of the cross and into communion with the crucified one."[120] Here, one might wonder if a problematic passivity has replaced a positive inclination toward pacifism. To suggest that discipleship entails unquestioning acceptance of the suffering inflicted by an enemy is hardly palatable to victims of violence and abuse. Indeed, Dahill notes this as a serious problem for Bonhoeffer.[121] While his insistence on selflessness and suffering proved liberating for him given his privilege, it does not hold forth such liberation for those for whom suffering and evacuation of self are daily realities.

Potentially giving such abuse a spiritual gloss by associating it with one's love of the enemy and participation in the suffering of Christ only deepens the problem in a manner that is otherwise wholly inconsistent with the logic driving Bonhoeffer's theology of discipleship. So, then, where does he go wrong? We see here not only a misalignment of the eschatological tension between death and resurrection in the life of the disciple, but also a devaluing of embodiment. Bonhoeffer's assumption seems to be that loving one's enemies will lead to suffering under the cross, but this suffering will be transformed by the resurrection and in this way love becomes unconquerable. In and of itself—as a path Christ may call his disciples down—this is not objectionable. However, insofar as Bonhoeffer asserts this in an unqualified manner, he fails to take fully into account the significance and implications of

---

119. On the topic of Bonhoeffer's peace ethic and his affinities with Anabaptist traditions, see DeJonge, *Bonhoeffer's Reception of Luther*, 142–82.

120. *DBWE* 4:141.

121. Dahill also confirms what we have suggested above—namely, that the resurrection provides a necessary corrective to Bonhoeffer's one-sidedness on this front. See "Con-Formation with Jesus Christ," 186–90.

Christ's resurrection body for bodily liberation from suffering. In other words, he rightly suggests that the suffering incurred in following after the crucified Christ is transformed by the fact that this Christ whom the disciple is bound to is also the risen one. Yet, he fails to acknowledge that not all suffering is cruciform, and when it comes to non-cruciform instances of suffering the resurrected Christ aims to liberate his disciples from their enemies. This does not mean that Christ at any point liberates his disciples from the law of love for enemies, but it does mean that there are, indeed, situations in which such "love for" is only possible in a "liberation from." A similar problem comes up in Bonhoeffer's exposition of Philemon. There he asserts: "Because this world is not in need of reform, but ripe to be demolished—that is why slaves are to remain slaves."[122] This strange sort of doom-and-gloom otherworldliness that ratifies problematic worldly orders is surely out of step with his thought on the whole.[123]

As we shall see, the second problem is related to the first and pertains to the inconsistent manner in which Bonhoeffer construes the relationship between the church and the world. On the one hand, he places the church in an oppositional relation to the world, saying that Christ's disciples "are to remain in the world in order to engage the world in a frontal assault."[124] On the other hand, he emphasizes the church's participation in the philanthropy of God.[125] As such, Jennifer McBride is certainly correct when she suggests that this is a genuine inconsistency within *Discipleship*.[126] The problem arises when simple obedience in following after Christ becomes saddled with conditions that are missing in Bonhoeffer's initial discussion of it. There he writes: "Jesus' concrete call and simple obedience have their own irrevocable meaning. Jesus calls us into a concrete situation in which we can believe in him. That is why he calls in such a concrete way and wants to be so understood, because he knows that people will become free for faith only in concrete obedience."[127] Here, Christ's call to concrete obedience is unconditioned. However, due to the intensity of Bonhoeffer's rhetoric, certain conditions come to subtly and implicitly shape discipleship so that it ceases to be a concrete response to Christ's call in a given situation. In this way, obedience to Christ becomes

---

122. *DBWE* 4:239. Stephen Plant notes of the wider passage, in which Bonhoeffer also advocates for obeying political authority as a matter of obedience to God's order: "It is perhaps telling that, when making his defense to the examining magistrate after his arrest, Bonhoeffer referred to this passage in *Discipleship* to help bolster the image he was attempting to paint of himself as a loyal citizen!" (*Bonhoeffer*, 104).

123. A rendering of this statement that comports with his broader theological legacy might read as follows: Because this world has been liberated unto a new creation, working for the liberation of the oppressed is an enactment of one's justificatory participation in Christ and the coming kingdom. Cf. Muers, *Keeping God's Silence*, 90–1.

124. *DBWE* 4:244.

125. *DBWE* 4:285.

126. McBride, *The Church for the World*, 88–91.

127. *DBWE* 4:81.

abstracted from concrete reality. The conditions that Bonhoeffer's rhetoric places on discipleship are suffering and opposition to the world. Suffering and opposition to the world are not problems per se, since Jesus surely names these as realities of discipleship.[128] Rather, the rub lies in what they preclude when they become conditions for discipleship: namely, responses to Christ's call which involve alleviation of or liberation from suffering, as well as worldly endeavors which are consonant with and genuinely in service of the vision of the Kingdom of God proclaimed by Christ.

What these preclusions indicate is that once simple obedience becomes conditioned by suffering and an expectation of opposition, the world easily becomes a negative cypher over against which the church stands. Indeed, the church stands in the midst of the world proclaiming Christ's lordship, but even as it does so it draws a clear line of division between itself and the world.[129] As the church makes its incursions into the world, it suffers and faces opposition, while in the safety of its own sphere it remains "[s]ecured from the world by an unbreakable seal" as it "awaits its final deliverance."[130] On this way of thinking, the sacred and the secular are distinct spheres and can remain so because the form of the disciple's obedience in the secular has already been dictated. Thus, the church need not engage with the world *as* the world which Christ has claimed, but only as that which stands in opposition to the church.

Of course, Bonhoeffer's inconsistent treatment of the relationship between the church and the world does not totally undermine his description of discipleship as participation in the reconciling work of Christ. In what follows, we shall see that, for Bonhoeffer, discipleship involves bearing and forgiving the sins of others, repentance, and real engagement with the world's troubles. Insofar as Bonhoeffer takes the separation between the church and the world to be generally permeable, this is grounded in the apocalyptic nature of the incarnation, Christ's death, and resurrection. "God does not abandon the earth. God created it. God sent God's Son to earth. God built a community on earth. Thus, the beginning is already made in this world's time."[131] The church-community through its very being as the body of Christ bears witness to the kingdom that has come and is coming. However, insofar as the church is made up of disciples, the witness which it bears to the kingdom is essentially active in nature and angled toward the world. Bonhoeffer sums this up when he writes:

---

128. Thus, it is only a problem when Mawson suggests that "suffering is integral to Christian discipleship" if by "integral" he intends suffering as a condition, rather than a consequence. See Michael Mawson, "Suffering Christ's Call: Discipleship and the Cross," *The Bonhoeffer Legacy: Australasian Journal of Bonhoeffer Studies,* Pre-Publication Version (2016): 18.

129. *DBWE* 4:26.

130. *DBWE* 4:260.

131. *DBWE* 4:105.

Proclamation becomes an event, and the event gives witness to the proclamation. The kingdom of God, Jesus Christ, forgiveness of sins, justification of the sinner by faith: all this is nothing other than the destruction of demonic power, healing, and raising the dead. As the word of the almighty God, it is deed, event, miracle. The *one* Jesus Christ goes through the country to his twelve messengers and does his work. The royal grace with which the disciples are equipped is the creative and redemptive word of God.[132]

Because discipleship is bodily participation in the living Christ, proclamation is necessarily embodied in deed, event, and miracle. Indeed, the work that disciples are called to is the enactment of Christ's victory over evil in his crucifixion and resurrection. "But what is work, if not this struggle with the powers of Satan, this struggle for the hearts of the people, this renunciation of [the disciple's] own reputation, possessions, and joys of the world, for the sake of serving the poor, the mistreated, and the miserable?"[133] The church, then, must proclaim the gospel of reconciliation as a witness to Christ and his kingdom, while also and always at the same time enacting the good news of that gospel in the world.

For Bonhoeffer, Christ's mediatorial work in and through the church is not aimed at separation, but genuine unity. Indeed, "it is precisely this same mediator who makes us into individuals, who becomes the basis for entirely *new community*. He stands in the center between the other person and me. He separates, but he also unites. He cuts off every direct path to someone else, but he guides everyone following him to the new and sole true way to the other person via the mediator."[134] Within the framework presented above, the church is a community of those who participate in Christ, and as such know the true way to the other person. That this true way to the other person is not only a reality within the church, but also orients the disciple toward the world is evident when we remember that to participate in Christ is to participate in his mission of reconciliation. "Inasmuch as we participate in Christ, the incarnate one, we also have a part in all of humanity, which is borne by him. Since we know ourselves to be accepted and borne within the humanity of Jesus, our new humanity now also consists in bearing the troubles and the sins of all others."[135] By bearing sins the disciple also bears witness to Christ, who bore the sins of the world in his body. In this way, she invites the world to abandon

---

132. *DBWE* 4:189.
133. *DBWE* 4:190.
134. *DBWE* 4:98.
135. *DBWE* 4:285. Christ's vicarious representative action [*Stellvertretung*] is a central theme throughout Bonhoeffer's theological writings, from *Sanctorum Communio* to *Ethics*. For a recent critical, but insightful assessment of the work this concept does theologically and ethically for Bonhoeffer, see Gerald McKenny, "Freedom, Responsibility, and Moral Agency," in *The Oxford Handbook of Dietrich Bonhoeffer*, ed. Michael Mawson and Philip G. Ziegler (Oxford: Oxford University Press, 2019), 315–20.

immediacy and enter into the mediated unity of the body of Christ.[136] Even though the church is separated from the world, it is separated by means of participation in Christ the mediator. As such, the means of its separation is also its commissioning to responsible action on behalf and for the sake of the world.

Bonhoeffer refers to this as participation in the philanthropy of God:

> The 'philanthropy' (Titus 3:4) of God that became evident in the incarnation of Christ is the reason for Christians to love every human being on earth as brother and sister. The form of the incarnate one transforms the church-community into the body of Christ upon which all of humanity's sin and trouble fall, and by which alone these troubles and sins are borne.[137]

Participation in Christ, then, both separates disciples from the world and enables them to engage in active service to the world on Christ's behalf. Here, we are pointed back to the ongoing baptismal character of participation.[138] Disciples who live from the resurrection participate in Christ's sufferings and do so for the sake of the world. "As Christ bears our burdens, so we are to bear the burden of our sisters and brothers. The law of Christ, which must be fulfilled, is to bear the cross."[139]

Furthermore, justificatory participation in Christ does, indeed, create the conditions necessary for reconciliation.[140] Throughout *Discipleship*, Bonhoeffer points to the fact that "[t]he way to one's neighbor leads only through Christ," and this means that "[t]here is no genuine gratitude for nation, family, history, and nature without deep repentance that honors Christ above all these gifts."[141] Repentance with respect to the disciple's worldly attachments simultaneously acknowledges her illicit claims to immediacy and the fact that her worth is externally grounded in Christ.[142] As such, "[d]isciples encounter other people only as those to whom Jesus himself comes."[143] Discipleship drives toward reconciliation in the social sphere because it sees all people in and through Christ as the one who bears humanity in the incarnation. "Jesus' struggle for the other person, his call, his love, his grace, his judgment are all that matters. Thus the disciples do not stand in a position from which the other person is attacked. Instead, in the truthfulness of Jesus' love they approach the other person with an unconditional offer of community."[144] If Christ's judgment according to his grace is the sole

---

136. Cf. *DBWE* 5:40–1.

137. *DBWE* 4:285.

138. On baptism as grafting, see Brian Bantum, *Redeeming Mulatto: A Theology of Race and Christian Hybridity* (Waco, TX: Baylor University Press, 2010), 154–55.

139. *DBWE* 4:88.

140. *DBWE* 4:117.

141. *DBWE* 4:96.

142. *DBWE* 4:189.

143. *DBWE* 4:170.

144. *DBWE* 4:170.

determination of worth, then for the disciple to assume superiority over another in any given situation is to forget that the historical dialectical unity of one's life is found only in Christ and never in oneself. In other words, it is to forget that one's basis for boasting is Christ alone.

Thus, we have seen that even as participation in Christ sets believers and the church apart from the world, it also orients the disciple toward the world in the service of Christ's mission of reconciliation. For the disciple, repentance is active turning from worldly immediacies toward Christ as the sole mediator. This repentance allows the disciple to see the other solely in and through Christ, as one for whom Christ became incarnate, died, and was raised from the dead. As a community of repentance, then, the church-community does not cordon itself off from the world but moves toward the world in order to bear witness to Christ through forgiveness and the bearing of sin. As such, the aim of discipleship is to proclaim and enact the reconciliation between God and humanity by bearing witness to the sole mediator between God and humanity, Jesus Christ.

In all of this, Bonhoeffer's vision for the disciple's participation in Christ's mission of reconciliation is clear. However, the inconsistent relationship he sketches between the church and the world prevents its full expression. Unlike the necessary theological tension between resurrection and suffering, this inconsistency is not theologically tenable and, as such, cannot be maintained. In the next chapter, we shall see how Bonhoeffer resolves the inconsistency in the direction of the philanthropy of God by rendering concrete the relationship between the church and the world in such a way that they are no longer relegated to separate spheres. However, insofar as *Ethics* corrects an inconsistency in *Discipleship*, we shall argue that it does so as the second step which Bonhoeffer had in mind even as he wrote *Discipleship*. That is, the purpose of *Discipleship* reflects the purpose of the preacher's seminary at Finkenwalde insofar as the goal of both was the formation of the disciple according to the Word of Christ. Bethge describes this as Bonhoeffer's turning "to the ultimate for the sake of the penultimate itself."[145] This is to both agree and disagree with Florian Schmitz, who has offered an insightful rebuttal to the most commonly posited discrepancies between *Discipleship* and *Ethics*.[146] By positing a genuine inconsistency in *Discipleship* that is resolved in *Ethics*, we are less keen to harmonize the two than is Schmitz.[147] However, Schmitz is certainly

---

145. Bethge, "The Challenge of Dietrich Bonhoeffer's Life and Theology," 52. Here, Bethge is making reference to a theological framework employed by Bonhoeffer in *Ethics*. See *DBWE* 6:151.

146. Florian Schmitz, *"Nachfolge": Zur Theologie Dietrich Bonhoeffers* (Göttingen: Vandenhoeck & Ruprecht, 2013). Schmitz asserts that there are three *"thematische Grundpfeiler* [thematic pillars]" which orient Bonhoeffer's theological reasoning in a manner that is consistent across his theology after 1931: "*Christologie* [Christology]," "*Weltverständnis* [understanding of the world]," and "*Verhältnis von Gemeinde und Welt* [the relationship between the church and the world]" (407).

147. See Schmitz, *"Nachfolge,"* 156–200.

right when he distinguishes between "*Grundannahmen* [basic assumptions]" and "*Aktualisierungen dieser Grundannahmen* [updates of these basics assumptions]" in Bonhoeffer's thought.[148] Indeed, *Ethics* resolves the inconsistency of *Discipleship* not by retreating from Bonhoeffer's basic assumptions but, rather, by updating those assumptions in a manner that casts new light on *Discipleship*'s tensions. *Ethics*, then, is the working out of the formation of the disciple in and for the world.[149] Thus, the inconsistency evident in *Discipleship* regarding the relationship between the church and the world is evidence that, while Bonhoeffer anticipated and felt the need for a second step, the concrete nature of discipleship in the world had yet to take shape for him.

VI Conclusion

We have seen that in *Discipleship* Bonhoeffer's primary goal is to unfold justification's intrinsic connection to works. In other words, he is keen to show the doctrine's formative social and ethical import. As such, he draws on justification in a way that certainly overlaps with, but is clearly distinct from, his early, academic theology. In order to show how justification disposes Christians to a certain form of social life, Bonhoeffer draws particularly on themes of participation and embodiment. Participation, as the content of discipleship, serves to locate Christ at the center of the believer's new existence, while its correlate—mediation—also locates Christ at the boundary of individual existence. This means that even as the disciple's new existence is determined by the baptismal logic of death and resurrection in a soteriological sense, so too is her embodied existence in the world shaped by the fact that the crucified and resurrected Christ mediates it to her. In other words, because the disciple participates in Christ in an embodied manner, when she moves toward the world her movement is, in fact, a following after Christ. Based on the eschatological tension that Bonhoeffer is generally successful in holding, this means that the disciple lives from her unity with the resurrected Christ as one who participates in the sufferings of Christ in this world. And this suffering is not meaningless but is distinctively Christian insofar as its ground is repentance, its form is the bearing and forgiveness of sin, and its aim is reconciliation. What remains to be seen, though, is exactly how justification establishes the disciple and the church in relation to the world as participants in Christ's reconciling work.

---

148. Schmitz, "*Nachfolge*," 410.
149. Cf. Hans Pfeifer, "The Forms of Justification: On the Question of the Structure in Dietrich Bonhoeffer's Theology," in *A Bonhoeffer Legacy: Essays in Understanding*, ed. A. J. Klassen (Grand Rapids, MI: Eerdmans, 1981), 14.

Chapter 6

Reconciling Church and World

Justification's Coordination of the Ultimate and Penultimate

I Introduction

Gaylon Barker offers an apt summary of the previous chapter's central point when he writes: "By linking justification and discipleship, Bonhoeffer provided the orientation that refuses to allow God to be separated from the world. Since God and the world are linked together, justification has an ethical component."[1] Indeed, we argued that justification entails embodied participation in Christ, which is, in turn, intrinsic to discipleship and formative for Christian living. What we also saw, however, is that the concrete nature of the ethical component of justification is obscured by the inconsistent manner in which Bonhoeffer articulates the relationship between the church and the world. As such, we must now attend to the way in which justification establishes the church in relation to the world as Christ's reconciling body. With respect to all that has come before in this study, the establishment of the church in the world follows the definition of the human being *coram Deo* and the formation of the disciple. Put another way, up to this point we have explored justification's implications for Christian self-understanding and other-understanding, as well as its implications for Christian formation. Now, we shall turn to consider the way in which justification establishes the disciple and the church in relation to the world, such that justification's social implications can be brought concretely to bear in daily life.

The chapter will proceed in two parts. First, we shall attend to the nature of the church's relationship to the world. Unsurprisingly, Christology features prominently in this discussion, highlighting the fact that the church's relationship to the world must be understood in light of the reconciliation between God and the world in Christ. In the second section, we shall focus on Bonhoeffer's *Ethics* manuscript, "Ultimate and Penultimate Things," in order to demonstrate how

---

1. H. Gaylon Barker, *The Cross of Reality: Luther's Theologia Crucis and Bonhoeffer's Christology* (Minneapolis, MN: Fortress Press, 2015), 324.

justification establishes the disciple in a world where the things before the last must be interpreted in light of the last things. Here, we shall work with Bonhoeffer's text, but we shall do so with an eye to how it might be seen as constructively synthesizing the central concerns of the book as a whole.

II Reconciling the Church and the World

If, in *Discipleship*, Bonhoeffer turned to the ultimate for the sake of the penultimate, then, in *Ethics*, Bonhoeffer is keen to show that the ultimate and penultimate are not rent apart, such that a turn to the ultimate entails an abandonment of or separation from the penultimate. Indeed, a turn to the ultimate is a turn to God's reconciliation of the world in Christ. For Bonhoeffer, *Discipleship*'s focus on the way in which justification forms and mobilizes disciples for obedience finds its necessary complement and second step in the proclamation and enactment of reconciliation in the world. However, the question that *Discipleship* leaves undecided is: Do disciples proclaim reconciliation between God and the world as a possibility or as a reality?[2] We shall return to Bonhoeffer's concept of the ultimate and penultimate later, and, in doing so, offer more precise definitions of both. Here, however, we shall focus on the reconciliation of God and the world in Christ as the basis for determining the relationship between the church and the world.

Kirsten Busch Nielsen highlights the import of reconciliation in Bonhoeffer's thought when she writes:

> Paul's words in 2 Corinthians that God reconciled us to himself through Christ and gave us the ministry of reconciliation (2 Cor 5:18–19) play a central role in Bonhoeffer's writings. . . . That reconciliation *has* taken place and that this must throw light on every part of theology is a strong conviction in Bonhoeffer's own theology, which has Christology as its center.[3]

That Bonhoeffer decisively identifies reconciliation between God and the world in Christ as a reality, rather than a possibility, is frequently commented upon.[4]

---

2. Cf. Clifford J. Green, "Editor's Introduction to the English Edition," in *Ethics*, ed. Clifford J. Green, trans. Reinhard Krauss, Charles C. West, and Douglas W. Stott (Minneapolis, MN: Fortress Press, 2005), 8–9.

3. Kirsten Busch Nielsen, "Community Turned Inside Out: Dietrich Bonhoeffer's Concept of the Church and of Humanity Reconsidered," in *Being Human, Becoming Human: Dietrich Bonhoeffer and Social Thought*, ed. Jens Zimmermann and Brian Gregor (Eugene, OR: Pickwick Publications, 2010), 91.

4. See recent discussions of this aspect of Bonhoeffer's thought in Eva Harasta, "Adam in Christ? The Place of Sin in Christ-Reality," in *Christ, Church, and World: New Studies in Bonhoeffer's Theology and Ethics*, ed. Michael G. Mawson and Philip G. Ziegler (New York: Bloomsbury T&T Clark, 2016), 71–4; Barry Harvey, *Taking Hold of the Real: Dietrich*

Indeed, Clifford Green calls it "Bonhoeffer's methodological starting point for *Ethics*."[5] As such, we shall only briefly outline the comprehensive nature of this reconciliation before commenting on Bonhoeffer's resultant rendering of the relationship between the church and the world. The section will then conclude by registering a brief concern with the manner in which the reality of reconciliation in Christ is sometimes articulated.

Bonhoeffer begins the manuscript, "Christ, Reality, and Good. Christ, Church, and World," by emphasizing that God's reality is the ultimate reality which trumps all others.[6] However, even to put it this way is deceiving. Indeed, God's reality is the *only* reality. On account of this, a theological ethic can be abstracted from neither the world's origin, nor its goal—namely, God.[7] Since God's reality is revealed only in and through Jesus Christ, the good can be known only via participation in what Bonhoeffer calls, "the Christ-reality [*Christuswirklichkeit*]."[8] In other words, participation in the *Christuswirklichkeit* opens one's eyes to God's reality as that which determines the reality of the world. Thus, Bonhoeffer writes: "In Christ we are invited to participate in the reality of God and the reality of the world at the same time, the one not without the other. The reality of God is disclosed only as it places me completely into the reality of the world."[9] What Bonhoeffer means by this is that, in the incarnation, Christ reveals what sort of God is laying claim to the world—namely, a God who is for the world in the person of his son who takes on human flesh.[10] Through the incarnate life, death, and resurrection of Jesus Christ, God and the world have been reconciled. Therefore, in Christ, human beings can once again understand themselves and the world according to their origin and goal.

For Bonhoeffer, this precludes the possibility of understanding the church and the world as "two realms bumping against and repelling each other."[11] If Christ has, in fact, reconciled all things in himself then properly Christian thinking about the world must begin with this *Einheitpunkt*. As such, the reconciliation of God and the world in Christ militates against understanding the world and church as two separate spheres. "The space of the church is not there in order to fight with the world for a piece of its territory, but precisely to testify to the world that it is

---

Bonhoeffer and the Profound Worldliness of Christianity. (Cambridge: James Clarke & Co, 2016), 40–1; Jennifer M. McBride, *The Church for the World: A Theology of Public Witness* (Oxford/New York: Oxford University Press, 2012), 101–4; Philip G. Ziegler, *Militant Grace: The Apocalyptic Turn and the Future of Christian Theology* (Grand Rapids, MI: Baker Academic, 2018), 175–80.

5. Green, "Editor's Introduction to the English Edition," 7.
6. *DBWE* 6:48.
7. *DBWE* 6:49.
8. *DBWE* 6:50, 58.
9. *DBWE* 6:55.
10. Cf. *DBWE* 2:90–91.
11. *DBWE* 6:57.

still the world, namely, the world that is loved and reconciled by God."[12] However, this is not to say that the church and the world have become identical. Indeed, Bonhoeffer recognizes that Scripture often deals in spatial imagery when it speaks of the church.[13] Yet, even if—given the necessary visibility of the church—spatial imagery is inevitable, "one must be aware that this space has already been broken through, abolished, and overcome in every moment by the witness of the church to Jesus Christ."[14] Framed in another, more explicitly Trinitarian way, reality is established in Jesus Christ and the "becoming real" [*Wirklichwerden*] of this reality in the world through the church is the work of the Spirit.[15] Thus, insofar as Christ became incarnate in and for the world, his body—the church—exists in and for the world, enacting and proclaiming reconciliation.

How, then, does this square with the apparent inconsistency, noted in the previous chapter, regarding *Discipleship*'s construal of the church–world relationship? Michael DeJonge's reading of the relationship between *Ethics* and *Discipleship* in light of the Lutheran doctrine of the two kingdoms is helpful here.[16] Rather than positing that the former corrects the latter's shortcomings, DeJonge suggests that the respective ways in which they depict the relationship between the church and the world reflect different emphases within Bonhoeffer's flexible use of the doctrine of the two kingdoms. "The church must attend to the historical situation and adjust the degree to which its proclamation focuses inwardly or outwardly."[17] As such, Bonhoeffer's inward focus in *Discipleship* gives rise to its oppositional framing of the church–world relationship, whereas his outward focus in *Ethics* gives rise to his emphasis on reconciliation in Christ. According to DeJonge, then, "this is a shift in emphasis rather than a fundamental change in the church's task or proclamation, for in any case the church's proclamation is to the whole world of which the church is a part."[18]

However, DeJonge's emphasis on the continuity of Bonhoeffer's thought under the rubric of the two kingdoms risks minimizing the fact that, as we have already noted, *Discipleship* and *Ethics* can also legitimately be read as a two-step development of the social implications of justification. A focus on the church's obedient participation in the risen Christ (*Discipleship*) must always

---

12. *DBWE* 6:63.
13. *DBWE* 6:62.
14. *DBWE* 6:64.
15. *DBWE* 6:50.
16. DeJonge has rehabilitated Bonhoeffer's perceived relationship to the two kingdoms doctrine in a way that helpfully sheds light on key aspects of his thought. In doing so, he provides a very specific definition of doctrine in relation to Bonhoeffer's use of it. With this in mind, I am not recommending the two kingdoms doctrine as such here, but, rather, DeJonge's use of it as a heuristic tool for disambiguating aspects of Bonhoeffer's thought.
17. Michael P. DeJonge, *Bonhoeffer's Reception of Luther* (Oxford: Oxford University Press, 2017), 119.
18. DeJonge, *Bonhoeffer's Reception of Luther*, 119.

lead to obedient enactment and proclamation of the gospel in the world (*Ethics*). Furthermore, while DeJonge makes a persuasive case for the governing logic of the two kingdoms in Bonhoeffer's thinking, *Discipleship*, when taken on its own, remains apparently inconsistent on the relationship between the church and the world. Yet, this apparent inconsistency points not to a problem which needs to be corrected, but, rather, to an intrinsic development which pushes toward a necessary second step.[19]

DeJonge's work on the doctrine of the two kingdoms also helps to highlight a concern regarding a prominent recent interpretation of Bonhoeffer's theology—namely, that of Jennifer McBride in *The Church for the World*.[20] In his analysis of the *Ethics* manuscript "Heritage and Decay," DeJonge discerns three misalignments of the two kingdoms which Bonhoeffer critiques:

> The German-Lutheran secularization process misunderstands the two kingdoms in terms of *Eigengesetzlichkeit* [autonomy], the French Catholic tradition turns the heresy of the "essential goodness of human beings" into the idolatry of liberation, and the Anglo-Saxon Calvinist and enthusiast attempt to build the kingdom of God on earth fails to distinguish between the two kingdoms.[21]

Bonhoeffer's focus in *Ethics* is the correction of the first, "pseudo-Lutheran" misalignment.[22] However, one might wonder if McBride's reading of Bonhoeffer's *Ethics* tends toward the third misalignment endorsed by the enthusiasts.

Core to her argument is a strongly apocalyptic reading of Bonhoeffer's theology of reconciliation in *Ethics*.[23] The problem is not her apocalyptic proclivities as such, but, rather, the way in which her stress on the ontological and cosmic unity of reality in Christ leads to an implicit identification of reconciliation's ultimacy with this-worldly penultimacy. This is most evident when, in describing *Discipleship*'s primary shortcoming, she poses a false opposition between "the cosmic impulse of Paul's apocalyptic gospel" and the justification of the sinner. Indeed, she implies

---

19. Contra McBride, *The Church for the World*, 96.

20. McBride's work is of particular interest here because, in a manner similar to the present study, it seeks to show the fruitfulness of Bonhoeffer's theology for the church's public witness in the world.

21. DeJonge, *Bonhoeffer's Reception of Luther*, 128.

22. Cf. *DBWE* 6:56, 224.

23. Both Barry Harvey (*Taking Hold of the Real*) and Philip Ziegler (*Militant Grace*) pick up on the apocalyptic valences present in *Ethics* as well. However, their respective studies both emphasize the justification of the sinner, forgiveness of sin, the work of the Holy Spirit, and the ongoing, albeit, relative duality of "being in Adam" and "being in Christ." We shall see below that McBride either neglects or rejects each of these aspects, and therefore tends toward an implicit identification of the Kingdom of God and the world.

that an emphasis on justification and the forgiveness of sin contributes to a "dualistic church/world conception."[24]

Her relentless focus on the unity of the church and the world also leads her to set Bonhoeffer's thinking in *Ethics* over against the "in Adam"–"in Christ" paradigm he develops in *Act and Being*:

> Bonhoeffer's claim in *Act and Being* that human beings are always either a part of "a community in 'Adam' or in 'Christ'" is much too rigid to square with his later understanding that all reality is Christ-reality: All of humanity is accepted, judged, and reconciled to Christ such that the church is simply the body in which Christ-reality is acknowledged, demonstrated, and proclaimed.[25]

The problem with this is that it erases the eschatological tension that Bonhoeffer is seeking to hold, as we shall see later, in his construal of the relationship between the ultimate and penultimate. The ultimate "is" of reconciliation swallows up the penultimate "will be" of redemption. Furthermore, McBride neglects the role of the Holy Spirit as the one who gathers individuals into the church and unites them to Christ in the formation of the church-community. As the basis for the union between Christ and the church, the Holy Spirit does much more than merely empower the church for good works and proper awareness of reality in Christ.[26] Indeed, it proleptically and militantly creates faith and draws individuals into the ontological reality of the world reconciled in the body of Christ.[27] Insofar as the unitive and gathering work of the Holy Spirit takes place in the penultimate and is a necessary ingredient in God's reconciliation of the world to himself in Christ, there is still a real sense in which we can and should meaningfully speak of two communities—one "in Adam" and one "in Christ"—even as we avoid speaking of them in terms of an oppositional duality.[28]

In her discussion of the manuscript, "Ultimate and Penultimate Things," McBride again implies that justification is somehow at odds with the unity of life in the *Christuswirklichkeit*. Even though, as we shall see later, Bonhoeffer clearly associates justification with the ultimate numerous times throughout the manuscript,[29]

---

24. McBride, *The Church for the World*, 96.

25. McBride, *The Church for the World*, 127.

26. These are the two roles that McBride ascribes to the Spirit in her description of apocalyptic theology (97–101).

27. See Ziegler, *Militant Grace*, 71–9, on the eschatological work of the Holy Spirit.

28. Of course, those who are united to Christ by the Spirit are both "in Adam" and "in Christ" according to the logic of the *simul*. On this, see Harasta, "Adam in Christ?" However, Harasta seems to share McBride's impulse, positing that, according to Bonhoeffer's logic of reconciliation in *Ethics*, the category of being "in Christ" envelops being "in Adam" (73–4).

29. DBWE 6:146, 149, 150, 151, 156, 160, 168; cf. DeJonge, *Bonhoeffer's Reception of Luther*, 138; Feil, *The Theology of Dietrich Bonhoeffer*, 143; Frick, "Bonhoeffer on the Social-Political Dimension of Grace," 244; Plant, *Bonhoeffer*, 116.

McBride insists that this identification is subordinate to his overarching intent—namely, the description of "the ontological unity of this-worldly Christ-reality that at once envelops both the ultimate and penultimate."[30] The crucial point she misses is that, for Bonhoeffer, justification is basic to both the ultimate unity of reality and that which properly aligns and describes the relationship between the penultimate and ultimate. When justification is marginalized in this equation the ultimate impinges on the penultimate in a way that compromises the latter's integrity. In this way, McBride unconsciously emulates the misalignment of the two kingdoms which Bonhoeffer attributes to the enthusiasts. Therefore, we might say, contra McBride, that justification is the necessary starting point for Christian ethics because only then is the extrinsic ultimacy of Christ granted its full reality in the life of the disciple without compromising her threefold simultaneity as creature, sinner, and reconciled.[31]

It would seem, then, that even if the ultimate reality of reconciliation in Christ is acknowledged, how one conceives of the penultimate distinction between the church and the world remains an open question. Indeed, there is a direct connection between how the ultimate and penultimate are aligned and how one conceives of the relationship between the church and the world. Insofar as Bonhoeffer's concern "*is God's reality revealed in Christ becoming real among God's creatures*," he points to the fact that even though the indispensable presupposition of Christian ethics is God's reconciliation of the world in Christ, its substance is Christ taking form in the world.[32] As such, Christian ethics is not centrally about the enveloping ontological unity of the *Christuswirklichkeit* as McBride would have it, but, instead, is concerned with its becoming real through Spirit-effected conformation to Christ. This is why Bonhoeffer chooses to employ the language of "taking form" to describe how Christ coordinates the ultimate and penultimate, rather than that of envelopment.

As such, even though Christ's form is most certainly nothing less than that of the reconciler, Bonhoeffer recognizes that its becoming real among real human beings requires exegeting "Christ the reconciler" according to "the concrete richness of the historical reality of a living human being."[33] In other words, "Christ the reconciler" becomes an abstraction if what it means for him to be the one who reconciles is not understood in terms of his incarnation, death, and resurrection. Thus, in the manuscript "Ethics as Formation," Bonhoeffer proposes that Pilate's "*ecce homo*" in John 19:5 identifies Christ as the reconciler, but then goes on to unpack it more specifically in this threefold manner.[34] When we consider the fact

30. McBride, *The Church for the World*, 109.
31. Cf. DeJonge, *Bonhoeffer's Reception of Luther*, 138.
32. *DBWE* 6:49.
33. *DBWE* 6:335.
34. *DBWE* 6:82–92. "Ecce homo—behold, what a human being! In Christ the reconciliation of the world with God took place" (82). "Ecce homo—behold God become human, the unfathomable mystery of the love of God for the world" (84). "Ecce homo—

that—in a manner that closely parallels his thinking in *Discipleship*—Bonhoeffer directly identifies justification with participation in this threefold form of Christ, it becomes clear that justification stands in closest relation to the becoming real of the *Christuswirklichkeit*.[35]

Furthermore, since "[t]*he church is the place where Jesus Christ's taking form is proclaimed and where it happens*," justification is also central to the church's penultimate distinction from the world. What prevents such a distinction from falling back into the church-world duality, against which McBride rightly cautions, is the fact that, for Bonhoeffer, justification is not something God does for some people and not for others, but is, rather, the Spirit-effected becoming real in the church of what God has done for all humanity in Jesus. Christ taking form in the church does not create saints that virtuously tower over against the sinful world. Rather, as those who participate in his incarnate, crucified, and risen body, Christians are enabled to embrace their full humanity *coram Deo* as those who are simultaneously creatures, sinners, and reconciled in Christ alone. There is a sense, then, in which justification is humanization.[36] "The church is the human being who has become human, has been judged, and has been awakened to new life in Christ. Therefore essentially its first concern is not with the so-called religious functions of human beings, but with the existence in the world of whole human beings in all their relationships."[37] As such, what distinguishes the church from the world is Christ's justificatory taking form within it. For Bonhoeffer, however, it is precisely in its distinguishing conformation that the church is enabled to recognize the fact that because of Christ all humanity stands *coram Deo* as creatures, sinners, and those who are reconciled in him alone.[38]

---

behold the *one whom God has judged*" (88)! "Ecce homo—behold the human being, accepted by God, judged by God, awakened by God to new life—see the Risen One" (91)!

35. *DBWE* 6:142.

36. The flip side of humanization, Bonhoeffer contends, is "the human being as self-creator, self-judge, and self-renewer; these people bypass their true humanity and therefore, sooner or later, destroy themselves" (*DBWE* 6:134). Even though in Christ the humanity of real human beings is preserved and affirmed, this does not negate the possibility of self-destruction, or, in Karl Barth's terms, the "impossible possibility" (*Church Dogmatics: The Doctrine of Reconciliation*, ed. G. W. Bromiley and T. F. Torrance, trans. G. W. Bromiley, vol. IV/1 [Peabody, MA: Hendrickson, 2010], 463). My thanks to Phil Ziegler for drawing my attention to the connection between humanization and justification for Bonhoeffer.

37. *DBWE* 6:97.

38. This not only subverts "good church"-"bad world" ways of thinking about the church-world relationship, but also valuations of human being employing a sliding scale between wickedness and goodness. "Christ belongs to the wicked and the good. Christ belongs to both only as sinners, which means as those who, in their wickedness and in their goodness, have fallen away from the origin. Christ calls them back to the origin so that they may be no longer be [sic] the wicked and the good, but justified and sanctified sinners" (*DBWE* 6:348).

Conformation to Christ as the incarnate, crucified, and risen one, then, structures both the self-understanding of the church and its understanding of its relation to the world, such that God's justificatory Yes and No govern both. Regarding the church's self-understanding, it errs deeply if it assumes the Yes for itself while forgetting the No, forgetting that, even as the body of Christ, it is made up of individuals who are simultaneously created, sinful, and reconciled. Rather, Bonhoeffer asserts: "We now live stretched between the Yes and the No. . . . Only in the Yes and the No can we recognize Christ as our life. It is the Yes of creation, reconciliation, and redemption, and the No of judgment and death over life that has fallen away from its origin, essence, and goal."[39] Thus, insofar as the church understands that God's justificatory Yes to real human beings is also a No to sin, it will recognize that it is a "community of people that has been led by the grace of Christ to acknowledge its guilt toward Christ."[40] In Christ, Christians truly are sinners, but being sinners in Christ means being those who confess their sins.[41] Because the church is where Christ takes form in the world and is called to serve this taking form, it must understand itself as a community of real human beings, bound to the Christ, participating in his reconciling work as embodied creatures and confessing sinners.

Regarding the church's relation to the world, its essential function is to bear witness to what is real and is becoming real in word and in deed. This too is governed by God's Yes to real human beings and the No to sin contained therein, such that the church may not, on the one hand, reserve Christ for itself "while granting the world only some law, Christian though it may be."[42] Neither, on the other hand, may it affirm the world in its sin.[43] As such, "it is certainly not the case that the law would apply to the world while the gospel would apply to the church-community. Instead, both law and gospel apply equally to the world and to the church-community. Whatever the message of the church to the world may be, it must be both *law and gospel*."[44] Because the church's mission is to serve Christ's taking form in the world, its bearing witness to the Yes of reconciliation and creation is not only compatible with, but also necessarily entails its proclamation and enactment of God's No to sin and death. The upshot of this is that the church

---

39. *DBWE* 6:251.
40. *DBWE* 6:135.
41. The seeds for Bonhoeffer's thinking about confession in the *Ethics* manuscript, "Guilt, Justification, Renewal," are evident in the chapter, "Confession and the Lord's Supper," in *Life Together*. "God wants to see you as you are, wants to be gracious to you. You do not have to go on lying to yourself and to other Christians as if you were without sin. You are allowed to be a sinner" (*DBWE* 5:108). Indeed, just as confession is the "form of Jesus Christ breaking through in the church" (*DBWE* 6:142), it is necessary preparation for Christ's taking form in the community through the Lord's Supper (*DBWE* 5:116–18).
42. *DBWE* 6:67.
43. *DBWE* 6:291.
44. *DBWE* 6:357.

must acknowledge and love the world in its current state, while also registering protest against its enslavement to sin and death. In doing so, the church bears witness to Christ's taking form because "[e]verything that actually exists receives from *the* Real One, whose name is Jesus Christ, both its ultimate foundation and its ultimate negation, its justification and its ultimate contradiction [*Aufhebung*], its ultimate Yes and its ultimate No."[45]

We have seen, then, that God's reconciliation of the world in the person of Jesus Christ is the point of unity that must ground any account of the relationship between the church and the world. As such, the penultimate distinction between the Christ's body and the rest of humanity is not indicative of an ultimate distinction such that Christ has been enthroned as Lord over one but not the other. Rather, the church is where Christ takes form in the world creating a community whose vocation is to bear witness to the ultimate reality of reconciliation and its penultimate becoming real in both word and deed. At each point—the threefold form of Christ, its becoming real in the church, and the church's witness to the world—the logic of justification by faith structures what it means to be a real human being and what it means to act humanly for the sake of the world. Indeed, the church's faithfulness to its vocation is measured by the degree to which its presence in the world is defined by Christ's taking form, thereby affirming its worldliness, prompting its confession of sin, and drawing it into Christ's love for the world. "It is as whole human beings, as thinking and acting human beings, that we are loved by God in Christ, that we are reconciled with God. And as whole human beings, thinking and acting, we love God and our brothers and sisters."[46] In all of this, we have caught glimpses of how *Ethics* draws together and integrates—under the rubric of Christ's reconciliation—Bonhoeffer's relational and tripartite anthropology with his later emphasis on discipleship as embodied participation in Christ. The next section will draw this out more explicitly in its consideration of the manuscript, "Ultimate and Penultimate Things."

III Ultimate Justification and Penultimate Action

In his overview of Bonhoeffer's life and theology, Stephen Plant gives special attention to the ethical substance of Bonhoeffer's thought. However, he does so with a critical edge, leading him to ask at several points "whether Bonhoeffer's strong convictions about the distinctiveness of Christian theology, knowledge and ethics, does not make it difficult for Christians to engage with reality."[47] Responding to his own rhetorical question, Plant writes: "In his categories of the penultimate and the ultimate, he offers his strongest explanation yet of how Christians are in

---

45. *DBWE* 6:261–2.
46. *DBWE* 6:338.
47. Plant, *Bonhoeffer*, 116.

but not of the world."⁴⁸ Likewise, in a manner that is consonant with the trajectory of our study thus far, Peter Frick turns to the manuscript in order to show that it "extends grace from a theological doctrine to the social-political realm without creating an artificial dichotomy between theology and praxis."⁴⁹ In light of all this, it is hardly surprising that Bonhoeffer's treatment of "the last things and the things before last" serves as a fitting framework within which to synthesize what we have argued for thus far concerning the social implications of justification by faith in his theology.⁵⁰

Bonhoeffer begins "Ultimate and Penultimate Things" with the following programmatic statement concerning the import of justification for the Christian life:

> The origin and essence of all Christian life are consummated in the one event that the Reformation has called the justification of the sinner by grace alone. It is not what a person is per se, but what a person is in this event, that gives us insight into the Christian life. Here the length and breadth of human life are concentrated in one moment, one point; the whole of life is embraced in this event.⁵¹

This, of course, must be understood under the broader umbrella of his earlier assertion, in the manuscript, "Guilt, Justification, Renewal," that, given the reality of the incarnation, "all thinking about human beings without Christ is unfruitful abstraction."⁵² Recall, then, that justification for Bonhoeffer is not merely something that happens to human beings, but is, rather, Spirit-effected, embodied participation in the justificatory person and work of Christ.⁵³ If this is the case, then we can say, broadly, that Christ's justificatory person and work are decisive for what it means to be human *coram Deo*, and, more specifically, that justification is decisive for the life of the Christian who is bound to Christ by the Holy Spirit. As such, human being, Christian and otherwise, is extrinsically grounded in Jesus Christ, the incarnate one who was crucified, is risen, and has ascended to intercede at the right hand of the Father on behalf of human beings.⁵⁴ Indeed, "[f]aith means

---

48. Plant, 116; cf. Rachel Muers, *Keeping God's Silence: Towards a Theological Ethics of Communication* (Malden, MA: Blackwell, 2004), 89.

49. Frick, "Bonhoeffer on the Social-Political Dimension of Grace," 238.

50. "Ultimate and Penultimate Things" is a rendering of the German—"*Die letzen und die vorletzten Dinge*"—which literally means "the last and the things before the last" (*DBW* 6:137).

51. *DBWE* 6:146.

52. *DBWE* 6:134; cf. 6:160.

53. See *DBWE* 6:142: "The justification of the church and the individual consists in their becoming participants in the form of Christ."

54. Bonhoeffer unfolds this in the manuscript, "Ethics as Formation," particularly in his theological exegesis of Pilate's utterance, "*ecce homo*," in John 19:5.

to base life on a foundation outside myself, on an eternal and holy foundation, on Christ."[55]

For the sake of clarity we shall, at this point, transition to speak specifically of Christians and the Christian life in a manner that reflects the orientation of Bonhoeffer's manuscript. However, the assumption remains that all human beings must be understood according to Christ's justificatory person and work—namely, as those who exist extrinsically in Christ *coram Deo* and are therefore simultaneously created, sinful, and reconciled to God in Christ alone. With that in mind, Bonhoeffer not only highlights that the Christian life is extrinsically sourced in the justificatory person of Christ, but he also notes that this has profound relational implications: "In this saving light, people recognize God and their neighbors for the first time."[56] Participation in Christ sets the Christian in right relationship to God, and this, in turn, has serious epistemic consequences. The person who is justified by grace is united to the mediatorial person of Christ by the Spirit in faith, and as such, Christ enables her to know God and her neighbor according to the *Christuswirklichkeit*.

Thus, borrowing Bonhoeffer's language, a person can see her way to the neighbor only when she is fully immersed in the penultimate as one who lives from the ultimate. But what does this mean? Here, it is useful to clarify, to the extent that it is possible, exactly what Bonhoeffer means by "ultimate" and "penultimate." As noted earlier, the ultimate simply is the justification of the sinner by grace though faith. However, Bonhoeffer identifies two aspects of this ultimate word: the qualitatively ultimate and the temporally ultimate.[57] Justification is qualitatively ultimate because it is a word which encounters the individual from the outside, causing a complete break with all that came before.[58] It is liberative unto new life in Christ, but it also "is the word of forgiveness, and only in forgiving does it justify."[59] Justification is also temporally ultimate insofar as it occurs in time. "Something penultimate always precedes it."[60] Because "[j]ustification presupposes that the creature became guilty," its qualitatively ultimate aspect does not envelop the penultimate in such a way that guilt ceases to be taken seriously.[61] DeJonge summarizes this dynamic well: "With these two senses of ultimate, Bonhoeffer establishes both the radical alterity and the this-worldliness of justification."[62]

The challenge of living fully in the penultimate as one whose existence is sourced from the ultimate is in navigating between the Scylla of radicalism and

---

55. *DBWE* 6:147.
56. *DBWE* 6:146.
57. See Rachel Muer's observation that these are "the terms in which Bonhoeffer elsewhere discusses the resurrection," in *Keeping God's Silence*, 87.
58. *DBWE* 6:149.
59. *DBWE* 6:150.
60. *DBWE* 6:150.
61. *DBWE* 6:151.
62. DeJonge, *Bonhoeffer's Reception of Luther*, 138.

the Charybdis of compromise. As Bonhoeffer sees it, compromise hates eternity, decision, simplicity, the immeasurable, and the word, whereas radicalism hates time, patience, wisdom, measure, and the real.[63] However, this strong language is tempered with the acknowledgment that "both contain truths and falsehoods." Indeed, the folly of compromise and radicalism is not an outright rejection of God, but, rather, an absolutizing of certain aspects of God; radicalism leans on God as judge and redeemer, while compromise looks to God as creator and preserver.[64] In the end, though, the presence of truth does not make the outcome of these extreme approaches any less destructive: "One absolutizes the end, the other absolutizes what exists. Thus creation and redemption, time and eternity, fall into an insoluble conflict; the very unity of God is itself dissolved, and faith in God is shattered."[65]

Charting a route between radicalism and compromise is possible only when one remembers that the temporal ultimacy of justification is both subjective *and* objective. It is subjectively temporal in the sense described earlier, as it claims human beings in time and at a certain point in time. However, it is also objectively temporal insofar as the objective ground of justification is the person of Jesus Christ who became incarnate in time, lived, died, was raised, and has ascended to the right hand of the Father. "It is faith alone that sets life on a new foundation, and only on this new foundation can I live justified before God. This foundation is the living, dying, and rising of Jesus Christ. Faith means to find, hold to, and cast my anchor on this foundation and so to be held by it."[66] Thus, justification by faith is, indeed, a qualitatively ultimate reality that effects a break with the penultimate by binding Christians to a new foundation. Yet, because this foundation is the incarnate Christ, "Christian life is participation [*Teilnahme*] in Christ's encounter with the world," that is, encounter with and in the penultimate realities of life.[67] In other words, the ultimacy of justification establishes a break *in* time, but not *with* time, because it binds the Christian to the God-man who entered time for the sake of the world's reconciliation.

Getting the relationship between the ultimate and penultimate right, then, is possible only in Christ and depends on holding together his humanity, death, and resurrection.[68] Bonhoeffer's emphasis on these three aspects of the incarnation takes on a heightened significance when we read it in light of the historical dialectic he ascribes to humanity in *Sanctorum Communio*.

> In the becoming human we recognize God's love toward God's creation, in the crucifixion God's judgment on all flesh, and in the resurrection God's purpose

---

63. *DBWE* 6:156.
64. *DBWE* 6:154.
65. *DBWE* 6:154.
66. *DBWE* 6:147.
67. *DBWE* 6:159.
68. On Bonhoeffer's consistent use of this threefold formula, see Green, "Editor's Introduction to the English Edition," 7.

for a new world. Nothing could be more perverse than to tear these three apart, because the whole is contained in each of them. Just as it is improper to pit against one another a theology of the incarnation, a theology of the cross, or a theology of the resurrection, by falsely absolutizing one of them, such a procedure is false as well in any consideration of Christian life. A Christian ethic built only on the incarnation would lead easily to the compromise solution; an ethic built only on the crucifixion or only on the resurrection of Jesus Christ would fall into radicalism and enthusiasm. The conflict is resolved only in their unity [*Einheit*].[69]

Recall that the real historical dialectic—in which human beings live as those who are simultaneously creatures, sinners, and reconciled in Christ alone—finds its point of unity (*Einheitspunkt*) extrinsically only through participation in Christ and the church.[70] Here, not only does Christ serve as the point of unity for the historical dialectic, but he also establishes a new way of being in the world in the threefold unity of his person.

The threefold unity of Christ's person, then, serves as the basis from which we can determine the relationship between the ultimate and penultimate. Because Christ takes on humanity, he "lets human reality exist as penultimate neither making it self-sufficient nor destroying it—a penultimate that will be taken seriously and not seriously in its own way, a penultimate that has become the cover of the ultimate."[71] In this way, Christ affirms the creatureliness of humanity, even as he reorients human existence in relation to himself. The crucifixion, then, is where the ultimate becomes real "as judgment on all that is penultimate, but at the same time as grace for the penultimate that bows to the judgment of the ultimate."[72] In other words, the cross is where human beings are judged for their sins. Yet, insofar as, in faith, they believe that they are really judged in the person of Christ, it is also the place where their penultimate existence is graciously reconfigured by the ultimate word of justification. On the cross of Christ the disruption of sin is countered and conquered by the disruption of grace. Finally, even as the resurrection "makes an end of death and calls a new creation into life," it does not abolish the penultimate.[73] Indeed, it serves as the inauguration of a new eschatological existence that inflects the lives of Christians in the present via their participation in the resurrected body of Christ. In this threefold manner, the form of the Christian life is radically contingent on the person of Christ. Bonhoeffer sums this up in the following way: "Christian life is life with Jesus Christ who became human, was crucified, and is risen, and whose word as a *whole* encounters us in the message of justification of the sinner by grace."[74]

---

69. *DBWE* 6:157; *DBW* 6:149.
70. Cf. *DBW* 10:358.
71. *DBWE* 6:158.
72. *DBWE* 6:158.
73. *DBWE* 6:158.
74. *DBWE* 6:159. Emphasis added.

Life with Jesus Christ is, then, life that is fully immersed in the penultimate even as it lives from the ultimate. Here, Bonhoeffer's concern for embodied participation in Christ's reconciling work is on full display. Insofar as justification is temporally ultimate and, as such, is essentially related to the penultimate, it can be genuinely harmed by the disintegrating effects of evil in the penultimate. In other words, when human beings are harmed or oppressed physically, mentally, or emotionally this can seriously hinder their ability to hear the word of justification.[75] As such, the call to discipleship is also always a call to prepare the way. This, however, must always be held in tension with the fact that justification is also qualitatively ultimate, and as such, is solely dependent on the presence of Christ's Spirit.

While Bonhoeffer spends little time speaking of the body as such, he clearly sees the correlation between human embodiment and what he calls the Christian's task of "preparing the way [*Wegbereitung*]."[76] Indeed, "[b]odiliness and being human belong indivisibly together."[77] As such, Jesus cares about bodiliness because he "is really human and wants us to be human beings."[78] The Christian, who is justified in and through her bodily participation in Christ, now encounters the world with Christ, paving the way to the ultimate by caring for her neighbors in their penultimate, bodily existence. Indeed, there is nothing abstract about the task of *Wegbereitung*:

> It is, instead, a commission of immeasurable responsibility given to all who know about the coming of Jesus Christ. The hungry person needs bread, the homeless person needs shelter, the one deprived of right needs justice, the lonely person needs community, the undisciplined one needs order, and the slave needs freedom. It would be blasphemy against God and our neighbor to leave the hungry unfed while saying that God is closest to those in deepest need. We break bread with the hungry and share our home with them for the sake of Christ's love, which belongs to the hungry as much as it does to us. If the hungry do not come to faith, the guilt falls on those who denied them bread. To bring bread to the hungry is preparing the way for the coming of grace.[79]

Thus, Christians must participate in the reconciling work of Christ not only by means of proclamation, but also through concretely caring for others in their embodied existence.

Christian life is, then, lived from and within grace, serving the relentless mission of God's grace in the world. The Christian lives from grace insofar as justification locates her existence extrinsically in Christ. Through his life, death,

---

75. *DBWE* 6:160.
76. *DWBE* 6:161; *DBW* 6:154. See also Bonhoeffer's extended meditation on the right to bodily life in the *Ethics* manuscript, "Natural Life" (*DBWE* 6:185–96).
77. *DBWE* 6:186.
78. *DBWE* 6:158.
79. *DBWE* 6:163.

and resurrection she lives *coram Deo* for others. Even as her very existence is defined by the ultimate, she lives fully in the penultimate, participating in the church-community where she is formed and sent out for the proclamation and enactment of reconciliation.[80] In this way, the Christian lives within grace. Finally, the Christian life is fundamentally marked by the task of *Wegbereitung*, which engages the church and the individuals that make it up in the proclamation and the enactment of God's reconciliation of the world in Christ. Alongside Christ, the Christian embodies reconciliation in the world. Therefore, the Christian lives from the ultimate, within the penultimate, loving and serving the penultimate for the sake of the ultimate.[81]

IV Conclusion

Recall Philip Ziegler's assertion, noted in the introduction to this study, that "Bonhoeffer's ethics [are] thoroughly *metaethical* in character."[82] Indeed, the goal throughout this book has been to show that, for Bonhoeffer, justification by faith in Christ is the basic theological presupposition that patterns the relational framework within which Christians live, move, and have their being. As such, we have seen that justification plays an important role not only in Bonhoeffer's ethics, but also in his theological anthropology and his theology of discipleship. Put another way, justification defines human being *coram Deo*, forms the Christian for discipleship by binding her to Christ, and establishes her in the church, for the world, as a witness to and participant in Christ's reconciling work.

In "Ultimate and Penultimate Things," Bonhoeffer draws these three strands together, showing that God's gracious justification of human beings in the person and work of Jesus Christ has profound social implications which govern Christian existence in the world. Yet, Bonhoeffer's theological insistence on the concrete over against the abstract beckons us to consider what real difference this might make for the life of church. As such, we shall, in the next chapter, turn to consider how retrieval of the social implications of justification serves to highlight the connection between white supremacy in the church a narrowed soteriological horizon. In order to properly address this problem, the church must confess its guilt and recognize afresh that its being, formation, and action are radically contingent on Christ's justifying grace.

---

80. Cf. Richard J. Perry, Jr., "African American Lutheran Ethical Action: The Will to Build," in *The Promise of Lutheran Ethics*, ed. Karen L. Bloomquist and John R. Stumme (Minneapolis, MN: Fortress Press, 1998), 86–7.

81. See *DBWE* 6:159.

82. Philip G. Ziegler, "'Completely Within God's Doing': Soteriology as Meta-Ethics in the Theology of Dietrich Bonhoeffer," in *Christ, Church, and World: New Studies in Bonhoeffer's Theology and Ethics*, ed. Michael Mawson and Philip G. Ziegler (London: Bloomsbury T&T Clark, 2016), 101.

Chapter 7

JUSTIFICATION AGAINST WHITE SUPREMACY

RETRIEVAL AS CRITICAL CORRECTIVE

I Introduction

Bonhoeffer's concern for harmonizing doctrinal and ethical considerations was evident early in his life, when, reflecting on his time and the people at Union Theological Seminary in 1930/1, he simultaneously expresses his respect for their commitment to social action and his deep frustration with their dearth of dogmatic sensibilities.[1] This is especially on display when he writes:

> I learned much from my own experiences in Harlem. The impressions I got of contemporary representatives of the social gospel will remain determinative for me for a long time to come. The sobriety and seriousness of a book such as that of H. Ward, *Which Way Religion?* is irrefutable; and yet the entire protest must repeatedly be raised if that is preached as *real* Christianity while abbreviating all the crucial Christian ideas. In many discussions and lectures I tried to show that Reformation Christianity does indeed include rather than exclude all these things, but that their assessment is different. But people basically didn't want to believe that.[2]

The book Bonhoeffer mentions, given to him by Marion and Paul Lehmann, was written by Harry F. Ward, a staunch advocate for the social gospel. Thus, as early as his time in New York, and perhaps partially on account of that time, Bonhoeffer believed that the ethical concerns of the social gospel were contained within the fundamental principles of the Reformation.

Throughout this study our central concern has been the distinctive manner in which the emblematic doctrine of the Reformation, justification by faith, shapes Bonhoeffer's understanding of what it means to be human and act humanly before God. By refusing a construal of justification that relegates it to soteriological abstraction, Bonhoeffer draws out the decisive nature of Christ's

---

1. *DBWE* 10:307–17.
2. *DBWE* 10:318–19.

justificatory person for human being in the world. In doing so, he holds forth a more comprehensive vision of the doctrine that is worthy of retrieval for the sake of the church today. However, it is important to recognize that such retrieval does not involve the transformation of justification into an ethical doctrine, such that its soteriological import is minimized. Rather, it involves an affirmation that God's justification of the ungodly is *both* salvific *and* socially meaningful. Or, perhaps more appropriately, it is socially meaningful *because* it is salvific.

The aim of this chapter is to point suggestively toward why this retrieval work is a matter of concrete import. In order to narrow our scope, we shall focus specifically on how, in turning afresh to the social implications of justification, we might locate tools *within* one of the white Western church's most cherished doctrines for challenging its disturbing complicity in the rise and perpetuation of white supremacy.[3] To this end, the chapter will unfold in two sections. The first section shall attend to the attunement of the black ecclesial traditions to the social implications of justification. Insofar as this attunement has not been present in predominantly white ecclesial traditions, its absence may help to explain the church's susceptibility to the allures of whiteness.[4] Thus, I will argue that retrieval of Bonhoeffer's thought in this regard provides a critical corrective in which the soteriological import of justification is seen to militate against the way whiteness has been grafted into the church's anthropology and ethics. The second section will then offer a case study that, in a sense, performs this critique by reading Bonhoeffer's description of the death-dealing work of Christ, the counter Logos, analogically in relation to the critique that black bodies level against whiteness. I will argue that, read in this manner, it offers a theological basis for embracing the black neighbor's critique as participant in the ongoing nature of Christ's justificatory work. The goal in all of this is not to suggest that a theological corrective will overcome the deeply

---

3. The history and dynamics of this complicity have been insightfully treated elsewhere, so we shall not address it here. See, for example, J. Kameron Carter, *Race: A Theological Account* (Oxford/New York: Oxford University Press, 2008); Kelly Brown Douglas, *What's Faith Got to Do With It? Black Bodies/Christian Souls* (Maryknoll, NY: Orbis Books, 2005); Willie James Jennings, *The Christian Imagination: Theology and the Origins of Race* (New Haven, CT: Yale University Press, 2010).

4. Whiteness must be distinguished from white skin color or European descent. Regarding the relationship between whiteness and white supremacy, whiteness is intrinsically connected to white supremacy insofar as whiteness is "an idolatrous form of being in the world which participates in white supremacy—whether actively or passively, explicitly or implicitly," and white supremacy is understood as "a specific and historically particular form of racism, which in turn refers to a general set of practices and beliefs embedded in institutions and practices that promote a hierarchical ordering of racial groups from best to worst." Johnny Ramírez-Johnson and Love L. Sechrest, "Introduction: Race and Missiology in Glocal Perspective," in *Can "White" People Be Saved? Triangulating Race, Theology, and Mission*, ed. Love L. Sechrest, Johnny Ramírez-Johnson, and Amos Yong (Downers Grove, IL: IVP Academic, 2018), 13.

entrenched and systemic nature of white supremacy in the church, but, rather, that the church's efforts in this regard will be severely limited as long as it operates with a narrowed soteriological horizon that has little or no significance for the embodied existence of real human beings.

II Justification in Black and White

As we begin, it is important to distinguish between white supremacy as a theological problem and white supremacy as a *solely* theological problem. To suggest the latter—besides cutting against common sense—implies that white supremacy is an issue that can be solved by *pura doctrina*. It seems patently obvious that this is certainly not the case. As such, it is better to say that white supremacy is a theological problem because, to the extent that it is present in the church, the church has failed theologically. Or, in James Cone's words: "They [are] wrong ethically because they [are] wrong *theologically*."[5] That is, the church has failed to hear the Holy Spirit bear witness to Christ's justifying grace through Scripture in important ways, and its proclamation and public presence in the world have suffered because of it.

While there are certainly other core doctrines which can and should be drawn upon as the church seeks to provide a prophetic response to white supremacy, justification is particularly ripe for such use in light of the social implications teased out in the preceding chapters. However, retrieval of the social implications of justification for the church's witness must, at this point, be qualified in two important ways. First, the very idea that the social implications of justification need to be retrieved invites two possible assessments of the relationship between theology and ethics. On the one hand, one might assume that the problem being addressed is one in which doctrine and ethics have become problematically detached. Accordingly, doctrine and ethics are two separate entities that can be thought and pursued independently of each other, even if to do so is not entirely desirable or advisable. On the other hand, one might assume that the failure to draw out the ethical significance of Christian doctrine results in distorted theology that shapes Christian life in problematic ways. As such, doctrinal reasoning is never bereft of ethical valences. In the words of James Cone, "Christian ethics is a natural child of theology, and the two have really never been separated."[6] When the problem is understood in this manner, then retrieval becomes an essentially corrective task. While a case could be made for the former view in certain cases, we shall proceed assuming the latter.[7] By ignoring the anthropological and ethical

---

5. James H. Cone, *God of the Oppressed*, Rev. Ed. (Maryknoll, NY: Orbis Books, 1997), 183.

6. Cone, *God of the Oppressed*, 185.

7. It is important to note that I am *not* suggesting that all work on doctrinal theology must make explicit the social implications of the various formulations proffered. However, I

implications of justification, the white Western church has settled for a soteriology distorted by individualism and spiritualization.[8] Far from being ethically neutral, this state of affairs creates a theological safe haven for (un)ethical complacency with respect to white supremacy. The goal of what follows is to show that retrieving Bonhoeffer's sensitivity to the social implications of justification can play an important role in critiquing and correcting this distortion.

Second, understood in the corrective manner just outlined retrieval implies that the church has forgotten, neglected, or rejected that which is being retrieved and, as a result, needs to attend to it afresh. However, it would be problematic to proceed on these terms, using the church as a monolithic referent, since ecclesial amnesia with respect to justification's social import is hardly an accurate characterization of *all* segments of the church. Indeed, highlighting the social implications of justification has always been, according to Richard J. Perry, more consonant with the African-American Christian tradition than it is with the white Christian tradition.[9] Speaking specifically of the Lutheran response to slavery during the Civil War, Perry writes that "white Lutherans were quite satisfied and even energetic as they took on questions about 'pure doctrine' and church polity. But they were remarkably passive when it came to working for justice and freedom on behalf of God's enslaved African-American sons and daughters."[10] In stark contrast, however, Perry suggests that, for the African-American, justification by

---

am suggesting that any work of doctrinal theology that is not deeply informed by reflection on these implications risks straying from theology's central purpose: to serve the church as the worshipping and missional body of Christ.

8. According to Elsa Tamez, these distortions require nothing short of a reformulation: "The need to reformulate the doctrine of justification is equally evident now that individualism, subjectivism, universalism, passivity, and general misinterpretation (whether explicit or implicit, conscious or unconscious) have contributed to the confusion of its meaning" (*The Amnesty of Grace: Justification by Faith from a Latin American Perspective* [Nashville, TN: Abingdon Press, 1993], 25).

9. This claim, in light of our study, perhaps lends heft to Reggie Williams' claim that "Bonhoeffer had formative experiences in New York in a key historical moment that inspired his efforts in Germany to uncouple the false connection between white imperialist identity and Jesus and its tragic imprint for Christianity." *Bonhoeffer's Black Jesus: Harlem Renaissance Theology and an Ethic of Resistance* (Waco, TX: Baylor University Press, 2014), 3. Likewise, Josiah U. Young III (*No Difference in the Fare: Dietrich Bonhoeffer and the Problem of Racism* [Grand Rapids, MI: Eerdmans, 1998], 121–2) sees a deep consonance between Bonhoeffer's insistence on justification by grace and the theology he encountered at Abyssinian Baptist Church in Harlem during his year at Union Theological Seminary.

10. Richard J. Perry, "Justification by Faith and Its Social Implications," in *Theology and the Black Experience: The Lutheran Heritage Interpreted by African and African-American Theologians*, ed. Albert Pero and Ambrose Moyo (Minneapolis, MN: Augsburg, 1988), 15.

faith entails self-affirmation, freedom, and justice.[11] "Justification leads justified women and men to act on behalf of and with others who are oppressed. This is what makes justification wholistic for African-Americans. . . . Justification is a process within God's purposeful activity to build a kingdom of justice, equity, and wholeness."[12] By emphasizing that justification is a process, Perry, like Bonhoeffer, is affirming that justification and sanctification are bound together and cannot be viewed sequentially or in isolation from one another. Furthermore, rather than emphasizing the forensic side of justification as pure act, Perry asserts that the being of the one who is justified is drawn into Christ's body, the church, thereby becoming a participant in Christ's reconciling work in the world.[13]

Similarly, James Cone roots Christian responsibility for the poor in the reality of justification. "Having come before God as nothing and being received by him into his Kingdom through grace, the Christian should know that he has been made righteous (justified) so that he can join God in the fight for justice."[14] For Cone, being made righteous must be thought alongside the liberative import of God's justice established in the death and resurrection of Christ. As such, he asserts that justification is "the removal of oppressed black people from the control of white power, thereby making it possible for the enslaved to be free."[15] The liberative dimensions of justification are likewise clear in Latin American articulations of the doctrine. After surveying Latin American rereadings of justification in contradistinction to a traditional Western framing, Elsa Tamez concludes that "the word 'liberation' best encompasses" their re-articulation of the doctrine.[16]

So, there is a sense in which retrieving Bonhoeffer's insights regarding the social implications of justification by faith is simply a retrieval of what many black and Latin American Christians have believed all along. For them, the belief that justification by faith has real implications for their embodied, social existence is

---

11. It is important to note that self-affirmation is not intended here in the sense of self-justification. Rather, it is the appropriate affirmation of self in which a person's worth is firmly located in her gracious reception of the Christ-gift.

12. Perry, "Justification by Faith and Its Social Implications," 18.

13. Perry, "Justification by Faith and Its Social Implications," 32. It is important to acknowledge Jennifer Harvey's recent critique of Christian reconciliation paradigms for addressing systemic racism in *Dear White Christians: For Those Still Longing for Racial Reconciliation* (Grand Rapids, MI: Eerdmans, 2014). However, the version of reconciliation she problematizes is based on a vision for "universal shared humanity" that seeks to overcome white supremacy with "interracial togetherness" (18–29). She takes issue with this approach because it fails to name and deconstruct whiteness. We shall see later that by locating justification at the heart of reconciliation, whiteness is necessarily critiqued and at least some of Harvey's concerns are mitigated.

14. James H. Cone, *Black Theology and Black Power*, 50th Anniversary Edition (Maryknoll, NY: Orbis Books, 2018), 53; See also Cone, *God of the Oppressed*, 212–15.

15. Cone, *God of the Oppressed*, 217.

16. Tamez, *The Amnesty of Grace*, 35.

part and parcel of the belief that the God who justifies does so by taking on human flesh, suffering, dying, and being raised from the dead. Christ stands in bodily solidarity with his suffering people, interceding on their behalf before God, and offering them a "horizon of hope" by laying claim to their embodied existence through his resurrected body.[17]

Has it been misguided, then, to ask after the social implications of justification in the theology of a white, German, bourgeois pastor-theologian? There are several reasons to think that this is not the case. First, recent years have seen a burgeoning interest in Bonhoeffer as a theologian against white supremacy.[18] Amidst the growing literature, Cone has set Dietrich Bonhoeffer alongside Martin Luther King Jr. as one of the few theologians to actively oppose and speak out against white supremacy.[19] Likewise, Reggie Williams identifies Bonhoeffer as the "only prominent white theologian of the twentieth century to speak about racism as a Christian problem."[20] Second, the focus of this study has been a retrieval of the

---

17. M. Shawn Copeland, *Enfleshing Freedom: Body, Race, and Being* (Minneapolis, MN: Fortress Press, 2010), 5–6; cf. Brian Bantum, *The Death of Race: Building a New Christianity in a Racial World* (Minneapolis, MN: Fortress Press, 2016), 90–2.

18. Some of the earliest work in this regard was carried out by John W. de Gruchy (*Bonhoeffer and South Africa: Theology in Dialogue* [Grand Rapids, MI: W.B. Eerdmans Pub. Co, 1984]) and Josiah U. Young III (*No Difference in the Fare*). More recent work includes Alan Aubrey Boesak, "Church, Racism, and Resistance: Bonhoeffer and the Critical Dimensions of Theological Integrity," in *Luther, Bonhoeffer, and Public Ethics: Re-Forming the Church of the Future*, ed. Michael P. DeJonge and Clifford J. Green (Lanham, MD: Lexington Books/Fortress Academic, 2018), 137–49; Peter Frick, "Notes On Bonhoeffer's Theological Anthropology: The Case of Racism," in *Understanding Bonhoeffer* (Tübingen: Mohr Siebeck, 2017), 185–200; Ross E. Halbach, "Preparing the Way: Dietrich Bonhoeffer in Dialogue with Contemporary Theologians of Race" (PhD, University of Aberdeen, 2017); Barry Harvey, *Taking Hold of the Real: Dietrich Bonhoeffer and the Profound Worldliness of Christianity.* (Cambridge: James Clarke & Co, 2016), 178–208; Willis Jenkins and Jennifer M. McBride, eds., *Bonhoeffer and King: Their Legacies and Import for Christian Social Thought* (Minneapolis, MN: Fortress Press, 2010); J. Deotis Roberts, *Bonhoeffer and King: Speaking Truth to Power* (Louisville, KY: Westminster John Knox Press, 2005); Williams, *Bonhoeffer's Black Jesus*; Josiah U. Young III, "Dietrich Bonhoeffer and Reinhold Niebuhr: Their Ethics, Views on Karl Barth and African-Americans," in *Bonhoeffer's Intellectual Formation: Theology and Philosophy in His Thought*, ed. Peter Frick (Tübingen: Mohr Siebeck, 2008), 283–300; Josiah U. Young III, "'On My Way to Freedom Land': Bonhoeffer and Three Bright Lights of the Civil Rights Movement," in *Luther, Bonhoeffer, and Public Ethics: Re-Forming the Church of the Future*, ed. Michael P. DeJonge and Clifford J. Green (Lanham, MD: Lexington Books/Fortress Academic, 2018), 151–60.

19. James Cone, "Theology's Great Sin: Silence in the Face of White Supremacy," in *The Cambridge Companion to Black Theology*, eds. Dwight N. Hopkins and Edward P. Antonio (Cambridge: Cambridge University Press, 2012), 143.

20. Williams, *Bonhoeffer's Black Jesus*, 139.

social implications of justification by faith in Bonhoeffer's thought. We have not suggested that Bonhoeffer is the only theologian to draw on justification in this way, but, rather, that his thought is particularly fruitful on this front given the coherence between his life and writing. Third, just as theologians have highlighted the liberative import of justification for the oppressed, the white church, with respect to its complicity in white supremacy, needs to hear the social implications of justification articulated in terms of a critical corrective. Bonhoeffer speaks as a critic from within the white ecclesial tradition, offering us just such a voice.

In light of the previous chapters, his critique might be framed as follows. First, the white, Western church has spiritualized justification, abstracting it from its decisive relevance for human being *coram Deo*. As such, it has more to do with eternal security and less to do with embodied existence. White privilege, then, is taken for granted as a fact of life and thus emerges from the baptismal pool unscathed, an implicit order of creation. Here, we see a misalignment of the historical dialectic in which creatureliness is minimized and, as such, sin and reconciliation are construed in spiritual terms that have no intrinsic bearing on bodily existence. Ironically, the minimization of justification's import for creatureliness results in the problematic valorization of creaturely particularities because they are not interpreted in light of God's Yes and No in Christ.

Second, the white, Western church has fallen prey to individualism, rejecting the relational and participative dimensions of what it means to be justified in Christ. White Christians have laid claim to God's declaration of righteousness without surrendering their existence to the one in whom righteousness is created, preserved, and restored *coram Deo*. Or, to draw on the titular concepts of Bonhoeffer's *habilitationschrift*, they have laid hold of God's justifying act apart from the claim it lays to human beings. The result of this has been that justification no longer means being drawn out self-incurvature and bound to Christ, but, rather, a drawing of Christ-as-an-idea into the individual.[21] As a person, Christ draws human beings into himself, challenging and reconfiguring how they relate to their particularities through conformation. As an idea, Christ is malleable, conforming to the identity markers of white Christians. Insofar as it is in and through Christ the mediator that Christians are led toward and encounter others as real human beings, treating Christ as an idea in this manner inevitably leads to a form of individualism, rendering white Christians incapable of what Willie Jennings calls "intimate joining."[22]

---

21. When this happens, Christ can be pressed into the service of ideologies and *Weltanschauungen*. In his account of the manner in which the Christ is stripped of his Jewish, covenantal flesh and rendered white, J. Kameron Carter makes this point, arguing that, in modernity, racial reasoning has developed into a full-fledged *Weltanschauung* (*Race*, 5).

22. While Jennings does not employ participation terminology, there is clearly a high degree of overlap between what he is describing here and what has traditionally been understood as participation in Christ. Describing his vision for Christian community in

Ultimately, spiritualizing and individualizing justification have allowed white Christians to evade one of its key aspects: embodied participation in Christ's death. They fail to take seriously the fact that justification is not God's No to sin in some abstract spiritual sense, such that its goal is simply rescuing individuals from hell. Rather, it is his No to the myriad of concrete ways human beings are bodily susceptible to and enact sin. Therefore, embodied participation in Christ's death is God's No to all that degrades and distorts God's Yes to real, embodied human beings. White Christians have tended to interpret this individualistically, such that the import of Christ's death is the preservation of their souls unto salvation. However, they have failed to reckon with the fact that their bodies are enmeshed in sinful structures and systems that degrade and distort God's Yes to humanity in Christ. They have appropriated Christ's death opportunistically on their own behalf, rather than entering into it. The tragic upshot of this is an understanding of God's justifying grace in Christ that neither meaningfully shapes embodied human existence nor paves the way to intimate joining. In the next section, we shall unfold the corrective import of justification's social implications further by means of a sort of case study. It reads Bonhoeffer's description of the death-dealing work of Christ, the counter Logos, as an analogical basis for embracing the critique leveled by the black neighbor against whiteness as participant in the ongoing nature of Christ's justificatory work.

III *The Counter Logos and the Black Neighbor*

We have seen earlier that all too often white Christians have failed to grasp the social implications of justification, even as their black sisters and brothers have

---

and through Christ the mediator, Jennings writes: "If Christian existence stands on nothing greater than the body of one person, then it could be that the only way for Christian communities to move beyond cultural fragmentation and segregated mentalities is to find a place that is also a person, a new person that each of us and all of us together can enter into and, possibly, can become" (Willie James Jennings, *The Christian Imagination: Theology and the Origins of Race* [New Haven, CT: Yale University Press, 2010], 249). For Jennings, participation in Christ means entering into a story of Israel *as gentiles*, thereby displacing preconceived notions of self and one's community (258). While this entering into Christ and the story of Israel does not erase particularities, it does call our knowledge and interpretation of them into question (258). Jennings' persistent focus on the central role of Israel in God's economy of salvation and the Jewishness of Christ is part and parcel of Bonhoeffer's insistence, in *Ethics*, that Christ became incarnate as a "real human being" (*DBWE* 6:94). However, Bonhoeffer's failure to draw this out and his inversion of the Jew-gentile relationship in his essay, "The Church and the Jewish Question," means that he cannot be absolved of the Christian supersessionism that Jennings intends to critique.

been keenly aware of the broader scope of soteriology. While the church's role in engendering and perpetuating white supremacy can certainly not be explained solely with reference to this factor, it is suggestive of the possibility that retrieval of these social implications in predominantly white ecclesial spheres can and should challenge the entrenchment of whiteness. In this section, we shall move from a theoretical consideration of how Bonhoeffer's justification-based construal human being and action might participate in this work to a more constructive proposal for how his account of encounter with Christ might shape the consciousness of the church over against whiteness. In order to frame this reading, we shall draw on the introduction to Bonhoeffer's 1933 Christology Lectures, which sets the stage for what Andreas Pangritz has referred to as Bonhoeffer's Christology of encounter.[23] However, it may be fitting to further specify the nature of this encounter and simply speak of Bonhoeffer's confrontational Christology. Indeed, this seems particularly fitting in light of Bonhoeffer's assertion that "[t]here are only two possibilities when a human being confronts Jesus: the human being must either die or kill Jesus."[24]

Christology, then, cannot be reduced to mere reflection on an object. The possibility of asking the Christological question rightly depends on a justifying encounter with Christ in which, according to the baptismal logic of participation, the human being dies and is resurrected in faith. As such, for Bonhoeffer, knowing Christ and speaking of him well necessarily involves a critique of one's being in which the self's claim to be its own center is denied. Instead, the self is dislocated and relocated extrinsically in Christ. By characterizing this critique as a beckoning to death or a putting to death, he highlights that the radical nature of humanity's ineptitude in knowing Christ is matched by an equally radical and gracious solution.

However, as Bonhoeffer sees it, sinful humanity is defined by the human logos. What this means is that they enthrone their reason and perception of the world over against Christ. As such, their natural tendency is to evade confrontation with Christ by reducing him to an idea. As an idea—rather than a transcendent, personal other—the human logos approaches Christ as one who is beholden to its prior categories and classifications. In other words, the human logos approaches Christ as an idea which is immanent to its intellect and proves what it already believes to be the case. Broadly speaking, then, reducing Christ to an idea yields two types of responses to him: the human logos can either reject Christ outright or self-negate. We shall focus here only on the latter.

Bonhoeffer writes that "what the [human] logos does under attack from the other Logos represents not philistine self-defense but rather a great insight into its power of self-negation, for self-negation signifies the self-affirmation of the

---

23. Andreas Pangritz, "'Who Is Jesus Christ, for Us, Today?'" in *The Cambridge Companion to Dietrich Bonhoeffer*, ed. John W. de Gruchy (Cambridge: Cambridge University Press, 1999), 136.

24. *DBWE* 12:307.

[human] logos."²⁵ But what is "self-negation"? In invoking the term Bonhoeffer references Hegel's philosophy. According to Hegel, something is always defined in relation to its other, its negative. However, this other-as-negation is not fixed in its otherness, but can also be negated via sublation of the self and other. For Hegel, sublation is the synthesis of a term and its negative which yields a new, third term. While aspects of the original two terms are destroyed in the synthesis, they are ultimately taken up into and preserved in the new, third term.

With this in mind, what Bonhoeffer means by self-negation seems to be a situation in which confrontation with Christ is avoided by means of a synthesis between Christ and self. Thus, rather than the proper, negating critique of justification leveled by the person of Christ against the sinful human logos in order reconcile it in himself, the human logos affirms itself by assimilating Christ's critique only to the extent that the self is preserved. In other words, self-negation allows the human logos to have its cake and eat it too. It evades death and preserves its autonomy, all the while accepting just enough of Christ's critique to deceive itself into believing that an actual confrontation has happened. By taking the idea of Christ into oneself, any subjection to Christ is, in reality, a subjection to the self.²⁶ And by partially performing and preempting the death-dealing act of Christ, self-negation deceives the human logos into believing that it has surrendered itself to Christ, thereby blinding it to the fact that it continues to lay claim idolatrously to its own identity.²⁷

After discussing these ways of evading confrontation while asking the Christological question, Bonhoeffer returns to the reality of Christology: namely, that Christ is the transcendent, incarnate one who encounters humanity as a person.²⁸ Christ is the counter Logos to the sinful human logos. Here, Bonhoeffer flips the nomenclature of the gospel of John's first chapter on its head. In the beginning was the Logos, but after the fall he has become, to humanity, the counter Logos: God's "no" to the totalizing impulses of a humanity trapped in the total reality of sin. As such, Bonhoeffer puts the following words into the mouth of the counter Logos: "'I am the truth,' I am the death of the human logos, I am the Alpha and the Omega. Human beings are those who must die and must fall, with their logos into my hands."²⁹

The counter Logos cannot be sublated and demands nothing less than the death of the human logos. The middle ground which self-negation supposedly creates is, in the end, an illusion. Christ is either Lord or he is rejected. When viewed in this way it becomes clear that, because the counter Logos is a person, he cannot *actually* be turned into an idea. Merely human persons that resist such reduction can be

---

25. *DBWE* 12:302.

26. *DBWE* 2:108.

27. Cf. Brian Bantum, *Redeeming Mulatto: A Theology of Race and Christian Hybridity* (Waco, TX: Baylor University Press, 2010), 26–7.

28. *DBWE* 12:302.

29. *DBWE* 12:302.

killed, but the resurrected God-man has conquered death. Here, however, there is a tension in Bonhoeffer's lectures because while he insists that the resurrected Christ cannot be killed by human beings, he also writes:

> Jesus Christ passes through our time, through different stations and occupations in life, always being asked anew, Who are you? and yet always, when some person is aware of having confronted this question, being killed anew. . . . Wanting to be finished with Christ means that now and then we kill him, crucify him, commit shameful acts against him, kneel before him with the scornful and say, "Greetings, Rabbi!"[30]

While Bonhoeffer believes that nothing can reverse the good news of the resurrection, he still wants to maintain that self-negation, reduction of the counter Logos to an idea, and evasion of confrontation do, in a real sense, make the human logos in the present just as guilty of killing Christ as the crowds who demanded his death in the first century.

The self-negation of the human logos, then, is nothing more than a denial of the justification-inflected reality that human beings exist extrinsically *coram Deo* according to the historical dialectic of creation, sin, and reconciliation, which finds its point of unity in the person of Christ alone. Furthermore, self-negation seeks to claim Christ even as it denies Christ's claim. In other words, the self-negating human logos wants Christ without mediation and alongside of the immediacies of self and world. Thus, the self-negating human logos cannot know Christ because it turns in on itself and refuses the baptismal logic of participation in Christ as the counter Logos. This fundamental denial of justification's import for what it means to be human also corresponds to a denial of justification's formative aspect since it refuses holistic participation in Christ as determinative of the believer's whole being. With this in mind, we shall now consider how Bonhoeffer's assertion that Christology begins with a justificatory confrontation in which Christ cannot be known apart from death forms the basis for drawing out an analogy between Bonhoeffer's Christology and the problem of white supremacy.

The following argument hangs on an analogy between the confrontation of the human logos by the counter Logos and the confrontation between the human logos trapped in whiteness—or, what we might call, the white logos—and the black neighbor. In the analogy, the self-negating white Christian is comparable to the human logos, while the critiquing work of the black neighbor makes her analogous to the counter Logos. The language of analogy is crucial here because it preserves the differences between the two scenarios. For instance, not every human logos is white and the incarnate Christ is not identical with the black neighbor.

However, what makes this analogy so helpful is that it is not *merely* an analogy. It bears within it an element of univocity as well. Although not every human logos is white, every self-negating white logos is a human logos. As such, the person

30. *DBWE* 12:307.

shackled to and blinded by whiteness simply is a sinner who consistently evades confrontation with Christ in order to keep the human logos intact. For the sake of clarity, it is important to stress that this univocity is not present in the analogous relationship between the counter Logos and the black neighbor. Insofar as the black neighbor levels a critique against whiteness which participates in and serves the counter Logos' critique of the human logos, we can say that she is *like* the counter Logos. Yet, the black neighbor, insofar as she is also a human logos, cannot be identified with the counter Logos in a univocal manner. In sum, the analogy has teeth because the white logos simply is a specific type of human logos, and this univocal relation provides a basis from which to assert that the critique of the black neighbor participates in or is an aspect of the death-dealing work of the counter Logos. We might say, then, based on this analogy, that the white Christian's inability to hear, see, and perceive the critique which the black neighbor levels against it is indicative of a self-negating resistance to the person of Christ.

How then does this analogy play out? Just as Bonhoeffer supposes that Christ cannot be known properly apart from a confrontation in which the human logos is put to death, so too must whiteness' supremacy die in order for the black neighbor to be known. Here, self-negation emerges as a particularly apt way of conceptualizing how and why so many white Christians are complicit in white supremacy. In self-negation, whiteness is not put to death. Rather, it is sublated with the critique of the black neighbor, and thereby preserved—and not merely preserved, but preserved in the most insidious way because self-negation is self-deception. As such, a blind spot is created which allows the white Christian to believe that their whiteness is conquered even as it continues to whitewash their reality.

In this way self-negation becomes an affirmation and an entrenchment of whiteness. This is, of course, symptomatic of an unwillingness to treat the black neighbor as other than oneself. As an idea, the black neighbor's self-revelation does not serve as the prerequisite for my thinking about it.[31] Instead, it is only useful insofar as it affirms and proves what one already believes to be the case. Therefore the critique of the black neighbor is neutralized because it is forced to conform to a system of categorization shaped by whiteness rather than disrupting and restructuring that system.[32]

We can stretch the analogy further in relation to the purpose of Christ's critique. For Bonhoeffer the confrontation between the counter Logos and the human logos is one in which the human logos dies so that it might be resurrected with new eyes that can see Christ for who he truly is in his otherness. Likewise, the purpose of the critique which the black neighbor levels against white people is to open their eyes to the reality of the black neighbor's otherness. However, just as the critique of the counter Logos diagnoses a problem— it reveals that humans are sinful and

---

31. Cf. *DBWE* 12:301.

32. Cf. Rachel Muers, *Keeping God's Silence: Towards a Theological Ethics of Communication* (Malden, MA: Blackwell, 2004), 94.

turned in on themselves (*cor curvum en se*)—so too does the critique of the black neighbor. It provides a vantage point from which the insufficiency of self-negation can be seen and whiteness' continuing supremacy can be unmasked.

How does the black neighbor provide this vantage point? Here we might think of how Reggie Williams—in *Bonhoeffer's Black Jesus*—picks up W. E. B. Du Bois's concept of the veiled corner as a way of describing Harlem during the Harlem Renaissance. Williams asserts that "[t]he veiled corner is hidden to the white majority. It gives the black observer residing on the border a truer representation of the dominant streams of consciousness on both sides of the color line than that which is offered by the one-history-fits-all, white-centered worldview."[33] It is no wonder then that, according to Williams, Bonhoeffer's time spent in Harlem's veiled corner had a powerful effect on Bonhoeffer's theology, including his Christology.

By offering a perspective from the veiled corner, the black neighbor's critique holds up a mirror in which the white logos can recognize that it has evaded the counter Logos via self-negation and established an idol, a white Christ in his place.[34] The critique of the black neighbor, then, acts in service of and is really part of the critique of the counter Logos. Therefore, clinging to whiteness—refusing genuine encounter with the black neighbor—signals self-negation and evasion of confrontation with Christ.

Through self-negation the human logos deceives itself by creating a secret space for the retention of aspects of its identity, all the while believing that "it is no longer I who live, but it is Christ who lives in me" (Gal 2:20). However, insofar as Christ lives in the human logos alongside of those retained aspects of its identity, Christ begins to look a lot like the human logos. This is Christ as an idea conformed to the human logos, rather than Christ as a person, as the counter Logos standing over against the human logos. Thus, insofar as white supremacy is present in the church, we can locate it in the secret space created by self-negation and affirmed by a Christ-idea, a white Christ, conformed to the white logos.[35] Furthermore, this state of affairs is enabled and empowered by a fundamental misunderstanding of what it means to be justified by grace through faith. Here, justification is merely the justification of sin rather than the justification of the sinner because there is no genuine encounter with the person of Christ.

---

33. Williams, *Bonhoeffer's Black Jesus*, 55; cf. Charles W. Mills, *Blackness Visible: Essays on Philosophy and Race* (Ithaca, NY: Cornell University Press, 1998), 99.

34. This parallels Charles Mills' suggestion regarding epistemic injustice—namely, that "[dominant groups] are generally materially advantaged while in crucial respects (at least in regard to seeing social truth) epistemically handicapped, while [minority groups] are generally materially handicapped while in crucial respects epistemically advantaged," Charles W. Mills, "Ideology," in *The Routledge Handbook of Epistemic Injustice*, ed. Ian James Kidd, Jośe Medina, and Gaile Pohlhaus, Jr. (London: Routledge, 2017), 103.

35. Cf. Nico Koopman, "Bonhoeffer and the Future of Public Theology in South Africa: The On-Going Quest for Life Together," *Nederduitse Gereformeerde Teologiese Tydskrif* 55, no. Supplementum 1 (2014): 994–5.

This is a grim picture, indeed. However, Bonhoeffer is helpful in reminding us that no matter how clever the white logos is in turning Christ into an idea, the present and resurrected counter Logos stands over against it at every turn. Even self-negation cannot ultimately protect the human logos from this reality. Because the church is the sphere in which Christ's lordship over the world is proclaimed, white supremacy obscured by self-negation will be rooted out there and everywhere. This is the promise of the resurrection. Yet even so, it is incumbent upon the church to prepare the way, to proclaim and enact the justifying grace of God which reconciles Jews and Gentiles in Christ's body by rebuking whiteness as idolatry and fearlessly naming white supremacy as incompatible with God's reconciling work in Christ.[36]

Insofar as the critique which the black neighbor levels against the white logos serves to illuminate whiteness' supremacy, it reveals a space in which Christ's Lordship has been denied. It is thus part and parcel of the critique of the counter Logos. In the form of black flesh, the counter Logos confronts human being with a critique that both makes possible and requires the death of whiteness and the dismantling of white supremacy.[37] Indeed, "black confrontation with white racism is Jesus meeting whites, providing them with the possibility of reconciliation."[38]

In sum, then, the analogy is clear and compelling at a number of points. First, just as the human logos resists the counter Logos through open opposition or self-negation, so too do white Christians resist the critique of the black neighbor. Second, just as self-negation offers the illusion that one isn't actively opposing Christ, so too does it provide reassurance for the white Christian. They proudly proclaim their opposition to the KKK, segregation, etc., but will only take on board those aspects of the black neighbor's critique which are compatible with their own comfort. Third, just as self-negation treats Christ as a malleable idea, so too does it reduce the black neighbor to an idea that must conform to the reality of whiteness. Fourth, just as the self-negating human logos is complicit in the crucifixion of Christ when it refuses death, it is increasingly apparent, especially in North America, that either whiteness must be put to death or the black neighbor will continue to be killed.

The white Christian's inability to hear the black neighbor's critique and act accordingly is indicative of a resistance to, and, if we follow the analogy with

---

36. Cf. Bantum, *Redeeming Mulatto*, 137; Love L. Sechrest, *A Former Jew: Paul and the Dialectics of Race* (London: T&T Clark, 2009), 227–31; Bernard Ukwuegbu, "'Neither Jew nor Greek': The Church in Africa and the Quest for Self-Understanding in the Light of the Pauline Vision and Today's Context of Cultural Pluralism," *International Journal for the Study of the Christian Church* 8, no. 4 (2008): 307–8.

37. Without mitigating the need for the death of whiteness, Brian Bantum goes further, calling for a Christological understanding that also entails the death of race. See *The Death of Race*, 127–42.

38. James H. Cone, *A Black Theology of Liberation* (Philadelphia, PA: J. B. Lippincott Company, 1970), 114.

Bonhoeffer far enough, even a killing of Christ. Thus, white Christians must surrender their whiteness to the killing work of the counter Logos in order to properly hear, respond to, and love their black neighbor.[39] Used in this way, Bonhoeffer's Christology forms an analogy which emphasizes that racism and white supremacy in the church are, indeed, a struggle that must involve death in order to stem the tide of violence. As such, there is no self-negating middle ground where white supremacy and Christ can peacefully coexist.

IV Conclusion

It is hardly revolutionary to claim that white supremacy and Christianity are incompatible. However, the fact that much of the Western church remains, to some extent, beholden to whiteness and white supremacy points to a fundamental misalignment within the theology being espoused in these spaces.[40] One such misalignment occurs when justification by faith is reduced to the personal salvation of the individual and grace becomes a badge of pride rather than a gift that grounds human worth extrinsically in Christ.[41] When grace becomes a spiritualized commodity that the individual can possess, then Christ becomes an idea that is imminent to the intellect. Here, Christ serves to ratify any *Weltanschauung* he is integrated into, rather than disrupting through the becoming real of his reality— the *Christuswirklichkeit*—as he takes form among real human beings by the power of the Spirit.[42]

In radical contrast to grace conceived of individualistically as a spiritual commodity and the justification of sin stands grace as a gift and the justification of the sinner with all its attendant social implications.[43] Here, Christ's person is the

---

39. Cf. Harvey, *Taking Hold of the Real*, 206.

40. Another important misalignment not addressed here is the perennial problem of Christian supersessionism. On the connections between this and white supremacy in the church generally, see Carter, *Race*; Jennings, *The Christian Imagination*. On Bonhoeffer and supersessionism, see Harvey, *Taking Hold of the Real*, 178–233; Halbach, "Preparing the Way," 117–47.

41. Our positive emphasis on justification theology here differs markedly from Douglas Campbell's generally negative reading. However, his recent essay ("Mass Incarceration: Pauline Problems and Pauline Solutions," *Interpretation: A Journal of Bible and Theology* 72, no. 3 [2018]: 282–92) concerning the manner in which certain interpretations of Paul have come to shape the American penal system in problematic ways is a notable and important attempt to correct soteriological misalignments in Christian theology.

42. Cf. Josiah U. Young III, "'Is the White Christ, Too, Distraught by These Dark Sins His Father Wrought?': Dietrich Bonhoeffer and the Problem of the White Christ," *Perspectives in Religious Studies* 26, no. 3 (1999): 325–8.

43. Cf. Barry Harvey, "The Wound of History: Reading Bonhoeffer after Christendom," in *Bonhoeffer for a New Day: Theology in a Time of Transition*, ed. John W. DeGruchy (Grand

extrinsic ground of all human beings and worth. Indeed, the ongoing presence of sin in the historical dialectic of human existence precludes the possibility of hierarchy and Christ as the mediator of all reality relativizes human particularity even as he affirms it in his recapitulation of *creatio ex nihilo*.[44] Likewise, the baptismal logic of participation means that critique and death can never be separated out from affirmation, liberation, and resurrection. When these implications of justification are neglected the church is made vulnerable to the valorization of hierarchies and the sanctification of particularities in a way that evades and turns a deaf ear to the critiquing and justifying word of the counter Logos. The *sanctorum communio* ceases to understand itself as simultaneously the *peccatorum communio*, and the possibility that the critique of black Christians—and all persons of color for that matter—might be received as the Word of Christ is precluded.[45]

Renewed attention to the social implications of justification by faith must certainly, then, begin with public confession.[46] Indeed, the church must be "that community of people that has been led by the grace of Christ to acknowledge its guilt toward Christ."[47] As such, the church and its individual members must confess that far too often they have lived only from the resurrection, failing to take seriously God's judgment on their sin in the cross and Christ's affirmation of the bodily existence of real human beings in the incarnation. According to Bonhoeffer, though, confession is not a verbal magic trick that lets the church off the hook. "Continuity with past guilt, which in the life of the church and the believer is broken off by repentance and forgiveness, remains in the historical life

---

Rapids, MI: Eerdmans, 1997), 289–92. Remarkably, Harvey here draws on the same insights regarding ancient gift-economies as John Barclay in *Paul and the Gift*, which was published eighteen years later in 2015.

44. This way of understanding Christ's mediating and justifying work provides a way of thinking about humanity in Christ that does not demand an erasure of particularity. For a recent critique of the correlation between Christian claims regarding the possibility of salvation for all people and the authorization of "compulsory mutability," see Denise Kimber Buell, "Early Christian Universalism and Modern Forms of Racism," in *The Origins of Racism in the West*, ed. Miriam Eliav-Feldon, Benjamin Isaac, and Joseph Ziegler (Cambridge: Cambridge University Press, 2009), 109–31. See also Mills, *Blackness Visible*, 92.

45. For a helpful recent critique of theologies that fail to take seriously the ongoing presence of sin in the church, see Michael Mawson, "The Spirit and the Community: Pneumatology and Ecclesiology in Jenson, Hütter and Bonhoeffer," *International Journal of Systematic Theology* 15, no. 4 (2013): 453–68; cf. *DBWE* 1:213.

46. Cf. Elizabeth Conde-Frazier, "*Siempre Lo Mismo*: Theology, Rhetoric, and Broken Praxis," in *Can "White" People Be Saved? Triangulating Race, Theology, and Mission*, ed. Love L. Sechrest, Johnny Ramírez-Johnson, and Amos Yong (Downers Grove, IL: IVP Academic, 2018), 128–31.

47. *DBWE* 6:135.

of nations."[48] The scars of historical guilt run deep. Because the church does not live in a bubble, isolated from history and the world, confession requires a full engagement with the hard, humbling, and embodied work of reconciliation.[49]

Thus, by retrieving the social implications of justification in Bonhoeffer's theology we are better able to name the theological misalignment according to which justification is spiritualized and individualistic, thereby commodifying grace and endorsing complacent, self-negating self-satisfaction on the part of white Christians. Yet, even as an understanding of justification which takes seriously its social import critiques the misalignment, it also provides a corrective: highlighting Christ as the gracious ground of human existence in the historical dialectic, making discipleship intrinsic to justification via the logic of participation, and casting a vision for the church as a community that lives from the ultimate in the penultimate as way preparers in word and deed. In this corrective, the all-encompassing import of Christ's justifying grace for human existence counteracts a thin understanding of justification as self-affirmation and, instead, decenters the white Christian's sense of self in such a way that Christ replaces the immediacy of whiteness. When this happens the white Christian is freed for intimate joining, not only hearing the critique of her black neighbor but also responding to it in confession, co-suffering solidarity, and embodied acts of reconciliation.

---

48. *DBWE* 6:144.

49. Some have rightly expressed reservations regarding the language of reconciliation due to the cheap and flippant way in which it is often employed by white Christians. However, if it is paired with a proper understanding of justification, James Cone seems to have the right of it when he writes: "White people must be made to realize that reconciliation is a costly experience. It is not holding hands and singing 'Black and white together' and 'We shall overcome.' Reconciliation means *death*, and only those who are prepared to die in the struggle for freedom will experience new life with God" (*God of the Oppressed*, 219).

BIBLIOGRAPHY

Adams, Samuel V. *The Reality of God and Historical Method: Apocalyptic Theology in Conversation with N. T. Wright*. Downers Grove, IL: IVP Academic, 2015.

Aidala, Angela A. "Worldviews, Ideologies and Social Experimentation: Clarification and Replication of 'The Consciousness Reformation.'" *Journal for the Scientific Study of Religion* 23, no. 1 (1984): 44–59.

Bantum, Brian. *Redeeming Mulatto: A Theology of Race and Christian Hybridity*. Waco, TX: Baylor University Press, 2010.

Bantum, Brian. *The Death of Race: Building a New Christianity in a Racial World*. Minneapolis, MN: Fortress Press, 2016.

Barclay, John M. G. *Paul and the Gift*. Grand Rapids, MI: Eerdmans, 2015.

Barclay, John M. G. "Paul's Story: Theology as Testimony." In *Narrative Dynamics in Paul: A Critical Assessment*, edited by Bruce W. Longenecker, 133–56. Louisville, KY: Westminster John Knox Press, 2002.

Barclay, John M. G. "Under Grace: The Christ-Gift and the Construction of a Christian Habitus." In *Apocalyptic Paul: Cosmos and Anthropos in Romans 5–8*, edited by Beverly Roberts Gaventa, 59–76. Waco, TX: Baylor University Press, 2013.

Barker, H. Gaylon. *The Cross of Reality: Luther's Theologia Crucis and Bonhoeffer's Christology*. Minneapolis, MN: Fortress Press, 2015.

Barth, Karl. *Church Dogmatics: The Doctrine of Reconciliation*. Edited by G. W. Bromiley and T. F. Torrance. Translated by G. W. Bromiley. Vol. IV/1. Peabody, MA: Hendrickson, 2010.

Barth, Karl. *The Epistle to the Romans*. Translated by Edwin C. Hoskyns. 6th ed. Oxford/New York: Oxford University Press, 1933.

Bates, Matthew W. *Salvation by Allegiance Alone: Rethinking Faith, Works, and the Gospel of Jesus the King*. Grand Rapids, MI: Baker Academic, 2017.

Batka, Ľubomír. "Luther's Teaching on Sin and Evil." In *The Oxford Handbook of Martin Luther's Theology*, edited by Robert Kolb, Irene Dingel, and Ľubomír Batka. Oxford/New York: Oxford University Press, 2014.

Bavinck, Herman. *Reformed Dogmatics: Holy Spirit, Church, and New Creation*. Edited by John Bolt. Translated by John Vriend. Vol. 4. 4 vols. Grand Rapids, MI: Baker Academic, 2008.

Bayer, Oswald. "Being in the Image of God." *Lutheran Quarterly* 27, no. 1 (2013): 76–88.

Bayer, Oswald. *Living by Faith: Justification and Sanctification*. Grand Rapids, MI: Eerdmans, 2003.

Bayer, Oswald. "Martin Luther's Conception of Human Dignity." In *The Cambridge Handbook of Human Dignity*, edited by Marcus Düwell, Jens Braarvig, Roger Brownsword, and Dietmar Mieth, translated by Naomi van Steenbergen, 101–7. Cambridge: Cambridge University Press, 2014.

Bayer, Oswald. *Martin Luther's Theology: A Contemporary Interpretation*. Translated by Thomas H. Trapp. Grand Rapids, MI: Eerdmans, 2008.

Bayer, Oswald. "The Doctrine of Justification and Ontology." Translated by Christine Helmer. *Neue Zeitschrift Für Systematische Theologie Und Religionsphilosophie* 43, no. 1 (2001): 44–53.

Bethge, Eberhard. *Dietrich Bonhoeffer: A Biography*. Edited by Victoria Barnett. Rev. Ed. Minneapolis, MN: Fortress Press, 2000.

Bethge, Eberhard. "The Challenge of Dietrich Bonhoeffer's Life and Theology." In *World Come of Age: A Symposium on Dietrich Bonhoeffer*, edited by Ronald Gregor Smith, 22–88. London: Collins, 1967.

Boesak, Alan Aubrey. "Church, Racism, and Resistance: Bonhoeffer and the Critical Dimensions of Theological Integrity." In *Luther, Bonhoeffer, and Public Ethics: Re-Forming the Church of the Future*, edited by Michael P. DeJonge and Clifford J. Green, 137–49. Lanham, MD: Lexington Books/Fortress Academic, 2018.

Bonhoeffer, Dietrich. *Dietrich Bonhoeffer Werke*. 17 vols. Edited by Eberhard Bethge et al. Munich: Chr. Kaiser/Gütersloher Verlagshaus, 1986–99.

Bonhoeffer, Dietrich. *Dietrich Bonhoeffer Works*. Edited by Victoria Barnett, Wayne Whitson Floyd Jr., and Barbara Wojhoski. 17 vols. Minneapolis, MN: Fortress, 1996–2013.

Bonhoeffer, Dietrich. DBWE 1: *Sanctorum Communio: A Theological Study of the Sociology of the Church*. Edited by Clifford J. Green. Translated by Reinhard Krauss and Nancy Lukens. Minneapolis, MN: Fortress Press, 2009.

Bonhoeffer, Dietrich. DBWE 2: *Act and Being: Transcendental Philosophy and Ontology in Systematic Theology*. Edited by Wayne Whitson Floyd, Jr. Translated by H. Martin Rumscheidt. Minneapolis, MN: Fortress Press, 1996.

Bonhoeffer, Dietrich. DBWE 3: *Creation and Fall: A Theological Exposition of Genesis 1–3*. Edited by John W. De Gruchy. Translated by Douglas S. Bax. Minneapolis, MN: Fortress Press, 1997.

Bonhoeffer, Dietrich. DBWE 4: *Discipleship*. Edited by Geffrey B. Kelly and John D. Godsey. Translated by Barbara Green and Reinhard Krauss. Minneapolis, MN: Fortress Press, 2001.

Bonhoeffer, Dietrich. DBWE 5: *Life Together and Prayerbook of the Bible*. Edited by Geffrey B. Kelly. Translated by Daniel W. Bloesch and James H. Burtness. Minneapolis, MN: Fortress Press, 2005.

Bonhoeffer, Dietrich. DBWE 6: *Ethics*. Edited by Clifford J. Green. Translated by Reinhard Krauss, Charles C. West, and Douglas W. Stott. Minneapolis, MN: Fortress Press, 2005.

Bonhoeffer, Dietrich. DBWE 8: *Letters and Papers from Prison*. Edited by John W. De Gruchy. Translated by Isabel Best, Lisa E. Dahill, Reinhard Krauss, and Nancy Lukens. Minneapolis, MN: Fortress Press, 2010.

Bonhoeffer, Dietrich. DBWE 9: *The Young Bonhoeffer: 1918–1927*. Edited by Paul Duane Matheny, Clifford J. Green, and Marshall D. Johnson. Translated by Mary C. Nebelsick and Douglas W. Stott. Minneapolis, MN: Fortress Press, 2003.

Bonhoeffer, Dietrich. DBWE 10: *Barcelona, Berlin, New York: 1928–1931*. Edited by Clifford J. Green. Translated by Douglas W. Stott. Minneapolis, MN: Fortress Press, 2008.

Bonhoeffer, Dietrich. DBWE 11: *Ecumenical, Academic, and Pastoral Work: 1931–1932*. Edited by Mark S. Brocker and Michael B. Lukens. Translated by Douglas W. Stott, Isabel Best, Anne Schmidt-Lange, Nicholas S. Humphrey, and Marion Pauck. Minneapolis, MN: Fortress Press, 2012.

Bonhoeffer, Dietrich. DBWE 12: *Berlin: 1932–1933*. Edited by Larry L. Rasmussen, Isabel Best, and David Higgins. Minneapolis, MN: Fortress Press, 2009.

Bonhoeffer, Dietrich. DBWE 13: *London: 1933–1935*. Edited by Keith Clements. Translated by Isabel Best. Minneapolis, MN: Fortress Press, 2007.
Bonhoeffer, Dietrich. DBWE 14: *Theological Education at Finkenwalde: 1935–1937*. Edited by H. Gaylon Barker and Mark S. Brocker. Translated by Douglas W. Stott. Minneapolis, MN: Fortress Press, 2013.
Bonhoeffer, Dietrich. DBWE 15: *Theological Education Underground: 1937–1940*. Edited by Victoria J. Barnett. Translated by Victoria J. Barnett, Claudia D. Bergmann, Peter Frick, and Scott A. Moore. Minneapolis, MN: Fortress Press, 2012.
Bonhoeffer, Dietrich. DBWE 16: *Conspiracy and Imprisonment: 1940–1945*. Edited by Mark S. Brocker. Translated by Lisa E. Dahill. Minneapolis, MN: Fortress Press, 2006.
Braaten, Carl E., and Robert W. Jenson, eds. *Union with Christ: The New Finnish Interpretation of Luther*. Grand Rapids, MI: Eerdmans, 1998.
Brock, Brian. "On Becoming Creatures: Being Called to Presence in a Distracted World." *International Journal of Systematic Theology* 18, no. 4 (2016): 432–52.
Buell, Denise Kimber. "Early Christian Universalism and Modern Forms of Racism." In *The Origins of Racism in the West*, edited by Miriam Eliav-Feldon, Benjamin Isaac, and Joseph Ziegler, 109–31. Cambridge: Cambridge University Press, 2009.
Campbell, Douglas A. "Mass Incarceration: Pauline Problems and Pauline Solutions." *Interpretation: A Journal of Bible and Theology* 72, no. 3 (2018): 282–92.
Carter, J. Kameron. *Race: A Theological Account*. Oxford/New York: Oxford University Press, 2008.
Chester, Stephen J. *Reading Paul with the Reformers: Reconciling Old and New Perspectives*. Grand Rapids, MI: Eerdmans, 2017.
Conde-Frazier, Elizabeth. "*Siempre Lo Mismo*: Theology, Rhetoric, and Broken Praxis." In *Can "White" People Be Saved? Triangulating Race, Theology, and Mission*, edited by Love L. Sechrest, Johnny Ramírez-Johnson, and Amos Yong, 123–49. Downers Grove, IL: IVP Academic, 2018.
Cone, James H. *A Black Theology of Liberation*. Philadelphia, PA: J. B. Lippincott Company, 1970.
Cone, James H. *Black Theology and Black Power*. 50th anniversary edn. Maryknoll, NY: Orbis Books, 2018.
Cone, James H. *God of the Oppressed*. Rev. edn. Maryknoll, NY: Orbis Books, 1997.
Copeland, M. Shawn. *Enfleshing Freedom: Body, Race, and Being*. Minneapolis, MN: Fortress Press, 2010.
Dahill, Lisa E. "Con-Formation with Jesus Christ: Bonhoeffer, Social Location, and Embodiment." In *Being Human, Becoming Human: Dietrich Bonhoeffer and Social Thought*, edited by Jens Zimmermann and Brian Gregor, 176–90. Eugene, OR: Pickwick Publications, 2010.
De Gruchy, John W. *Bonhoeffer and South Africa: Theology in Dialogue*. Grand Rapids, MI: Eerdmans, 1984.
DeJonge, Michael P. *Bonhoeffer on Resistance: The Word Against the Wheel*. Oxford: Oxford University Press, 2018.
DeJonge, Michael P. *Bonhoeffer's Reception of Luther*. Oxford: Oxford University Press, 2017.
DeJonge, Michael P. *Bonhoeffer's Theological Formation: Berlin, Barth, and Protestant Theology*. Oxford: Oxford University Press, 2012.
Douglas, Kelly Brown. *What's Faith Got to Do With It? Black Bodies/Christian Souls*. Maryknoll, NY: Orbis Books, 2005.

Dunn, James D. G. *The Theology of Paul the Apostle*. Edinburgh: T&T Clark, 1998.
Eastman, Susan. *Recovering Paul's Mother Tongue: Language and Theology in Galatians*. Grand Rapids, MI: Eerdmans, 2007.
Eastman, Susan Grove. "Apocalypse and Incarnation: The Participatory Logic of Paul's Gospel." In *Apocalyptic and the Future of Theology: With and Beyond J. Louis Martyn*, edited by Joshua B. Davis and Douglas Harink, 165–82. Eugene, OR: Cascade Books, 2012.
Eastman, Susan Grove. *Paul and the Person: Reframing Paul's Anthropology*. Grand Rapids, MI: Eerdmans, 2017.
Ebeling, Gerhard. *Die Theologische Definition Des Menschen: Kommentar Zu These 20–40*. Vol. 2:3. Lutherstudien. Tübingen: Mohr Siebeck, 1989.
Ebeling, Gerhard. *Luther: An Introduction to His Thought*. London: Collins, 1970.
Ebeling, Gerhard. "Luther's Understanding of Reality." Translated by Scott Celsor. *Lutheran Quarterly* 27, no. 1 (2013): 56–75.
Elshtain, Jean Bethke. "Bonhoeffer on Modernity: 'Sic et Non.'" *Journal of Religious Ethics* 29, no. 3 (2001): 345–66.
Fackenheim, Emil L. "Holocaust and *Weltanschauung*: Philosophical Reflections on Why They Did It." In *The God Within: Kant, Schelling, and Historicity*, edited by John Burbidge, 172–85. Toronto: University of Toronto Press, 1996.
Feil, Ernst. *The Theology of Dietrich Bonhoeffer*. Translated by Martin Rumscheidt. Philadelphia, PA: Fortress Press, 1985.
Fichte, J. G. *Science of Knowledge*. Edited and translated by Peter Heath and John Lachs. New York: Meredith Corporation, 1970.
Flett, John G. "Justification contra Mission: The Isolation of Justification in the History of Reconciliation." *Zeitschrift Für Dialektische Theologie* Supplement Series 6 (2014): 105–27.
Floyd, Wayne Whitson. "Encounter with an Other: Immanuel Kant and G. W. F. Hegel in the Theology of Dietrich Bonhoeffer." In *Bonhoeffer's Intellectual Formation: Theology and Philosophy in His Thought*, edited by Peter Frick, 83–119. Tübingen: Mohr Siebeck, 2008.
Frick, Peter. "Bonhoeffer and Philosophy." In *Understanding Bonhoeffer*, 166–82. Tübingen: Mohr Siebeck, 2017.
Frick, Peter. "Bonhoeffer on the Social-Political Dimension of Grace." In *Understanding Bonhoeffer*. Tübingen: Mohr Siebeck, 2017.
Frick, Peter. "Notes On Bonhoeffer's Theological Anthropology: The Case of Racism." In *Understanding Bonhoeffer*, 185–200. Tübingen: Mohr Siebeck, 2017.
Frierson, Patrick R. *Freedom and Anthropology in Kant's Moral Philosophy*. Cambridge: Cambridge University Press, 2003.
Garcia, Javier A. *Recovering the Ecumenical Bonhoeffer: Thinking After the Tradition*. Lanham, MD: Lexington Books/Fortress Academic, 2019.
Green, Clifford J. *Bonhoeffer: A Theology of Sociality*. Rev. Ed. Grand Rapids, MI: Eerdmans, 1999.
Green, Clifford J. "Editor's Introduction to the English Edition." In *Ethics*, edited by Clifford J. Green, translated by Reinhard Krauss, Charles C. West, and Douglas W. Stott, 1–44. Minneapolis, MN: Fortress Press, 2005.
Greggs, Tom. *Dogmatic Ecclesiology: The Priestly Catholicity of the Church*. Vol. 1. Grand Rapids, MI: Baker Academic, 2019.
Gregor, Brian. *A Philosophical Anthropology of the Cross: The Cruciform Self*. Bloomington, IN: Indiana University Press, 2013.

Gremmels, Christian, ed. *Bonhoeffer Und Luther: Zur Sozialgestalt Des Luthertums in Der Moderne*. München: C. Kaiser, 1983.

Grünwaldt, Klaus, Christiane Tietz, and Udo Hahn, eds. *Bonhoeffer Und Luther: Zentrale Themen Ihrer Theologie*. Hannover: Amt der VELKD, 2007.

Gunton, Colin E. *The Actuality of Atonement: A Study of Metaphor, Rationality and the Christian Tradition*. Edinburgh: T&T Clark, 1988.

Halbach, Ross E. "Preparing the Way: Dietrich Bonhoeffer in Dialogue with Contemporary Theologians of Race." PhD, University of Aberdeen, 2017.

Hamilton, Nadine. "Dietrich Bonhoeffer and the Necessity of Kenosis for Scriptural Hermeneutics." *Scottish Journal of Theology* 71, no. 4 (2018): 441–59.

Harasta, Eva. "Adam in Christ? The Place of Sin in Christ-Reality." In *Christ, Church, and World: New Studies in Bonhoeffer's Theology and Ethics*, edited by Michael G. Mawson and Philip G. Ziegler, 61–75. London: Bloomsbury T&T Clark, 2016.

Harvey, Barry. *Taking Hold of the Real: Dietrich Bonhoeffer and the Profound Worldliness of Christianity*. Cambridge, UK: James Clarke & Co, 2016.

Harvey, Barry. "The Wound of History: Reading Bonhoeffer after Christendom." In *Bonhoeffer for a New Day: Theology in a Time of Transition*, edited by John W. DeGruchy, 72–93. Grand Rapids, MI: Eerdmans, 1997.

Harvey, Jennifer. *Dear White Christians: For Those Still Longing for Racial Reconciliation*. Grand Rapids, MI: Eerdmans, 2014.

Hays, Richard B. *The Faith of Jesus Christ: The Narrative Substructure of Galatians 3:1–4:11*. 2nd ed. Grand Rapids, MI/Dearborn, MI: Eerdmans/Dove Booksellers, 2002.

Hegel, G. W. F. *Phenomenology of Spirit*. Translated by A. V. Miller. Oxford: Oxford University Press, 1977.

Herms, Eilert. "*Weltanschauung* (Worldview)." In *Religion Past and Present*, edited by Hans Dieter Betz, Don S. Browning, Bernd Janowski, and Eberhard Jüngel. Vol. 13. Leiden: Brill, 2012.

Heuvel, Steven C. van den. *Bonhoeffer's Christocentric Theology and Fundamental Debates in Environmental Ethics*. Eugene, OR: Pickwick Publications, 2017.

Holm, Jacob. "G. W. F. Hegel's Impact on Dietrich Bonhoeffer's Early Theology." *Studia Theologica* 56, no. 1 (2002): 64–75.

Holmes, Christopher R. J. "The Holy Spirit." In *The Oxford Handbook of Dietrich Bonhoeffer*, edited by Michael Mawson and Philip G. Ziegler, 168–178. Oxford: Oxford University Press, 2019.

Insole, Christopher J. *The Intolerable God: Kant's Theological Journey*. Grand Rapids, MI: Eerdmans, 2016.

Jäckel, Eberhard. *Hitler's World View: A Blueprint for Power*. Translated by Herbert Arnold. Cambridge, MA: Harvard University Press, 1981.

Jenkins, Willis, and Jennifer M. McBride, eds. *Bonhoeffer and King: Their Legacies and Import for Christian Social Thought*. Minneapolis, MN: Fortress Press, 2010.

Jennings, Willie James. *The Christian Imagination: Theology and the Origins of Race*. New Haven, CT: Yale University Press, 2010.

Jenson, Matt. *The Gravity of Sin: Augustine, Luther and Barth on* Homo Incurvatus in Se. London: T&T Clark, 2006.

Jüngel, Eberhard. "Humanity in Correspondence to God: Remarks on the Image of God as a Basic Concept of Theological Anthropology." In *Theological Essays*, translated by John Webster, 124–53. Edinburgh: T&T Clark, 1989.

Jüngel, Eberhard. *Karl Barth: A Theological Legacy*. Translated by Garrett E. Paul. Philadelphia, PA: Westminster Press, 1986.

Jüngel, Eberhard. "On Becoming Truly Human: The Significance of the Reformation Distinction Between Person and Works for the Self-Understanding of Modern Humanity." In *Theological Essays II*, edited by J. B. Webster, translated by Arnold Neufeldt-Fast and J. B. Webster, 216–40. Edinburgh: T&T Clark, 1995.

Jüngel, Eberhard. "The World as Possibility and Actuality: The Ontology of the Doctrine of Justification." In *Theological Essays*, translated by John Webster, 95–123. Edinburgh: T&T Clark, 1989.

Kahl, Brigitte. "Justification, Ethics, and the 'Other': Paul, Luther, and Bonhoeffer in Trialogue." In *Luther, Bonhoeffer, and Public Ethics: Re-Forming the Church of the Future*, edited by Michael P. DeJonge and Clifford J. Green, 63–82. Lanham, MD: Lexington Books/Fortress Academic, 2018.

Kant, Immanuel. "Anthropology from a Pragmatic Point of View." In *Anthropology, History, and Education*, edited by Günter Zöller and Robert B. Louden, translated by Robert B. Louden, 231–429. Cambridge: Cambridge University Press, 2007.

Kant, Immanuel. "Idea for a Universal History with a Cosmopolitan Aim." In *Anthropology, History, and Education*, edited by Günter Zöller and Robert B. Louden, translated by Allen W. Wood, 108–19. Cambridge: Cambridge University Press, 2007.

Kant, Immanuel. "Lecture of the Winter Semester 1775–1776 Based on the Transcriptions Friedländer 3.3 (Ms 400), Friedländer 2 (Ms 399) and Prieger." In *Lectures on Anthropology*, edited by Allen W. Wood, translated by G. Felicitas Munzel, 43–255. Cambridge: Cambridge University Press, 2015.

Kant, Immanuel. *Religion Within the Boundaries of Mere Reason and Other Writings*. Edited and translated by Allen W. Wood and George Di Giovanni. Cambridge: Cambridge University Press, 1998.

Kant, Immanuel. "Review of J. G. Herder's *Ideas for the Philosophy of the History of Humanity* Parts 1 and 2." In *Anthropology, History, and Education*, edited by Günter Zöller and Robert B. Louden, translated by Allen W. Wood, 124–42. Cambridge: Cambridge University Press, 2007.

Käsemann, Ernst. *Commentary on Romans*. Translated by G. W. Bromiley. London: SCM Press, 1980.

Käsemann, Ernst. "Corporeality in Paul." In *On Being a Disciple of the Crucified Nazarene: Unpublished Lectures and Sermons*, edited by Rudolf Landau and Wolfgang Kraus, translated by Roy A. Harrisville, 38–51. Grand Rapids, MI: Eerdmans, 2010.

Käsemann, Ernst. "Justification and Freedom." In *On Being a Disciple of the Crucified Nazarene: Unpublished Lectures and Sermons*, edited by Rudolf Landau and Wolfgang Kraus, translated by Roy A. Harrisville, 52–60. Grand Rapids, MI: Eerdmans, 2010.

Käsemann, Ernst. "Justification and Salvation History." In *Perspectives on Paul*, 60–78. London: SCM Press, 1971.

Käsemann, Ernst. *Leib Und Leib Christi: Eine Untersuchung Zur Paulinischen Begrifflichkeit*. Tübingen: J. C. B. Mohr, 1933.

Käsemann, Ernst. "On Paul's Anthropology." In *Perspectives on Paul*, 1–31. London: SCM Press, 1971.

Keck, Leander E. *Romans. Abingdon New Testament Commentaries*. Nashville, TN: Abingdon Press, 2005.

Kelly, Geffrey B., and John D. Godsey. "Editor's Introduction to the English Edition." In *Discipleship*, edited by Geffrey B. Kelly and John D. Godsey, translated by Barbara Green and Reinhard Krauss. Minneapolis, MN: Fortress Press, 2001.

Kierkegaard, Søren. *Philosophical Fragments*. Edited and translated by Howard V. Hong and Edna H. Hong. Princeton, NJ: Princeton University Press, 1985.

Kirkpatrick, Matthew D. *Attacks on Christendom in a World Come of Age: Kierkegaard, Bonhoeffer, and the Question of "Religionless Christianity."* Eugene, OR: Pickwick Publications, 2011.
Knight, M. J. "Christ Existing in Ordinary: Dietrich Bonhoeffer and Sanctification." *International Journal of Systematic Theology* 16, no. 4 (2014): 414–35.
Kolb, Robert. "God and His Human Creatures in Luther's Sermons on Genesis: The Reformer's Early Use of His Distinction of Two Kinds of Righteousness." *Concordia Journal* 33, no. 22 (2007): 166–84.
Kolb, Robert. "Luther's View of Being Human: The Relationship of God and His Human Creatures as the Core of Wittenberg Anthropology." *Word & World* 37, no. 4 (2017): 330–8.
Kolb, Robert. *Martin Luther: Confessor of the Faith.* Oxford: Oxford University Press, 2009.
Koopman, Nico. "Bonhoeffer and the Future of Public Theology in South Africa. The On-Going Quest for Life Together." *Nederduitse Gereformeerde Teologiese Tydskrif* 55, no. Supplementum 1 (2014): 985–98.
Kroner, Richard. *Kant's* Weltanschauung. Translated by John E. Smith. Chicago, IL: University of Chicago Press, 1956.
Krötke, Wolf. "Dietrich Bonhoeffer and Martin Luther." In *Bonhoeffer's Intellectual Formation: Theology and Philosophy in His Thought*, edited by Peter Frick, 53–82. Tübingen: Mohr Siebeck, 2008.
Krumwiede, Hans-Walter. *Glaubenszuversicht Und Weltgestaltung Bei Martin Luther: Mit Einem Ausblick Auf Dietrich Bonhoeffer.* Göttingen: Vandenhoeck & Ruprecht, 1983.
Kuehn, Manfred. *Kant: A Biography.* Cambridge: Cambridge University Press, 2001.
Kuske, Martin. *The Old Testament as the Book of Christ: An Appraisal of Bonhoeffer's Interpretation.* Translated by S. T. Kimbrough. Philadelphia, PA: The Westminster Press, 1976.
Kuske, Martin, and Ilse Tödt. "Editor's Afterword to the German Edition." In *Discipleship*, edited by Geffrey B. Kelly and John D. Godsey, translated by Barbara Green and Reinhard Krauss, 289–314. Minneapolis, MN: Fortress Press, 2001.
Lang, Berel. *Act and Idea in the Nazi Genocide.* Syracuse, NY: Syracuse University Press, 2003.
Lehmann, Helmut T. "Editor's Introduction to the Disputation Concerning Justification." In *Luther's Works: Career of the Reformer IV*, 147–49. Philadelphia, PA: Fortress Press, 1960.
Lienhard, Marc. *Luther, Witness to Jesus Christ: Stages and Themes of the Reformer's Christology.* Translated by Edwin H. Robertson. Minneapolis, MN: Augsburg Publishing House, 1982.
Linebaugh, Jonathan. "The Grammar of the Gospel: Justification as a Theological Criterion in the Reformation and in Paul's Letter to the Galatians." *Scottish Journal of Theology* 71, no. 3 (2018): 287–307.
Linebaugh, Jonathan A. "The Christo-Centrism of Faith in Christ: Martin Luther's Reading of Galatians 2.16, 19–20." *New Testament Studies* 59, no. 4 (2013): 535–44.
Lohse, Bernhard. *Martin Luther's Theology: Its Historical and Systematic Development.* Edited and translated by Roy A. Harrisville. Minneapolis, MN: Fortress Press, 1999.
Louden, Robert B. "General Introduction." In *Anthropology, History, and Education*, edited by Günter Zöller and Robert B. Louden, 1–17. Cambridge: Cambridge University Press, 2007.
Louden, Robert B. *Kant's Human Being: Essays on His Theory of Human Nature.* Oxford: Oxford University Press, 2011.

Lugioyo, Brian. "Martin Luther's Eucharistic Christology." In *The Oxford Handbook of Christology*, edited by Francesca Murphy, 267–83. Oxford: Oxford University Press, 2015.

Luther, Martin. *Disputationen Dr. Martin Luthers in Den Jahren 1535–1545 an Der Universität Wittenberg Gehalten*. Edited by Paul Drews. Göttingen: Vandenhoeck und Ruprecht, 1895.

Luther, Martin. *Luther's Works*. Edited by Jaroslav Pelikan and Helmut Lehmann. 55 vols. St. Louis/Philadelphia, PA: Concordia Press/Fortress Press, 1955–1986.

Macaskill, Grant. *Living in Union with Christ: Paul's Gospel and Christian Moral Identity*. Grand Rapids, MI: Baker Academic, 2019.

Mack, Michael. *German Idealism and the Jew: The Inner Anti-Semitism of Philosophy and German Jewish Responses*. Chicago, IL: The University of Chicago Press, 2003.

Malysz, Piotr J. "Luther and Dionysius: Beyond Mere Negations." *Modern Theology* 24, no. 4 (2008): 679–92.

Mannermaa, Tuomo. *Christ Present in Faith: Luther's View of Justification*. Edited by Kirsi Irmeli Stjerna. Minneapolis, MN: Fortress Press, 2005.

Marsh, Charles. "Human Community and Divine Presence: Dietrich Bonhoeffer's Theological Critique of Hegel." *Scottish Journal of Theology* 45, no. 4 (1992): 427–48.

Mattes, Mark. "Luther on Justification as Forensic and Effective." In *The Oxford Handbook of Martin Luther's Theology*, edited by L'ubomír Batka, Irene Dingel, and Robert Kolb, 264–73. Oxford: Oxford University Press, 2014.

Mawson, Michael. *Christ Existing as Community: Bonhoeffer's Ecclesiology*. Oxford: Oxford University Press, 2018.

Mawson, Michael. "Suffering Christ's Call: Discipleship and the Cross." *The Bonhoeffer Legacy: Australasian Journal of Bonhoeffer Studies* Pre-Publication Version (2016): 1–20.

Mawson, Michael. "The Spirit and the Community: Pneumatology and Ecclesiology in Jenson, Hütter and Bonhoeffer." *International Journal of Systematic Theology* 15, no. 4 (2013): 453–68.

Mawson, Michael. "The Weakness of the Word and the Reality of God: Luther and Bonhoeffer on the Cross of Discipleship." *Studies in Christian Ethics* 31, no. 4 (2018): 452–62.

Mawson, Michael. "Theology and Social Theory—Reevaluating Bonhoeffer's Approach." *Theology Today* 71, no. 1 (2014): 69–80.

McBride, Jennifer M. *The Church for the World: A Theology of Public Witness*. Oxford: Oxford University Press, 2012.

McFarland, Ian A. *From Nothing: A Theology of Creation*. Louisville, KY: Westminster John Knox Press, 2014.

McGarry, Joseph. "Bridging the Gap: Dietrich Bonhoeffer's Early Theology and Its Influence on Discipleship." *Bonhoeffer Legacy: Australasian Journal of Bonhoeffer Studies* 2, no. 1 (2014): 13–31.

McGrath, Alister E. *Iustitia Dei: A History of the Christian Doctrine of Justification*. Vol. 2. Cambridge: Cambridge University Press, 1986.

McKenny, Gerald. "Freedom, Responsibility, and Moral Agency." In *The Oxford Handbook of Dietrich Bonhoeffer*, edited by Michael Mawson and Philip G. Ziegler, 306–20. Oxford: Oxford University Press, 2019.

Mills, Charles W. *Blackness Visible: Essays on Philosophy and Race*. Ithaca, NY: Cornell University Press, 1998.

Mills, Charles W. "Ideology." In *The Routledge Handbook of Epistemic Injustice*, edited by Ian James Kidd, José Medina, and Gaile Pohlhaus, Jr., 100–12. London: Routledge, 2017.

Muers, Rachel. *Keeping God's Silence: Towards a Theological Ethics of Communication*. Malden, MA: Blackwell, 2004.

Nielsen, Kirsten Busch. "Community Turned Inside Out: Dietrich Bonhoeffer's Concept of the Church and of Humanity Reconsidered." In *Being Human, Becoming Human: Dietrich Bonhoeffer and Social Thought*, edited by Jens Zimmermann and Brian Gregor, 91–101. Eugene, OR: Pickwick Publications, 2010.

Nielsen, Kirsten Busch. "Sünde." In *Bonhoeffer Und Luther: Zentrale Themen Ihrer Theologie*, edited by Klaus Grünwaldt, Christiane Tietz, and Udo Hahn, 105–21. Hannover: Amt der VELKD, 2007.

Pangritz, Andreas. "Bonhoeffer and the Jews." In *The Oxford Handbook of Dietrich Bonhoeffer*, edited by Michael Mawson and Philip G. Ziegler, 91–107. Oxford: Oxford University Press, 2019.

Pangritz, Andreas. *Karl Barth in the Theology of Dietrich Bonhoeffer*. Grand Rapids, MI: Eerdmans, 2000.

Pangritz, Andreas. "'Who Is Jesus Christ, for Us, Today?'" In *The Cambridge Companion to Dietrich Bonhoeffer*, edited by John W. de Gruchy, 134–53. Cambridge: Cambridge University Press, 1999.

Pannenberg, Wolfhart. *Anthropology in Theological Perspective*. Translated by Matthew J. O'Connell. Philadelphia, PA: The Westminster Press, 1985.

Pannenberg, Wolfhart. "Hintergründe Des Streites Um Die Rechtfertigungslehre in Der Evangelischen Theologie," Vol. 3. München: Verlag der Bayerischen Akademie der Wissenschaften, 2000.

Peerbolte, Bert Jan Lietaert. "A New Perspective on Justification: Recent Developments in the Study of Paul." *Zeitschrift Für Dialektische Theologie* Supplement Series 6 (2014): 128–52.

Perry, Jr., Richard J. "African American Lutheran Ethical Action: The Will to Build." In *The Promise of Lutheran Ethics*, edited by Karen L. Bloomquist and John R. Stumme, 75–96. Minneapolis, MN: Fortress Press, 1998.

Perry, Richard J. "Justification by Faith and Its Social Implications." In *Theology and the Black Experience: The Lutheran Heritage Interpreted by African and African-American Theologians*, edited by Albert Pero and Ambrose Moyo, 11–34. Minneapolis, MN: Augsburg, 1988.

Pfeifer, Hans. "The Forms of Justification: On the Question of the Structure in Dietrich Bonhoeffer's Theology." In *A Bonhoeffer Legacy: Essays in Understanding*, edited by A. J. Klassen, 14–47. Grand Rapids, MI: Eerdmans, 1981.

Pinkard, Terry. "Idealism." In *The Oxford Handbook of German Philosophy in the Nineteenth Century*, edited by Michael N. Forster and Kristin Gjesdal, 231–57. Oxford: Oxford University Press, 2015.

Plant, Stephen. *Bonhoeffer*. London: Continuum, 2004.

Rädes, Jorg. "Bonhoeffer and Hegel from *Sanctorum Communio* to the Hegel Seminar with Some Perspectives for the Later Works." PhD Thesis, Chapter Draft. University of St Andrews, 1988.

Ramírez-Johnson, Johnny, and Love L. Sechrest. "Introduction: Race and Missiology in Glocal Perspective." In *Can "White" People Be Saved? Triangulating Race, Theology, and Mission*, edited by Love L. Sechrest, Johnny Ramírez-Johnson, and Amos Yong, 1–24. Downers Grove, IL: IVP Academic, 2018.

Reuter, Hans-Richard. "Editor's Afterword to the German Edition." In *Act and Being: Transcendental Philosophy and Ontology in Systematic Theology*, edited by Wayne

Whitson Floyd, Jr., translated by H. Martin Rumscheidt, 162–83. Minneapolis, MN: Fortress Press, 2009.
Roberts, J. Deotis. *Bonhoeffer and King: Speaking Truth to Power*. Louisville, KY: Westminster John Knox Press, 2005.
Robinson, David S. *Christ and Revelatory Community in Bonhoeffer's Reception of Hegel*. Tübingen: Mohr Siebeck, 2018.
Rupp, Gordon. "Miles Emeritus? Continuity and Discontinuity Between the Young and the Old Luther." In *Luther: Theologian for Catholics and Protestants*, edited by George Yule, 75–86. Edinburgh: T&T Clark, 1985.
Schlingensiepen, Ferdinand. *Dietrich Bonhoeffer, 1906–1945: Martyr, Thinker, Man of Resistance*. Translated by Isabel Best. London: T&T Clark, 2010.
Schmitz, Florian. *"Nachfolge": Zur Theologie Dietrich Bonhoeffers*. Göttingen: Vandenhoeck & Ruprecht, 2013.
Schwanke, Johannes. "Luther's Theology of Creation." In *The Oxford Handbook of Martin Luther's Theology*, edited by Robert Kolb, Irene Dingel, and L'ubomír Batka, 201–11. Oxford: Oxford University Press, 2014.
Schwanke, Johannes. "Martin Luther's Theology of Creation." Translated by Carsten Card-Hyatt. *International Journal of Systematic Theology* 18, no. 4 (2016): 399–413.
Schwarzwäller, Klaus. "Justification and Reality." *Lutheran Quarterly* 24, no. 3 (2010): 292–309.
Schwöbel, Christoph. "Human Being as Relational Being: Twelve Theses for a Christian Anthropology." In *Persons, Divine and Human: King's College Essays in Theological Anthropology*, edited by Christoph Schwöbel and Colin E. Gunton, 141–70. Edinburgh: T&T Clark, 1999.
Sechrest, Love L. *A Former Jew: Paul and the Dialectics of Race*. London: T&T Clark, 2009.
Slenczka, Notger. "Luther's Anthropology." In *The Oxford Handbook of Martin Luther's Theology*, edited by Robert Kolb, Irene Dingel, and L'ubomír Batka, 212–32. Oxford: Oxford University Press, 2014.
Smith, James K. A. *Desiring the Kingdom: Worship, Worldview, and Cultural Formation*. Grand Rapids, MI: Baker Academic, 2009.
Soosten, Joachim von. "Editor's Afterword to the German Edition." In *Sanctorum Communio: A Theological Study of the Sociology of the Church*, edited by Clifford J. Green, translated by Reinhard Krauss and Nancy Lukens, 290–306. Minneapolis, MN: Fortress Press, 2009.
Sorum, Jonathan D. "Bonhoeffer's Early Interpretation of Luther as the Source of His Basic Theological Paradigm." *Fides et Historia* 29, no. 2 (1997): 35–51.
Sorum, Jonathan D. "The Eschatological Boundary in Dietrich Bonhoeffer's *Nachfolge*." PhD Thesis, Luther Northwestern Theological Seminary, 1994.
Stayer, James M. *Martin Luther, German Saviour: German Evangelical Theological Factions and the Interpretation of Luther, 1917–1933*. Montreal & Kingston: McGill-Queen's University Press, 2000.
Tamez, Elsa. *The Amnesty of Grace: Justification by Faith from a Latin American Perspective*. Nashville, TN: Abingdon Press, 1993.
Tappert, Theodore G., ed. *The Book of Concord: The Confessions of the Evangelical Lutheran Church*. Translated by Theodore G. Tappert. Philadelphia, PA: Fortress Press, 1959.
Tietz, Christiane. "Rechtfertigung Und Heiligung." In *Bonhoeffer Und Luther: Zentrale Themen Ihrer Theologie*, edited by Klaus Grünwaldt, Christiane Tietz, and Udo Hahn, 79–103. Hannover: Amt der VELKD, 2007.

Tietz, Christiane. *Theologian of Resistance: The Life and Thought of Dietrich Bonhoeffer*. Translated by Victoria Barnett. Minneapolis, MN: Fortress Press, 2016.

Torrance, James B. *Worship, Community and the Triune God of Grace*. Downers Grove, IL: IVP Academic, 1996.

Torrance, T. F. "Justification: Its Radical Nature and Place in Reformed Doctrine and Life." In *Theology in Reconstruction*, 150–68. London: SCM Press, 1965.

Trelstad, Marit. "The Way of Salvation in Luther's Theology: A Feminist Evaluation." *Dialog: A Journal of Theology* 45, no. 3 (2006): 236–45.

Trigg, Jonathan. "Luther on Baptism and Penance." In *The Oxford Handbook of Martin Luther's Theology*, edited by Robert Kolb, Irene Dingel, and L'ubomír Batka, 310–21. Oxford: Oxford University Press, 2014.

Ukwuegbu, Bernard. "'Neither Jew nor Greek': The Church in Africa and the Quest for Self-Understanding in the Light of the Pauline Vision and Today's Context of Cultural Pluralism." *International Journal for the Study of the Christian Church* 8, no. 4 (2008): 305–18.

Vainio, Olli-Pekka. *Justification and Participation in Christ: The Development of the Lutheran Doctrine of Justification from Luther to the Formula of Concord (1580)*. Leiden: Brill, 2008.

Vosloo, Robert. "Body and Health in the Light of the Theology of Dietrich Bonhoeffer." *Religion & Theology* 13, no. 1 (2006): 23–37.

Walker, Hamish. "The Incarnation and Crucifixion in Bonhoeffer's *Cost of Discipleship*." *Scottish Journal of Theology* 21, no. 4 (1968): 407–15.

Webster, John. "Discipleship and Obedience." *Scottish Bulletin of Evangelical Theology* 24, no. 1 (2006): 4–18.

Webster, John. "Justification, Analogy and Action: Barth and Luther in Jüngel's Anthropology." In *Barth's Moral Theology: Human Action in Barth's Thought*, 179–214. Edinburgh: T&T Clark, 1998.

Westerholm, Martin. "Creation and the Appropriation of Modernity." *International Journal of Systematic Theology* 18, no. 2 (2016): 210–32.

Westphal, Kenneth R. "Hegel's Critique of Kant's Moral Worldview." *Philosophical Topics* 19, no. 2 (1991): 133–76.

Williams, Reggie L. *Bonhoeffer's Black Jesus: Harlem Renaissance Theology and an Ethic of Resistance*. Waco, TX: Baylor University Press, 2014.

Woelfel, James W. *Bonhoeffer's Theology: Classical and Revolutionary*. Nashville, TN: Abingdon Press, 1970.

Wright, N. T. *Paul and the Faithfulness of God*. Christian Origins and the Question of God. Minneapolis, MN: Fortress Press, 2013.

Young III, Josiah U. "Dietrich Bonhoeffer and Reinhold Niebuhr: Their Ethics, Views on Karl Barth and African-Americans." In *Bonhoeffer's Intellectual Formation: Theology and Philosophy in His Thought*, edited by Peter Frick, 283–300. Tübingen: Mohr Siebeck, 2008.

Young III, Josiah U. "'Is the White Christ, Too, Distraught by These Dark Sins His Father Wrought?': Dietrich Bonhoeffer and the Problem of the White Christ." *Perspectives in Religious Studies* 26, no. 3 (1999): 317–30.

Young III, Josiah U. *No Difference in the Fare: Dietrich Bonhoeffer and the Problem of Racism*. Grand Rapids, MI: Eerdmans, 1998.

Young III, Josiah U. "'On My Way to Freedom Land': Bonhoeffer and Three Bright Lights of the Civil Rights Movement." In *Luther, Bonhoeffer, and Public Ethics: Re-Forming the Church of the Future*, edited by Michael P. DeJonge and Clifford J. Green, 151–60. Lanham, MD: Lexington Books/Fortress Academic, 2018.

Ziegler, Philip G. "'Completely Within God's Doing': Soteriology as Meta-Ethics in the Theology of Dietrich Bonhoeffer." In *Christ, Church, and World: New Studies in Bonhoeffer's Theology and Ethics*, edited by Michael Mawson and Philip G. Ziegler, 101–17. London: Bloomsbury T&T Clark, 2016.

Ziegler, Philip G. *Militant Grace: The Apocalyptic Turn and the Future of Christian Theology*. Grand Rapids, MI: Baker Academic, 2018.

Ziegler, Philip G. "'Not to Abolish, but to Fulfil': The Person of the Preacher and the Claim of the Sermon on the Mount." *Studies in Christian Ethics* 22, no. 3 (2009): 275–89.

Zimmermann, Jens. "Being Human, Becoming Human: Dietrich Bonhoeffer's Christological Humanism." In *Being Human, Becoming Human: Dietrich Bonhoeffer and Social Thought*, edited by Jens Zimmermann and Brian Gregor, 25–48. Eugene, OR: Pickwick Publications, 2010.

Zizioulas, John D. *Communion and Otherness: Further Studies in Personhood and the Church*. Edited by Paul McPartlan. London: T&T Clark, 2006.

INDEX

Act and Being   36, 43, 81, 128, 145
Adam, being in   37–41, 81–3, 88, 128
analogia relationis   43
anthropology
    Kant's pragmatic   55, 59
    of National Socialism   73
    philosophical   24–5, 31, 62
    theological   *passim*
Aristotle   24
Augustine   22

baptism   29, 100–1, 106–11, 113, 119, 145, 147, 149, 154
Barclay, John M. G.   81–2, 88–9
Barker, Gaylon H.   8, 9, 120
Barth, Karl   6, 36–8, 45, 47–9, 97
Bayer, Oswald   12, 20, 61
Bethel Confession   36
Bethge, Eberhard   7, 28, 68–9, 95, 97, 103, 108, 120
body/embodiment   84–90, 96, 111–15, 131–3, 136, 143–6, 155

Creation and Fall   36, 40, 62, 84, 111
Christ   *passim*
    being in   38–40, 45, 81–3, 88, 128
    the counter Logos   146, 148–54
    intercession of   112–13, 133
    Lordship of   83–4
    as mediator   105–7, 110, 118, 120, 134, 145, 149, 154
    mission of   95, 105, 120, 131
    as moral exemplar   60
    threefold unity of   43, 90, 112, 125, 135–6
Christology lectures   105, 147–53
Christuswirklichkeit   73, 125, 128–30, 134, 153
church   7, 9, 11, 34, 65, 67–8, 86, 89, 95–6, 102, 104, 113–14, 118, 126, 128, 131, 136, 138, 143, 152–5
    church-world relationship   116–21, 124–32
collective person   33, 37
    of Adam   34
    of Christ   34, 47
Cone, James H.   141, 143–4
confession   131–2, 154–5
confessing church   69, 95–6, 98, 101
Cor curvum en se   22, 34, 36–7, 81, 84, 145, 151
Coram deo existence   20–2, 25, 30, 32–3, 64, 66, 74, 80, 84, 90, 94, 130, 133–4, 138, 145, 149
creation   17–19, 21, 23, 35, 40, 61, 81, 85, 102
    in the historical dialectic   40–5
    ex nihilo   19, 41–2, 44, 66, 154
creatureliness   40, 43, 83, 136, 145
crucifixion   101, 107–8, 115, 118, 143

Dahill, Lisa E.   111, 115
Disputation Concerning Man   16, 22–3, 28–9, 62
Dejonge, Michael P.   6–9, 126, 134
Deutsche Christen   98, 101, 103
dialectic of personhood   33, 37, 47–8
Discipleship   94–121, 124, 126, 130
discipleship, theology and ethics of   94–121, 132, 137, 155
doctrine   99–101
    as *pura doctrina*   112, 141
Dunn, James D. G.   85–7

Eastman, Susan Grove   79–81, 83
Ebeling, Gerhard   7
Elshtain, Jean Bethke   51, 74
Ethics   72–3, 94, 112, 120–1, 124–38
ethics   77–155

Fackenheim, Emil L. 69–70, 73–4
faith 14, 17, 21–2, 24–5, 36, 38, 40, 43,
    46–9, 66–7, 96, 101–2, 105, 114,
    128, 134, 136
Finkenwalde 94–6, 98, 101, 120
forgiveness 120, 128, 134
formation 95, 99, 120, 131
freedom 41–2, 55, 58, 64, 143
    God's 65–6
Frick, Peter 133

Geschlossenheit 70, 74
grace 21, 32, 34, 47, 71, 74, 82, 102, 119–
    20, 137–8, 141, 146, 153, 155
    as cheap 96, 101, 103–4
    as costly 103–5
Green, Clifford J. 30–2, 48, 125

Hegel, G. W. F. 52, 56, 67, 70, 148
heteronomy 66
historical dialectic of creation, sin, and
    reconciliation 120, 129–31,
    145, 149, 154–5
    in Luther 16, 20–1, 25, 34
    in Bonhoeffer 34–5, 39–40, 43–4, 46,
        67, 74, 80, 89, 132, 134–6
    in Paul 84–90
Hitler, Adolf 69, 95
Holl, Karl 28
Holy Spirit 21–2, 29, 83, 90, 98–100,
    102–3, 105, 107, 109, 126, 128,
    130, 133–4, 141, 153
human logos 148–51

idealism, German 31–2, 48, 52–4, 60,
    63–7, 74–5, 103
ideology 51, 69–70, 74
image of God 20, 30, 42–3
incarnation 66, 112, 114, 125, 133, 148,
    154
Insole, Christopher J. 60
intimate joining 145–6, 155

Jennings, Willie James 145
justification by faith *passim*
    as forensic and/or effective 13–15,
        46–8, 102, 143

by works 24, 32, 34

Kant, Immanuel 52–68, 70, 73
    on autonomous reason 60–1, 64
    on cosmopolitanism 56–8, 65, 67
    on morality 56–7, 59–60, 65, 67
    on teleology 56–8, 60, 65, 67
    on unsociable sociability 56–7,
        67
Käsemann, Ernst 80, 88–9
Kierkegaard, Søren 8, 32, 113
King, Jr., Martin Luther 144
Kingdom of God 65, 72, 104, 117–18
Kirchenkampf 68
Kolb, Robert 15
Krötke, Wolf 7–10

Life Together 94
Lohse 12–13
Louden, Robert B. 54–5, 58
love 115–16, 119, 123, 153
Letters and Papers from Prison 95
Luther 5–26, 28–9, 33–6, 39, 61–2, 82,
    85, 88, 98, 110
    on justification 10–15
    on theological anthropology 15–25
Luther Renaissance 6, 8, 28

Mannermaa, Tuomo/Finnish School 14–
    15
Mawson, Michael 33, 35
McBride, Jennifer M. 116, 127–30
McGrath, Alister E. 13–14

national socialism 68, 72–3, 75, 96
new creation 19, 21, 38–9, 46, 89
Nielsen, Kirsten Busch 124

pacifism 115
participation in Christ
    in Bonhoeffer 46, 96, 102, 105–7,
        109–15, 118–20, 126, 130,
        133–4, 136, 145–7, 149, 154–5
    in Luther 14
    in Paul 79, 83–4, 90
Paul, the Apostle 5, 10, 19, 79–91, 97,
    103–4

Perry, Richard J.   142–3
philosophy   16–17, 23, 25, 32, 54, 62–3
Plant, Stephen   95–6, 132
point of unity (*Einheitspunkt*)   45, 48, 125, 136, 149
preservation   40–1, 102

reality   124–5, 128, 131–2
reconciliation   23, 35, 43, 46, 66, 83–5, 89–90, 103, 111, 115, 118–20, 125–6, 128–9, 131, 135, 145, 155
   in the historical dialectic   38–40
   proclamation and enactment of   124, 127, 138
   as recapitulation of creation   38, 43, 82, 154
relationality   20, 22, 30, 36, 66, 79, 81, 83, 85, 132, 134, 145
repentance   117, 119–20, 154
resurrection   41–3, 83, 86, 107–12, 114–15, 118, 125, 135–6, 143, 149, 152, 154
retrieval, theological   141–4, 147
revelation   24–5, 40, 44

sanctification   102–3, 112, 143
Sanctorum Communio   31–2, 34, 52, 66, 80, 135
Schlingensiepen, Ferdinand   96
Schmitz, Florian   120
Schwöbel, Christoph   68
Scripture   10–11, 99, 101, 103, 126, 141
Seeberg, Reinhold   52
self-determination   62, 66, 72
self-justification   22, 72
self-negation   147–52, 155
Sermon on the Mount   97–8
simple obedience   112, 116–17
Simul justus et peccator   17, 35, 38–40, 88

sin   17, 19, 21–2, 24, 35–8, 62–3, 66–7, 74, 82, 86, 101, 107, 109, 114–15, 131, 146, 148, 154
   in the historical dialectic   35–8
Slenczka, Notger   20
sociality   30–2
Sōma   83, 86–9
soteriology   29, 39–40, 83, 88, 90, 142, 147
   as spiritualized and individualistic   142, 145–6, 153, 155
suffering   108–11, 116–17, 155

Tamez, Elsa   143
Theologia crucis   7, 110
Tietz, Christiane   96
Trelstad, Marit   108
two kingdoms   7, 126–7, 129

ultimate and penultimate   95, 120, 124, 127–30, 132–8, 155

Vainio, Olli-Peka   11
Vischer, Wilhelm   41

way-preparing (*Wegbereitung*)   137–8, 155
Weltanschauung   52–3, 56, 61, 68–75, 153
white privilege   145
white supremacy   141–2, 144–5, 147, 149–51, 153
whiteness   146–7, 149–50, 152, 155
William, Reggie L.   144, 151
witness-bearing   100–1, 103, 117–18, 120, 131–2, 141
Wright, N. T.   87–8

Ziegler, Philip G.   138
Zinn, Elizabeth   97–8

www.ingramcontent.com/pod-product-compliance
Lightning Source LLC
Chambersburg PA
CBHW061837300426
44115CB00013B/2426